The Best American Humorous Short Stories

Ed. Alexander Jessup

Dear Daddy,

I may not always say this but you have made a difference in my life. Everything from teaching me how to ride a bike to teaching me the value of spending time at libraries.

It reminds me of a saying by Groucho Max — "Outside a dog, a book is man's best friend. Inside a dog, it's too dark to read."

— Love
Rishi 12/24/2012

Contents

THE
BEST AMERICAN
HUMOROUS SHORT
STORIES

by

Ed. Alexander Jessup

Edited by ALEXANDER JESSUP, *Editor of "Representative American Short Stories," "The Book of the Short Story," the "Little French Masterpieces" Series, etc.*

INTRODUCTION

This volume does not aim to contain all "the best American humorous short stories"; there are many other stories equally as good, I suppose, in much the same vein, scattered through the range of American literature. I have tried to keep a certain unity of aim and impression in selecting these stories. In the first place I determined that the pieces of brief fiction which I included must first of all be not merely good stories, but good short stories. I put myself in the position of one who was about to select the best short stories in the whole range of American literature,[1] but who, just before he started to do this, was notified that he must refrain from selecting any of the best American short stories that did not contain the element of humor to a marked degree. But I have kept in mind the wide boundaries of the term humor, and also the fact that the humorous standard should be kept second—although a close second—to the short story standard.

In view of the necessary limitations as to the volume's size, I could not hope to represent all periods of American literature adequately, nor was this necessary in order to give examples of the best that has been done in the short story in a humorous vein in American literature. Probably all types of the short story of humor are included here, at any rate. Not only copyright restrictions but in a measure my own opinion have combined to exclude anything by Joel Chandler Harris— *Uncle Remus*—from the collection. Harris is primarily—in his best work—a humorist, and only secondarily a short story writer. As a humorist he is of the first rank; as a writer of short stories his place is hardly so high. His humor is not mere funniness and diversion; he is a humorist in the fundamental and large sense, as are Cervantes,

---

1   This I have attempted in *Representative American Short Stories* (Allyn & Bacon: Boston, 1922).

Rabelais, and Mark Twain.

No book is duller than a book of jokes, for what is refreshing in small doses becomes nauseating when perused in large assignments. Humor in literature is at its best not when served merely by itself but when presented along with other ingredients of literary force in order to give a wide representation of life. Therefore "professional literary humorists," as they may be called, have not been much considered in making up this collection. In the history of American humor there are three names which stand out more prominently than all others before Mark Twain, who, however, also belongs to a wider classification: "Josh Billings" (Henry Wheeler Shaw, 1815-1885), "Petroleum V. Nasby" (David Ross Locke, 1833-1888), and "Artemus Ward" (Charles Farrar Browne, 1834-1867). In the history of American humor these names rank high; in the field of American literature and the American short story they do not rank so high. I have found nothing of theirs that was first-class both as humor and as short story. Perhaps just below these three should be mentioned George Horatio Derby (1823-1861), author of *Phoenixiana* (1855) and the *Squibob Papers* (1859), who wrote under the name "John Phoenix." As has been justly said, "Derby, Shaw, Locke and Browne carried to an extreme numerous tricks already invented by earlier American humorists, particularly the tricks of gigantic exaggeration and calm-faced mendacity, but they are plainly in the main channel of American humor, which had its origin in the first comments of settlers upon the conditions of the frontier, long drew its principal inspiration from the differences between that frontier and the more settled and compact regions of the country, and reached its highest development in Mark Twain, in his youth a child of the American frontier, admirer and imitator of Derby and Browne, and eventually a man of the world and one of its greatest humorists."[2] Nor have such later writers who were essentially humorists as "Bill Nye" (Edgar Wilson Nye, 1850-1896) been considered, because their work does not attain the literary standard and the short story standard as creditably as it does the humorous one. When we come to the close of the nineteenth century the work of such men as "Mr. Dooley" (Finley Peter Dunne, 1867-) and George Ade (1866-) stands out. But while these two writers successfully conform to the exacting critical requirements of good humor and—especially the

---

2   Will D. Howe, in *The Cambridge History of American Literature*, Vol. II, pp. 158-159 (G.P. Putnam's Sons, 1918).

former—of good literature, neither—though Ade more so—attains to the greatest excellence of the short story. Mr. Dooley of the Archey Road is essentially a wholesome and wide-poised humorous philosopher, and the author of *Fables in Slang* is chiefly a satirist, whether in fable, play or what not.

This volume might well have started with something by Washington Irving, I suppose many critics would say. It does not seem to me, however, that Irving's best short stories, such as *The Legend of Sleepy Hollow* and *Rip Van Winkle*, are essentially humorous stories, although they are o'erspread with the genial light of reminiscence. It is the armchair geniality of the eighteenth century essayists, a constituent of the author rather than of his material and product. Irving's best humorous creations, indeed, are scarcely short stories at all, but rather essaylike sketches, or sketchlike essays. James Lawson (1799-1880) in his *Tales and Sketches: by a Cosmopolite* (1830), notably in *The Dapper Gentleman's Story*, is also plainly a follower of Irving. We come to a different vein in the work of such writers as William Tappan Thompson (1812-1882), author of the amusing stories in letter form, *Major Jones's Courtship* (1840); Johnson Jones Hooper (1815-1862), author of *Widow Rugby's Husband, and Other Tales of Alabama* (1851); Joseph G. Baldwin (1815-1864), who wrote *The Flush Times of Alabama and Mississippi* (1853); and Augustus Baldwin Longstreet (1790-1870), whose *Georgia Scenes* (1835) are as important in "local color" as they are racy in humor. Yet none of these writers yield the excellent short story which is also a good piece of humorous literature. But they opened the way for the work of later writers who did attain these combined excellences.

The sentimental vein of the midcentury is seen in the work of Seba Smith (1792-1868), Eliza Leslie (1787-1858), Frances Miriam Whitcher ("Widow Bedott," 1811-1852), Mary W. Janvrin (1830-1870), and Alice Bradley Haven Neal (1828-1863). The well-known work of Joseph Clay Neal (1807-1847) is so all pervaded with caricature and humor that it belongs with the work of the professional humorist school rather than with the short story writers. To mention his *Charcoal Sketches, or Scenes in a Metropolis* (1837-1849) must suffice. The work of Seba Smith is sufficiently expressed in his title, *Way Down East, or Portraitures of Yankee Life* (1854), although his *Letters of Major Jack Downing* (1833) is better known. Of his single stories may be mentioned *The General Court and Jane Andrews' Firkin of Butter* (October, 1847, *Graham's Magazine*). The work of Frances Miriam Whitcher ("Widow

Bedott") is of somewhat finer grain, both as humor and in other literary qualities. Her stories or sketches, such as *Aunt Magwire's Account of Parson Scrantum's Donation Party* (March, 1848, *Godey's Lady's Book*) and *Aunt Magwire's Account of the Mission to Muffletegawmy* (July, 1859, *Godey's*), were afterwards collected in *The Widow Bedott Papers* (1855-56-80). The scope of the work of Mary B. Haven is sufficiently suggested by her story, *Mrs. Bowen's Parlor and Spare Bedroom* (February, 1860, *Godey's*), while the best stories of Mary W. Janvrin include *The Foreign Count; or, High Art in Tattletown* (October, 1860, *Godey's*) and *City Relations; or, the Newmans' Summer at Clovernook* (November, 1861, *Godey's*). The work of Alice Bradley Haven Neal is of somewhat similar texture. Her book, *The Gossips of Rivertown, with Sketches in Prose and Verse* (1850) indicates her field, as does the single title, *The Third-Class Hotel* (December, 1861, *Godey's*). Perhaps the most representative figure of this school is Eliza Leslie (1787-1858), who as "Miss Leslie" was one of the most frequent contributors to the magazines of the 1830's, 1840's and 1850's. One of her best stories is *The Watkinson Evening* (December, 1846, *Godey's Lady's Book*), included in the present volume; others are *The Batson Cottage* (November, 1846, *Godey's Lady's Book*) and *Juliet Irwin; or, the Carriage People* (June, 1847, *Godey's Lady's Book*). One of her chief collections of stories is *Pencil Sketches* (1833-1837). "Miss Leslie," wrote Edgar Allan Poe, "is celebrated for the homely naturalness of her stories and for the broad satire of her comic style." She was the editor of *The Gift* one of the best annuals of the time, and in that position perhaps exerted her chief influence on American literature When one has read three or four representative stories by these seven authors one can grasp them all. Their titles as a rule strike the keynote. These writers, except "the Widow Bedott," are perhaps sentimentalists rather than humorists in intention, but read in the light of later days their apparent serious delineations of the frolics and foibles of their time take on a highly humorous aspect.

George Pope Morris (1802-1864) was one of the founders of *The New York Mirror*, and for a time its editor. He is best known as the author of the poem, *Woodman, Spare That Tree*, and other poems and songs. *The Little Frenchman and His Water Lots* (1839), the first story in the present volume, is selected not because Morris was especially prominent in the field of the short story or humorous prose but because of this single story's representative character. Edgar Allan Poe (1809-1849) follows with *The Angel of the Odd* (October, 1844, *Columbian Magazine*), perhaps the best of his humorous stories. *The System of Dr. Tarr and Prof. Fether* (November, 1845, *Graham's Magazine*) may be rated higher, but it is not essentially a humorous story. Rather it is incisive satire, with too biting an undercurrent to pass muster in the company of the genial in literature. Poe's humorous stories as a whole have tended to belittle rather than increase his fame, many of them verging on the inane. There are some, however, which are at least excellent fooling; few more than that.

Probably this is hardly the place for an extended discussion of Poe, since the present volume covers neither American literature as a whole nor the American short story in general, and Poe is not a humorist in his more notable productions. Let it be said that Poe invented or perfected—more exactly, perfected his own invention of—the modern short story; that is his general and supreme achievement. He also stands superlative for the quality of three varieties of short stories, those of terror, beauty and ratiocination. In the first class belong *A Descent into the Maelstrom* (1841), *The Pit and the Pendulum* (1842), *The Black Cat* (1843), and *The Cask of Amontillado* (1846). In the realm of beauty his notable productions are *The Assignation* (1834), *Shadow: a Parable* (1835), *Ligeia* (1838), *The Fall of the House of Usher* (1839), *Eleonora* (1841), and *The Masque of the Red Death* (1842). The tales of ratiocination—what are now generally termed detective stories—include *The Murders in the Rue Morgue* (1841) and its sequel, *The Mystery of Marie Roget* (1842-1843), *The Gold-Bug* (1843), *The Oblong Box* (1844), *"Thou Art the Man"* (1844), and *The Purloined Letter* (1844).

Then, too, Poe was a master of style, one of the greatest in English prose, possibly the greatest since De Quincey, and quite the most remarkable among American authors. Poe's influence on the short story form has been tremendous. Although the *effects* of structure may be astounding in their power or unexpectedness, yet the *means* by which these effects are brought about are purely mechanical. Any student of fiction can comprehend them, almost any practitioner of fiction with a bent toward form can fairly master them. The merit of any short story production depends on many other elements as well—the value of the structural element to the production as a whole depends first on the selection of the particular sort of structural scheme best suited to the story in hand, and secondly, on the way in which this is *combined* with the piece of writing to form a well-balanced whole. Style is more difficult to imitate than structure, but on the other hand *the origin of structural influence* is more difficult to trace than that of style. So while, in a general way, we feel that Poe's influence on structure in the short story has been great, it is difficult rather than obvious to trace particular instances. It is felt in the advance of the general level of short story art. There is nothing personal about structure—there is everything personal about style. Poe's style is both too much his own and too superlatively good to be successfully imitated—whom have we had who, even if he were a master of structural effects, could be a second Poe? Looking at the matter in another way, Poe's style is not his own at all. There is nothing "personal" about it in the petty sense of that term. Rather we feel that, in the case of this author, universality has been attained. It was Poe's good fortune to be himself in style, as often in content, on a plane of universal appeal. But in some general characteristics of his style his work can be, not perhaps imitated, but emulated. Greater vividness, deft impressionism, brevity that strikes instantly to a telling effect—all these an author may have without imitating any one's style but rather imitating excellence. Poe's "imitators" who have amounted to anything have not tried to imitate him but to vie with him. They are striving after perfectionism. Of course the sort of good style in which Poe indulged is not the kind of style—or the varieties of style—suited for all purposes, but for the purposes to which it is adapted it may well be called supreme.

Then as a poet his work is almost or quite as excellent in a somewhat more restricted range. In verse he is probably the best artist in American letters. Here his sole pursuit was beauty, both of form and thought; he is vivid and apt, intensely lyrical but without much range of thought. He has deep intuitions but no comprehensive grasp of life.

His criticism is, on the whole, the least important part of his work. He had a few good and brilliant ideas which came at just the right time to make a stir in the world, and these his logical mind and telling style enabled him to present to the best advantage. As a critic he is neither broad-minded, learned, nor comprehensive. Nor is he, except in the few ideas referred to, deep. He is, however, limitedly original—perhaps intensely original within his narrow scope. But the excellences and limitations of Poe in any one part of his work were his limitations and excellences in all.

As Poe's best short stories may be mentioned: *Metzengerstein* (Jan. 14, 1832, Philadelphia *Saturday Courier*), *Ms. Found in a Bottle* (October 19, 1833, *Baltimore*

Saturday Visiter), *The Assignation* (January, 1834, *Godey's Lady's Book*), *Berenice* (March, 1835, *Southern Literary Messenger*), *Morella* (April, 1835, *Southern Literary Messenger*), *The Unparalleled Adventure of One Hans Pfaall* (June, 1835, *Southern Literary Messenger*), *King Pest: a Tale Containing an Allegory* (September, 1835, *Southern Literary Messenger*), *Shadow: a Parable* (September, 1835, *Southern Literary Messenger*), *Ligeia* (September, 1838, *American Museum*), *The Fall of the House of Usher* (September, 1839, *Burton's Gentleman's Magazine*), *William Wilson* (1839: *Gift for* 1840), *The Conversation of Eiros and Charmion* (December, 1839, *Burton's Gentleman's Magazine*), *The Murders in the Rue Morgue* (April, 1841, *Graham's Magazine*), *A Descent into the Maelstrom* (May, 1841, *Graham's Magazine*), *Eleonora* (1841: *Gift* for 1842), *The Masque of the Red Death* (May, 1842, *Graham's Magazine*), *The Pit and the Pendulum* (1842: *Gift for 1843*), *The Tell-Tale Heart* (January, 1843, *Pioneer*), *The Gold-Bug* (June 21 and 28, 1843, *Dollar Newspaper*), *The Black Cat* (August 19, 1843, *United States Saturday Post*), *The Oblong Box* (September, 1844, *Godey's Lady's Book*), *The Angel of the Odd* (October, 1844, *Columbian Magazine*), *"Thou Art the Man"* (November, 1844, *Godey's Lady's Book*), *The Purloined Letter* (1844: *Gift* for 1845), *The Imp of the Perverse* (July, 1845, *Graham's Magazine*), *The System of Dr. Tarr and Prof. Fether* (November, 1845, *Graham's Magazine*), *The Facts in the Case of M. Valdemar* (December, 1845, *American Whig Review*), *The Cask of Amontillado* (November, 1846, *Godey's Lady's Book*), and *Lander's Cottage* (June 9, 1849, *Flag of Our Union*). Poe's chief collections are: *Tales of the Grotesque and Arabesque* (1840), *Tales* (1845), and *The Works of the Late Edgar Allan Poe* (1850-56). These titles have been dropped from recent editions of his works, however, and the stories brought together under the title *Tales*, or under subdivisions furnished by his editors, such as *Tales of Ratiocination*, etc.

Caroline Matilda Stansbury Kirkland (1801-1864) wrote of the frontier life of the Middle West in the mid-nineteenth century. Her principal collection of short stories is *Western Clearings* (1845), from which *The Schoolmaster's Progress*, first published in *The Gift* for 1845 (out in 1844), is taken. Other stories republished in that collection are *The Ball at Thram's Huddle* (April, 1840, *Knickerbocker Magazine*), *Recollections of the Land-Fever* (September, 1840, *Knickerbocker Magazine*), and *The Bee-Tree* (*The Gift* for 1842; out in 1841). Her description of the country schoolmaster, "a puppet cut out of shingle and jerked by a string," and the local color in general of this and other stories give her a leading place among the writers of her period who combined fidelity in delineating frontier life with sufficient fictional interest to make a pleasing whole of permanent value.

George William Curtis (1824-1892) gained his chief fame as an essayist, and probably became best known from the department which he conducted, from 1853, as *The Editor's Easy Chair* for *Harper's Magazine* for many years. His volume, *Prue and I* (1856), contains many fictional elements, and a story from it, *Titbottom's Spectacles*, which first appeared in Putnam's Monthly for December, 1854, is given in this volume because it is a good humorous short story rather than because of its author's general eminence in this field. Other stories of his worth noting are *The Shrouded Portrait* (in *The Knickerbocker Gallery*, 1855) and *The Millenial Club* (November, 1858, *Knickerbocker Magazine*).

Edward Everett Hale (1822-1909) is chiefly known as the author of the short story, *The Man Without a Country* (December, 1863, *Atlantic Monthly*), but his venture in the comic vein, *My Double; and How He Undid Me* (September, 1859, *Atlantic Monthly*), is equally worthy of appreciation. It was his first published story of importance. Other noteworthy stories of his are: *The Brick Moon* (October, November and December, 1869, *Atlantic Monthly*), *Life in the Brick Moon* (February, 1870, *Atlantic Monthly*), and *Susan's Escort* (May, 1890, *Harper's Magazine*). His chief volumes of short stories are: *The Man Without a Country, and Other Tales* (1868); *The Brick Moon, and Other Stories* (1873); *Crusoe in New York, and Other Tales* (1880); and *Susan's Escort, and Others* (1897). The stories by Hale which have made his fame all show ability of no mean order; but they are characterized by invention and ingenuity rather than by suffusing imagination. There is not much homogeneity about Hale's work. Almost any two stories of his read as if they might have been written by different authors. For the time being perhaps this is an advantage—his stories charm by their novelty and individuality. In the long run, however, this proves rather a handicap. True individuality, in literature as in the other arts, consists not in "being different" on different occasions—in different works—so much as in being *samely* different from other writers; in being *consistently* one's self, rather than diffusedly various selves. This does not lessen the value of particular stories, of course. It merely injures Hale's fame as a whole. Perhaps some will chiefly feel not so much that his stories are different among themselves, but that they are not strongly anything—anybody's—in particular, that they lack strong personality. The pathway to fame is strewn with stray exhibitions of talent. Apart from his purely literary productions, Hale was one of the large moral forces of his time, through "uplift" both in speech and the written word.

Oliver Wendell Holmes (1809-1894), one of the leading wits of American literature, is not at all well known as a short story writer, nor did he write many brief pieces of fiction. His fame rests chiefly on his poems and on the *Breakfast-Table* books (1858-1860-1872-1890). *Old Ironsides*, *The Last Leaf*, *The Chambered Nautilus* and *Homesick in Heaven* are secure of places in the anthologies of the future, while his lighter verse has made him one of the leading American writers of "familiar verse." Frederick Locker-Lampson in the preface to the first edition of his *Lyra Elegantiarum* (1867) declared that Holmes was "perhaps the best living writer of this species of verse." His trenchant attack on *Homeopathy and Its Kindred Delusions* (1842) makes us wonder what would have been his attitude toward some of the beliefs of our own day; Christian Science, for example. He might have "exposed" it under some such title as *The Religio-Medical Masquerade*, or brought the batteries of his humor to bear on it in the manner of Robert Louis Stevenson's fable, *Something In It*: "Perhaps there is not much in it, as I supposed; but there is something in it after all. Let me be thankful for that." In Holmes' long works of fiction, Elsie Venner (1861), *The Guardian Angel* (1867) and *A Mortal Antipathy* (1885), the method is still somewhat that of the essayist. I have found a short piece of fiction by him in the March, 1832, number of *The New England Magazine*, called *The Debut*, signed O.W.H. *The Story of Iris* in *The Professor at the Breakfast Table*, which ran in *The Atlantic* throughout 1859, and *A Visit to the Asylum for Aged and Decayed Punsters* (January, 1861, *Atlantic*) are his only other brief fictions of which I am aware. The last named has been given place in the present selection because it is characteristic of a certain type and period of American humor, although its short story qualities are not particularly strong.

Samuel Langhorne Clemens (1835-1910), who achieved fame as "Mark Twain," is only incidentally a short story writer, although he wrote many short pieces of fiction. His humorous quality, I mean, is so preponderant, that one hardly thinks of the form. Indeed, he is never very strong in fictional construction, and of the modern short story art he evidently knew or cared little. He is a humorist in the large sense, as are Rabelais and Cervantes, although he is also a humorist in various restricted applications of the word that are wholly American. *The Celebrated*

Jumping Frog of Calaveras County was his first publication of importance, and it saw the light in the Nov. 18, 1865, number of *The Saturday Press*. It was republished in the collection, *The Celebrated Jumping Frog of Calaveras County, and Other Sketches*, in 1867. Others of his best pieces of short fiction are: *The Canvasser's Tale* (December, 1876, *Atlantic Monthly*), *The L1,000,000 Bank Note* (January, 1893, *Century Magazine*), *The Esquimau Maiden's Romance* (November, 1893, *Cosmopolitan*), *Traveling with a Reformer* (December, 1893, *Cosmopolitan*), *The Man That Corrupted Hadleyburg* (December, 1899, *Harper's*), *A Double-Barrelled Detective Story* (January and February, 1902, *Harper's*) *A Dog's Tale* (December, 1903, *Harper's*), and *Eve's Diary* (December, 1905, *Harper's*). Among Twain's chief collections of short stories are: *The Celebrated Jumping Frog of Calaveras County, and Other Sketches* (1867); *The Stolen White Elephant* (1882), *The L1,000,000 Bank Note* (1893), and *The Man That Corrupted Hadleyburg, and Other Stories and Sketches* (1900).

Harry Stillwell Edwards (1855-), a native of Georgia, together with Sarah Barnwell Elliott (? -) and Will N. Harben (1858-1919) have continued in the vein of that earlier writer, Augustus Baldwin Longstreet (1790-1870), author of *Georgia Scenes* (1835). Edwards' best work is to be found in his short stories of black and white life after the manner of Richard Malcolm Johnston. He has written several novels, but he is essentially a writer of human-nature sketches. "He is humorous and picturesque," says Fred Lewis Pattee, "and often he is for a moment the master of pathos, but he has added nothing new and nothing commandingly distinctive."[3] An exception to this might be made in favor of *Elder Brown's Backslide* (August, 1885, *Harper's*), a story in which all the elements are so nicely balanced that the result may well be called a masterpiece of objective humor and pathos. Others of his short stories especially worthy of mention are: *Two Runaways* (July, 1886, *Century*), *Sister Todhunter's Heart* (July, 1887, *Century*), *"De Valley an' de Shadder"* (January, 1888, *Century*), *An Idyl of "Sinkin' Mount'in"* (October, 1888, *Century*), *The Rival Souls* (March, 1889, *Century*), *The Woodhaven Goat* (March, 1899, *Century*), and *The Shadow* (December, 1906, *Century*). His chief collections are *Two Runaways, and Other Stories* (1889) and *His Defense, and Other Stories* (1898).

The most notable, however, of the group of short story writers of Georgia life is perhaps Richard Malcolm Johnston (1822-1898). He stands between Longstreet

---

3   *A History of American Literature Since 1870*, p. 317 (The Century Co.: 1915).

and the younger writers of Georgia life. His first book was Georgia Sketches, by an Old Man (1864). *The Goose Pond School*, a short story, had been written in 1857; it was not published, however, till it appeared in the November and December, 1869, numbers of a Southern magazine, *The New Eclectic*, over the pseudonym "Philemon Perch." His famous *Dukesborough Tales* (1871-1874) was largely a republication of the earlier book. Other noteworthy collections of his are: *Mr. Absalom Billingslea and Other Georgia Folk* (1888), *Mr. Fortner's Marital Claims, and Other Stories* (1892), and *Old Times in Middle Georgia* (1897). Among individual stories stand out: *The Organ-Grinder* (July, 1870, *New Eclectic*), *Mr. Neelus Peeler's Conditions* (June, 1879, *Scribner's Monthly*), *The Brief Embarrassment of Mr. Iverson Blount* (September, 1884, *Century*); *The Hotel Experience of Mr. Pink Fluker* (June, 1886, *Century*), republished in the present collection; *The Wimpy Adoptions* (February, 1887, *Century*), *The Experiments of Miss Sally Cash* (September, 1888, *Century*), and *Our Witch* (March, 1897, *Century*). Johnston must be ranked almost with Bret Harte as a pioneer in "local color" work, although his work had little recognition until his *Dukesborough Tales* were republished by Harper & Brothers in 1883.

Bret Harte (1839-1902) is mentioned here owing to the late date of his story included in this volume, *Colonel Starbottle for the Plaintiff* (March, 1901, *Harper's*), although his work as a whole of course belongs to an earlier period of our literature. It is now well-thumbed literary history that *The Luck of Roaring Camp* (August, 1868, *Overland*) and *The Outcasts of Poker Flat* (January, 1869, *Overland*) brought him a popularity that, in its suddenness and extent, had no precedent in American literature save in the case of Mrs. Stowe and *Uncle Tom's Cabin*. According to Harte's own statement, made in the retrospect of later years, he set out deliberately to add a new province to American literature. Although his work has been belittled because he has chosen exceptional and theatric happenings, yet his real strength came from his contact with Western life.

Irving and Dickens and other models served only to teach him his art. "Finally," says Prof. Pattee, "Harte was the parent of the modern form of the short story. It was he who started Kipling and Cable and Thomas Nelson Page. Few indeed have surpassed him in the mechanics of this most difficult of arts. According to his own belief, the form is an American product ... Harte has described the genesis of his own art. It sprang from the Western humor and was developed by the circumstances that surrounded him. Many of his short stories are models. They contain not a su-perfluous word, they handle a single incident with grapic power, they close without moral or comment. The form came as a natural evolution from his limitations and powers. With him the story must of necessity be brief.... Bret Harte was the artist of impulse, the painter of single burning moments, the flashlight photographer who caught in lurid detail one dramatic episode in the life of a man or a community and left the rest in darkness."[4]

Harte's humor is mostly "Western humor" There is not always uproarious mer-riment, but there is a constant background of humor. I know of no more amusing scene in American literature than that in the courtroom when the Colonel gives his version of the deacon's method of signaling to the widow in Harte's story included in the present volume, *Colonel Starbottle for the Plaintiff*. Here is part of it:

"True to the instructions she had received from him, her lips part in the musi-cal utterance (the Colonel lowered his voice in a faint falsetto, presumably in fond imitation of his fair client) 'Kerree!' Instantly the night becomes resonant with the impassioned reply (the Colonel here lifted his voice in stentorian tones), 'Kerrow!' Again, as he passes, rises the soft 'Kerree!'; again, as his form is lost in the distance, comes back the deep 'Kerrow!'"

While Harte's stories all have in them a certain element or background of hu-mor, yet perhaps the majority of them are chiefly romantic or dramatic even more than they are humorous.

Among the best of his short stories may be mentioned: *The Luck of Roaring Camp* (August, 1868, *Overland*), *The Outcasts of Poker Flat* (January, 1869, *Overland*), *Ten-nessee's Partner* (October, 1869, *Overland*), *Brown of Calaveras* (March, 1870, *Over-land*), *Flip: a California Romance* (in *Flip, and Other Stories*, 1882), *Left Out on Lone Star Mountain* (January, 1884, *Longman's*), *An Ingenue of the Sierras* (July, 1894, *Mc-Clure's*), *The Bell-Ringer of Angel's* (in *The Bell-Ringer of Angel's, and Other Stories*, 1894), *Chu Chu* (in *The Bell-Ringer of Angel's, and Other Stories*, 1894), *The Man and the Mountain* (in *The Ancestors of Peter Atherly, and Other Tales*, 1897), *Salomy Jane's Kiss* (in *Stories in Light and Shadow*, 1898), *The Youngest Miss Piper* (February, 1900, *Les-lie's Monthly*), *Colonel Starbottle for the Plaintiff* (March, 1901, *Harper's*), *A Mercury of the Foothills* (July, 1901, *Cosmopolitan*), *Lanty Foster's Mistake* (December, 1901, *New*

---

4   *A History of American Literature Since 1870*, pp 79-81.

England), *An Ali Baba of the Sierras* (January 4, 1902, *Saturday Evening Post*), and *Dick Boyle's Business Card* (in *Trent's Trust, and Other Stories*, 1903). Among his notable collections of stories are: *The Luck of Roaring Camp, and Other Sketches* (1870), *Flip, and Other Stories* (1882), *On the Frontier* (1884), *Colonel Starbottle's Client, and Some Other People* (1892), *A Protege of Jack Hamlin's, and Other Stories* (1894), *The Bell-Ringer of Angel's, and Other Stories* (1894), *The Ancestors of Peter Atherly, and Other Tales* (1897), *Openings in the Old Trail* (1902), and *Trent's Trust, and Other Stories* (1903). The titles and makeup of several of his collections were changed when they came to be arranged in the complete edition of his works.[5]

Henry Cuyler Bunner (1855-1896) is one of the humorous geniuses of American literature. He is equally at home in clever verse or the brief short story. Prof. Fred Lewis Pattee has summed up his achievement as follows: "Another [than Stockton] who did much to advance the short story toward the mechanical perfection it had attained to at the close of the century was Henry Cuyler Bunner, editor of *Puck* and creator of some of the most exquisite *vers de societe* of the period. The title of one of his collections, *Made in France: French Tales Retold with a U.S. Twist* (1893), forms an introduction to his fiction. Not that he was an imitator; few have been more original or have put more of their own personality into their work. His genius was Gallic. Like Aldrich, he approached the short story from the fastidious standpoint of the lyric poet. With him, as with Aldrich, art was a matter of exquisite touches, of infinite compression, of almost imperceptible shadings. The lurid splashes and the heavy emphasis of the local colorists offended his sensitive taste: he would work with suggestion, with microscopic focussings, and always with dignity and elegance. He was more American than Henry James, more even than Aldrich. He chose always distinctively American subjects—New York City was his favorite theme—and his work had more depth of soul than Stockton's or Aldrich's. The story may be trivial, a mere expanded anecdote, yet it is sure to be so vitally treated that, like Maupassant's work, it grips and remains, and, what is more, it lifts and chastens or explains. It may be said with assurance that *Short Sixes* marks one of the high places which have been attained by the American short story."[6]

---

5 "The Works of Bret Harte," twenty volumes. The Houghton Mifflin Company, Boston.

6 *The Cambridge History of American Literature*, Vol. II, p. 386.

Among Bunner's best stories are: *Love in Old Cloathes* (September, 1883, Century), A Successful Failure (July, 1887, *Puck*), *The Love-Letters of Smith* (July 23, 1890, *Puck*) *The Nice People* (July 30, 1890, *Puck*), *The Nine Cent-Girls* (August 13, 1890, *Puck*), *The Two Churches of 'Quawket* (August 27, 1890, *Puck*), *A Round-Up* (September 10, 1890, *Puck*), *A Sisterly Scheme* (September 24, 1890, *Puck*), *Our Aromatic Uncle* (August, 1895, *Scribner's*), *The Time-Table Test* (in *The Suburban Sage*, 1896). He collaborated with Prof. Brander Matthews in several stories, notably in *The Documents in the Case* (Sept., 1879, *Scribner's Monthly*). His best collections are: *Short Sixes: Stories to be Read While the Candle Burns* (1891), *More Short Sixes* (1894), and *Love in Old Cloathes, and Other Stories* (1896).

After Poe and Hawthorne almost the first author in America to make a vertiginous impression by his short stories was Bret Harte. The wide and sudden popularity he attained by the publication of his two short stories, *The Luck of Roaring Camp* (1868) and *The Outcasts of Poker Flat* (1869), has already been noted.[7] But one story just before Harte that astonished the fiction audience with its power and art was Harriet Prescott Spofford's (1835-) *The Amber Gods* (January and February, 1860, Atlantic), with its startling ending, "I must have died at ten minutes past one." After Harte the next story to make a great sensation was Thomas Bailey Aldrich's *Marjorie Daw* (April, 1873, *Atlantic*), a story with a surprise at the end, as had been his *A Struggle for Life* (July, 1867, *Atlantic*), although it was only *Marjorie Daw* that attracted much attention at the time. Then came George Washington Cable's (1844-) "*Posson Jone',*" (April 1, 1876, *Appleton's Journal*) and a little later Charles Egbert Craddock's (1850-) *The Dancin' Party at Harrison's Cove* (May, 1878, *Atlantic*) and *The Star in the Valley* (November, 1878, *Atlantic*). But the work of Cable and Craddock, though of sterling worth, won its way gradually. Even Edward Everett Hale's (1822-1909) *My Double; and How He Undid Me* (September, 1859, *Atlantic*) and *The Man Without a Country* (December, 1863, *Atlantic*) had fallen comparatively still-born. The truly astounding short story successes, after Poe and Hawthorne, then, were Spofford, Bret Harte and Aldrich. Next came Frank Richard Stockton (1834-1902). "The interest created by the appearance of *Marjorie Daw*," says Prof. Pattee, "was mild compared with that accorded to Frank R. Stockton's *The Lady or the Tiger?* (1884). Stockton had not the technique of Aldrich nor his naturalness and ease. Certainly he had not

---

7   See this Introduction.

his atmosphere of the *beau monde* and his grace of style, but in whimsicality and unexpectedness and in that subtle art that makes the obviously impossible seem perfectly plausible and commonplace he surpassed not only him but Edward Everett Hale and all others. After Stockton and *The Lady or the Tiger?* it was realized even by the uncritical that short story writing had become a subtle art and that the master of its subtleties had his reader at his mercy."[8] The publication of Stockton's short stories covers a period of over forty years, from *Mahala's Drive* (November, 1868, *Lippincott's*) to *The Trouble She Caused When She Kissed* (December, 1911, *Ladies' Home Journal*), published nine years after his death. Among the more notable of his stories may be mentioned: *The Transferred Ghost* (May, 1882, *Century*), *The Lady or the Tiger?* (November, 1882, *Century*), *The Reversible Landscape* (July, 1884, *Century*), *The Remarkable Wreck of the "Thomas Hyke"* (August, 1884, *Century*), *"His Wife's Deceased Sister"* (January, 1884, *Century*), *A Tale of Negative Gravity* (December, 1884, *Century*), *The Christmas Wreck* (in *The Christmas Wreck, and Other Stories*, 1886), *Amos Kilbright* (in *Amos Kilbright, His Adscititious Experiences, with Other Stories*, 1888), *Asaph* (May, 1892, *Cosmopolitan*), *My Terminal Moraine* (April 26, 1892, Collier's *Once a Week Library*), *The Magic Egg* (June, 1894, *Century*), *The Buller-Podington Compact* (August, 1897, *Scribner's*), and *The Widow's Cruise* (in *A Story-Teller's Pack*, 1897). Most of his best work was gathered into the collections: *The Lady or the Tiger?, and Other Stories* (1884), *The Bee-Man of Orn, and Other Fanciful Tales* (1887), *Amos Kilbright, His Adscititious Experiences, with Other Stories* (1888), *The Clocks of Rondaine, and Other Stories* (1892), *A Chosen Few* (1895), *A Story-Teller's Pack* (1897), and *The Queen's Museum, and Other Fanciful Tales* (1906).

After Stockton and Bunner come O. Henry (1862-1910) and Jack London (1876-1916), apostles of the burly and vigorous in fiction. Beside or above them stand Henry James (1843-1916)—although he belongs to an earlier period as well—Edith Wharton (1862-), Alice Brown (1857-), Margaret Wade Deland (1857-), and Katharine Fullerton Gerould (1879-), practitioners in all that O. Henry and London are not, of the finer fields, the more subtle nuances of modern life. With O. Henry and London, though perhaps less noteworthy, are to be grouped George Randolph Chester (1869-) and Irvin Shrewsbury Cobb (1876-). Then, standing rather each by himself, are Melville Davisson Post (1871-), a master of psychological mystery

---

8 *The Cambridge History of American Literature*, Vol. II, p. 385.

stories, and Wilbur Daniel Steele (1886-), whose work it is hard to classify. These ten names represent much that is best in American short story production since the beginning of the twentieth century (1900). Not all are notable for humor; but inasmuch as any consideration of the American humorous short story cannot be wholly dissociated from a consideration of the American short story in general, it has seemed not amiss to mention these authors here. Although Sarah Orne Jewett (1849-1909) lived on into the twentieth century and Mary E. Wilkins Freeman (1862-) is still with us, the best and most typical work of these two writers belongs in the last two decades of the previous century. To an earlier period also belong Charles Egbert Craddock (1850-), George Washington Cable (1844-), Thomas Nelson Page (1853-), Constance Fenimore Woolson (1848-1894), Harriet Prescott Spofford (1835-), Hamlin Garland (1860-), Ambrose Bierce (1842-?), Rose Terry Cooke (1827-1892), and Kate Chopin (1851-1904).

"O. Henry" was the pen name adopted by William Sydney Porter. He began his short story career by contributing *Whistling Dick's Christmas Stocking* to *McClure's Magazine* in 1899. He followed it with many stories dealing with Western and South- and Central-American life, and later came most of his stories of the life of New York City, in which field lies most of his best work. He contributed more stories to the *New York World* than to any other one publication—as if the stories of the author who later came to be hailed as "the American Maupassant" were not good enough for the "leading" magazines but fit only for the sensation-loving public of the Sunday papers! His first published story that showed distinct strength was perhaps *A Black- jack Bargainer* (August, 1901, *Munsey's*). He followed this with such masterly stories as: *The Duplicity of Hargraves* (February, 1902, *Junior Munsey*), *The Marionettes* (April, 1902, *Black Cat*), *A Retrieved Reformation* (April, 1903, *Cosmopolitan*), *The Guardian of the Accolade* (May, 1903, *Cosmopolitan*), *The Enchanted Kiss* (February, 1904, *Metropolitan*), *The Furnished Room* (August 14, 1904, *New York World*), *An Unfinished Story* (August, 1905, *McClure's*), *The Count and the Wedding Guest* (October 8, 1905, *New York World*), *The Gift of the Magi* (December 10, 1905, *New York World*), *The Trimmed Lamp* (August, 1906, *McClure's*), *Phoebe* (November, 1907, *Everybody's*), *The Hiding of Black Bill* (October, 1908, *Everybody's*), *No Story* (June, 1909, *Metropolitan*), *A Municipal Report* (November, 1909, *Hampton's*), *A Service of Love* (in *The Four Million*, 1909), *The Pendulum* (in *The Trimmed Lamp*, 1910), *Brickdust Row* (in *The Trimmed*

Lamp, 1910), and *The Assessor of Success* (in *The Trimmed Lamp*, 1910). Among O. Henry's best volumes of short stories are: *The Four Million* (1909), *Options* (1909), *Roads of Destiny* (1909), *The Trimmed Lamp* (1910), *Strictly Business: More Stories of the Four Million* (1910), *Whirligigs* (1910), and *Sixes and Sevens* (1911).

"Nowhere is there anything just like them. In his best work—and his tales of the great metropolis are his best—he is unique. The soul of his art is unexpectedness. Humor at every turn there is, and sentiment and philosophy and surprise. One never may be sure of himself. The end is always a sensation. No foresight may predict it, and the sensation always is genuine. Whatever else O. Henry was, he was an artist, a master of plot and diction, a genuine humorist, and a philosopher. His weakness lay in the very nature of his art. He was an entertainer bent only on amusing and surprising his reader. Everywhere brilliancy, but too often it is joined to cheapness; art, yet art merging swiftly into caricature. Like Harte, he cannot be trusted. Both writers on the whole may be said to have lowered the standards of American literature, since both worked in the surface of life with theatric intent and always without moral background, O. Henry moves, but he never lifts. All is fortissimo; he slaps the reader on the back and laughs loudly as if he were in a barroom. His characters, with few exceptions, are extremes, caricatures. Even his shop girls, in the limning of whom he did his best work, are not really individuals; rather are they types, symbols. His work was literary vaudeville, brilliant, highly amusing, and yet vaudeville."[9] *The Duplicity of Hargraves*, the story by O. Henry given in this volume, is free from most of his defects. It has a blend of humor and pathos that puts it on a plane of universal appeal.

George Randolph Chester (1869-) gained distinction by creating the genial modern business man of American literature who is not content to "get rich quick" through the ordinary channels. Need I say that I refer to that amazing compound of likeableness and sharp practices, Get-Rich-Quick Wallingford? The story of his included in this volume, *Bargain Day at Tutt House* (June, 1905, *McClure's*), was nearly his first story; only two others, which came out in *The Saturday Evening Post* in 1903 and 1904, preceded it. Its breathless dramatic action is well balanced by humor. Other stories of his deserving of special mention are: *A Corner in Farmers* (February,

---

9   Fred Lewis Pattee, in The Cambridge History of American Literature,
    Vol. II, p. 394.

29, 1908, *Saturday Evening Post*), *A Fortune in Smoke* (March 14, 1908, *Saturday Evening Post*), *Easy Money* (November 14, 1908, *Saturday Evening Post*), *The Triple Cross* (December 5, 1908, *Saturday Evening Post*), *Spoiling the Egyptians* (December 26, 1908, *Saturday Evening Post*), *Whipsawed!* (January 16, 1909, *Saturday Evening Post*), *The Bubble Bank* (January 30 and February 6, 1909, *Saturday Evening Post*), *Straight Business* (February 27, 1909, *Saturday Evening Post*), *Sam Turner: a Business Man's Love Story* (March 26, April 2 and 9, 1910, *Saturday Evening Post*), *Fundamental Justice* (July 25, 1914, *Saturday Evening Post*), *A Scropper Patcher* (October, 1916, *Everybody's*), and *Jolly Bachelors* (February, 1918, *Cosmopolitan*). His best collections are: *Get-Rich-Quick Wallingford* (1908), *Young Wallingford* (1910), *Wallingford in His Prime* (1913), and *Wallingford and Blackie Daw* (1913). It is often difficult to find in his books short stories that one may be looking for, for the reason that the titles of the individual stories have been removed in order to make the books look like novels subdivided into chapters.

Grace MacGowan Cooke (1863-) is a writer all of whose work has interest and perdurable stuff in it, but few are the authors whose achievements in the American short story stand out as a whole. In *A Call* (August, 1906, *Harper's*) she surpasses herself and is not perhaps herself surpassed by any of the humorous short stories that have come to the fore so far in America in the twentieth century. The story is no less delightful in its fidelity to fact and understanding of young human nature than in its relish of humor. Some of her stories deserving of special mention are: *The Capture of Andy Proudfoot* (June, 1904, *Harper's*), *In the Strength of the Hills* (December, 1905, *Metropolitan*), *The Machinations of Ocoee Gallantine* (April, 1906, *Century*), *A Call* (August, 1906, *Harper's*), *Scott Bohannon's Bond* (May 4, 1907, *Collier's*), and *A Clean Shave* (November, 1912, *Century*). Her best short stories do not seem to have been collected in volumes as yet, although she has had several notable long works of fiction published, such as *The Power and the Glory* (1910), and several good juveniles.

William James Lampton (?-1917), who was known to many of his admirers as Will Lampton or as W.J.L. merely, was one of the most unique and interesting characters of literary and Bohemian New York from about 1895 to his death in 1917. I remember walking up Fifth Avenue with him one Sunday afternoon just after he had shown me a letter from the man who was then Comptroller of the Currency. The letter was signed so illegibly that my companion was in doubts as to the sender, so he suggested that we stop at a well-known hotel at the corner of 59th Street, and ask the manager who the Comptroller of the Currency then was, so that he might know whom the letter was from. He said that the manager of a big hotel like that, where many prominent people stayed, would be sure to know. When this problem had been solved to our satisfaction, John Skelton Williams proving to be the man, Lampton said, "Now you've told me who he is, I'll show you who I am." So he asked for a copy of *The American Magazine* at a newsstand in the hotel corridor, opened it, and showed the manager a full-page picture of himself clad in a costume suggestive of the time of Christopher Columbus, with high ruffs around his neck, that happened to appear in the magazine the current month. I mention this incident to illustrate the lack of conventionality and whimsical originality of the man, that stood out no less forcibly in his writings than in his daily life. He had little use for "doing the usual thing in the usual sort of way." He first gained prominence by his book of verse, *Yawps* (1900). His poems were free from convention in technique as well as in spirit, although their chief innovation was simply that as a rule there was no regular number of syllables in a line; he let the lines be any length they wanted to be, to fit the sense or the length of what he had to say. He once said to me that if anything of his was remembered he thought it would be his poem, *Lo, the Summer Girl*. His muse often took the direction of satire, but it was always good-natured even when it hit the hardest. He had in his makeup much of the detached philosopher, like Cervantes and Mark Twain.

There was something cosmic about his attitude to life, and this showed in much that he did. He was the only American writer of humorous verse of his day whom I always cared to read, or whose lines I could remember more than a few weeks. This was perhaps because his work was never *merely* humorous, but always had a big sweep of background to it, like the ruggedness of the Kentucky mountains from which he came. It was Colonel George Harvey, then editor of *Harper's Weekly*, who had started the boom to make Woodrow Wilson President. Wilson afterwards, at least seemingly, repudiated his sponsor, probably because of Harvey's identification with various moneyed interests. Lampton's poem on the subject, with its refrain, "Never again, said Colonel George," I remember as one of the most notable of his poems on current topics. But what always seemed to me the best of his poems dealing with matters of the hour was one that I suggested he write, which dealt with gift-giving to the public, at about the time that Andrew Carnegie was making a big stir with his gifts for libraries, beginning:

> Dunno, perhaps
> One of the yaps
> Like me would make
> A holy break
> Doing his turn
> With money to burn.
>   Anyhow, I
>   Wouldn't shy
>   Making a try!

and containing, among many effective touches, the pathetic lines,

> ... I'd help
> The poor who try to help themselves,
> Who have to work so hard for bread
> They can't get very far ahead.

When James Lane Allen's novel, *The Reign of Law*, came out (1900), a little quatrain by Lampton that appeared in *The Bookman* (September, 1900) swept like wildfire across the country, and was read by a hundred times as many people as the book itself:

> "The Reign of Law"?
>   Well, Allen, you're lucky;
> It's the first time it ever
>   Rained law in Kentucky!

The reader need not be reminded that at that period Kentucky family feuds were well to the fore. As Lampton had started as a poet, the editors were bound to keep him pigeon-holed as far as they could, and his ambition to write short stories was not at first much encouraged by them. His predicament was something like that of the chief character of Frank R. Stockton's story, "*His Wife's Deceased Sister*" (January, 1884, *Century*), who had written a story so good that whenever he brought the editors another story they invariably answered in substance, "We're afraid it won't do. Can't you give us something like '*His Wife's Deceased Sister*'?" This was merely Stockton's turning to account his own somewhat similar experience with the editors after his story, *The Lady or the Tiger?* (November, 1882, *Century*) appeared. Likewise the editors didn't want Lampton's short stories for a while because they liked his poems so well.

Do I hear some critics exclaiming that there is nothing remarkable about *How the Widow Won the Deacon*, the story by Lampton included in this volume? It handles an amusing situation lightly and with grace. It is one of those things that read easily and are often difficult to achieve. Among his best stories are: *The People's Number of the Worthyville Watchman* (May 12, 1900, *Saturday Evening Post*), *Love's Strange Spell* (April 27, 1901, *Saturday Evening Post*), *Abimelech Higgins' Way* (August 24, 1001, *Saturday Evening Post*), *A Cup of Tea* (March, 1902, *Metropolitan*), *Winning His Spurs* (May, 1904, *Cosmopolitan*), *The Perfidy of Major Pulsifer* (November, 1909, *Cosmopolitan*), *How the Widow Won the Deacon* (April, 1911, *Harper's Bazaar*), and *A Brown Study* (December, 1913, *Lippincott's*). There is no collection as yet of his short stories. Although familiarly known as "Colonel" Lampton, and although of Kentucky, he was not merely a "Kentucky Colonel," for he was actually appointed Colonel on the staff of the governor of Kentucky. At the time of his death he was about to be made a brigadier-general and was planning to raise a brigade of Kentucky mountaineers for service in the Great War. As he had just struck his stride in short story writing, the loss to literature was even greater than the patriotic loss.

Gideon (April, 1914, *Century*), by Wells Hastings (1878-), the story with which this volume closes, calls to mind the large number of notable short stories in American literature by writers who have made no large name for themselves as short story writers, or even otherwise in letters. American literature has always been strong in its "stray" short stories of note. In Mr. Hastings' case, however, I feel that the fame is sure to come. He graduated from Yale in 1902, collaborated with Brian

Hooker (1880-) in a novel, *The Professor's Mystery* (1911) and alone wrote another novel, *The Man in the Brown Derby* (1911). His short stories include: *The New Little Boy* (July, 1911, *American*), *That Day* (September, 1911, *American*), *The Pick-Up* (December, 1911, *Everybody's*), and *Gideon* (April, 1914, *Century*). The last story stands out. It can be compared without disadvantage to the best work, or all but the very best work, of Thomas Nelson Page, it seems to me. And from the reader's standpoint it has the advantage—is this not also an author's advantage?—of a more modern setting and treatment. Mr. Hastings is, I have been told, a director in over a dozen large corporations. Let us hope that his business activities will not keep him too much away from the production of literature—for to rank as a piece of literature, something of permanent literary value, *Gideon* is surely entitled.

ALEXANDER JESSUP.

ACKNOWLEDGMENTS

The Nice People, by Henry Cuyler Bunner, is republished from his volume, *Short Sixes*, by permission of its publishers, Charles Scribner's Sons. *The Buller-Podington Compact*, by Frank Richard Stockton, is from his volume, *Afield and Afloat*, and is republished by permission of Charles Scribner's Sons. *Colonel Starbottle for the Plaintiff*, by Bret Harte, is from the collection of his stories entitled *Openings in the Old Trail*, and is republished by permission of the Houghton Mifflin Company, the authorized publishers of Bret Harte's complete works. *The Duplicity of Hargraves*, by O. Henry, is from his volume, *Sixes and Sevens*, and is republished by permission of its publishers, Doubleday, Page & Co. These stories are fully protected by copyright, and should not be republished except by permission of the publishers mentioned. Thanks are due Mrs. Grace MacGowan Cooke for permission to use her story, *A Call*, republished here from *Harper's Magazine*; Wells Hastings, for permission to reprint his story, *Gideon*, from *The Century Magazine*; and George Randolph Chester, for permission to include *Bargain Day at Tutt House*, from *McClure's Magazine*. I would also thank the heirs of the late lamented Colonel William J. Lampton for permission to use his story, *How the Widow Won the Deacon*, from *Harper's Bazaar*. These stories are all copyrighted, and cannot be republished except by authorization of their authors or heirs. The editor regrets that their publishers have seen fit to refuse him permission to include George W. Cable's story, "*Posson Jone'*," and Irvin S. Cobb's story, *The Smart Aleck*. He also regrets he was unable to obtain a copy of Joseph C. Duport's story, *The Wedding at Timber Hollow*, in time for inclusion, to which its merits—as he remembers them—certainly entitle it. Mr. Duport, in addition to his literary activities, has started an interesting "back to Nature" experiment at Westfield, Massachusetts.

*   *   *   *   *

To: CHARLES GOODRICH WHITING, Critic, Poet, Friend

THE LITTLE FRENCHMAN AND HIS WATER LOTS
By George Pope Morris (1802-1864)

[From *The Little Frenchman and His Water Lots, with Other Sketches of the Times* (1839),
by George Pope Morris.]

Look into those they call unfortunate,
And, closer view'd, you'll find they are unwise.— Young.

Let wealth come in by comely thrift,
And not by any foolish shift:
   'Tis haste
   Makes waste:
Who gripes too hard the dry and slippery sand
Holds none at all, or little, in his hand.— *Herrick*.

Let well alone.— *Proverb*.

HOW much real comfort every one might enjoy if he would be content-ed with the lot in which heaven has cast him, and how much trouble would be avoided if people would only "let well alone." A moderate independence, quietly and honestly procured, is certainly every way preferable even to immense possessions achieved by the wear and tear of mind and body so necessary to procure them. Yet there are very few individuals, let them be doing ever so well in the world, who are not always straining every nerve to do better; and this is one of the many causes why failures in business so frequently oc-cur among us. The present generation seem unwilling to "realize" by slow and sure degrees; but choose rather to set their whole hopes upon a single cast, which either makes or mars them forever!

Gentle reader, do you remember Monsieur Poopoo? He used to keep a small toy-store in Chatham, near the corner of Pearl Street. You must recollect him, of course. He lived there for many years, and was one of the most polite and accom-modating of shopkeepers. When a juvenile, you have bought tops and marbles of him a thousand times. To be sure you have; and seen his vinegar-visage lighted up with a smile as you flung him the coppers; and you have laughed at his little straight queue and his dimity breeches, and all the other oddities that made up the every-day apparel of my little Frenchman. Ah, I perceive you recollect him now.

Well, then, there lived Monsieur Poopoo ever since he came from "dear, de-lightful Paris," as he was wont to call the city of his nativity—there he took in the pennies for his kickshaws—there he laid aside five thousand dollars against a rainy day—there he was as happy as a lark—and there, in all human probability, he would have been to this very day, a respected and substantial citizen, had he been willing to "let well alone." But Monsieur Poopoo had heard strange stories about the prodigious rise in real estate; and, having understood that most of his neighbors had become suddenly rich by speculating in lots, he instantly grew dissatisfied with his own lot, forthwith determined to shut up shop, turn everything into cash, and set about making money in right-down earnest. No sooner said than done; and our quondam storekeeper a few days afterward attended an extensive sale of real estate, at the Merchants' Exchange.

There was the auctioneer, with his beautiful and inviting lithographic maps—all the lots as smooth and square and enticingly laid out as possible—and there were the speculators—and there, in the midst of them, stood Monsieur Poopoo.

"Here they are, gentlemen," said he of the hammer, "the most valuable lots ever offered for sale. Give me a bid for them!"

"One hundred each," said a bystander.

"One hundred!" said the auctioneer, "scarcely enough to pay for the maps. One hundred—going—and fifty—gone! Mr. H., they are yours. A noble purchase. You'll sell those same lots in less than a fortnight for fifty thousand dollars profit!"

Monsieur Poopoo pricked up his ears at this, and was lost in astonishment. This was a much easier way certainly of accumulating riches than selling toys in Chatham Street, and he determined to buy and mend his fortune without delay.

The auctioneer proceeded in his sale. Other parcels were offered and disposed of, and all the purchasers were promised immense advantages for their enterprise. At last came a more valuable parcel than all the rest. The company pressed around the stand, and Monsieur Poopoo did the same.

"I now offer you, gentlemen, these magnificent lots, delightfully situated on Long Island, with valuable water privileges. Property in fee—title indisputable—terms of sale, cash—deeds ready for delivery immediately after the sale. How much for them? Give them a start at something. How much?" The auctioneer looked around; there were no bidders. At last he caught the eye of Monsieur Poopoo. "Did you say one hundred, sir? Beautiful lots—valuable water privileges—shall I say one hundred for you?"

"*Oui, monsieur*; I will give you von hundred dollar apiece, for de lot vid de valu-arble vatare privalege; *c'est ca*."

"Only one hundred apiece for these sixty valuable lots—only one hundred—going—going—going—gone!"

Monsieur Poopoo was the fortunate possessor. The auctioneer congratulated him—the sale closed—and the company dispersed.

"*Pardonnez-moi, monsieur*," said Poopoo, as the auctioneer descended his pedestal, "you shall *excusez-moi*, if I shall go to *votre bureau*, your counting-house, ver quick to make every ting sure wid respec to de lot vid de valuarble vatare privalege. Von leetle bird in de hand he vorth two in de tree, *c'est vrai*—eh?"

"Certainly, sir."

"Vell den, *allons*."

And the gentlemen repaired to the counting-house, where the six thousand dollars were paid, and the deeds of the property delivered. Monsieur Poopoo put these carefully in his pocket, and as he was about taking his leave, the auctioneer made him a present of the lithographic outline of the lots, which was a very liberal thing on his part, considering the map was a beautiful specimen of that glorious art. Poopoo could not admire it sufficiently. There were his sixty lots, as uniform as possible, and his little gray eyes sparkled like diamonds as they wandered from one end of the spacious sheet to the other.

Poopoo's heart was as light as a feather, and he snapped his fingers in the very wantonness of joy as he repaired to Delmonico's, and ordered the first good French dinner that had gladdened his palate since his arrival in America.

After having discussed his repast, and washed it down with a bottle of choice old claret, he resolved upon a visit to Long Island to view his purchase. He consequently immediately hired a horse and gig, crossed the Brooklyn ferry, and drove along the margin of the river to the Wallabout, the location in question.

Our friend, however, was not a little perplexed to find his property. Everything on the map was as fair and even as possible, while all the grounds about him were as undulated as they could well be imagined, and there was an elbow of the East River thrusting itself quite into the ribs of the land, which seemed to have no business there. This puzzled the Frenchman exceedingly; and, being a stranger in those parts, he called to a farmer in an adjacent field.

"*Mon ami*, are you acquaint vid dis part of de country—eh?"

"Yes, I was born here, and know every inch of it."

"Ah, *c'est bien*, dat vill do," and the Frenchman got out of the gig, tied the horse, and produced his lithographic map.

"Den maybe you vill have de kindness to show me de sixty lot vich I have bought, vid de valuarble vatere privalege?"

The farmer glanced his eye over the paper.

"Yes, sir, with pleasure; if you will be good enough to *get into my boat, I will row you out to them*!"

"Vat dat you say, sure?"

"My friend," said the farmer, "this section of Long Island has recently been bought up by the speculators of New York, and laid out for a great city; but the principal street is only visible *at low tide*. When this part of the East River is filled up, it will be just there. Your lots, as you will perceive, are beyond it; *and are now all under water*."

At first the Frenchman was incredulous. He could not believe his senses. As the facts, however, gradually broke upon him, he shut one eye, squinted obliquely at the heavens—-the river—the farmer—and then he turned away and squinted at them all over again! There was his purchase sure enough; but then it could not be perceived for there was a river flowing over it! He drew a box from his waistcoat pocket, opened it, with an emphatic knock upon the lid, took a pinch of snuff and restored it to his waistcoat pocket as before. Poopoo was evidently in trouble, having "thoughts which often lie too deep for tears"; and, as his grief was also too big for words, he untied his horse, jumped into his gig, and returned to the auctioneer in hot haste.

It was near night when he arrived at the auction-room—his horse in a foam and himself in a fury. The auctioneer was leaning back in his chair, with his legs stuck out of a low window, quietly smoking a cigar after the labors of the day, and humming the music from the last new opera.

"Monsieur, I have much plaisir to fin' you, *chez vous*, at home."

"Ah, Poopoo! glad to see you. Take a seat, old boy."

"But I shall not take de seat, sare."

"No—why, what's the matter?"

"Oh, *beaucoup* de matter. I have been to see de gran lot vot you sell me to-day."

"Well, sir, I hope you like your purchase?"

"No, monsieur, I no like him."

"I'm sorry for it; but there is no ground for your complaint."

"No, sare; dare is no *ground* at all—de ground is all vatare!"

"You joke!"

"I no joke. I nevare joke; *je n'entends pas la raillerie*, Sare, *voulez-vous* have de kindness to give me back de money vot I pay!"

"Certainly not."

"Den vill you be so good as to take de East River off de top of my lot?"

"That's your business, sir, not mine."

"Den I make von *mauvaise affaire*—von gran mistake!"

"I hope not. I don't think you have thrown your money away in the *land*."

"No, sare; but I tro it avay in de *vatare!*"

"That's not my fault."

"Yes, sare, but it is your fault. You're von ver gran rascal to swindle me out of *de l'argent*."

"Hello, old Poopoo, you grow personal; and if you can't keep a civil tongue in your head, you must go out of my counting-room."

"Vare shall I go to, eh?"

"To the devil, for aught I care, you foolish old Frenchman!" said the auctioneer, waxing warm.

"But, sare, I vill not go to de devil to oblige you!" replied the Frenchman, waxing warmer. "You sheat me out of all de dollar vot I make in Shatham Street; but I vill not go to de devil for all dat. I vish you may go to de devil yourself you dem yankee-doo-dell, and I vill go and drown myself, *tout de suite*, right avay."

"You couldn't make a better use of your water privileges, old boy!"

"Ah, *misericorde!* Ah, *mon dieu, je suis abime*. I am ruin! I am done up! I am break all into ten sousan leetle pieces! I am von lame duck, and I shall vaddle across de gran ocean for Paris, vish is de only valuarble vatare privalege dat is left me *a present!*"

Poor Poopoo was as good as his word. He sailed in the next packet, and arrived in Paris almost as penniless as the day he left it.

Should any one feel disposed to doubt the veritable circumstances here recorded, let him cross the East River to the Wallabout, and farmer J—— will *row him out* to the very place where the poor Frenchman's lots still remain *under water*.

THE ANGEL OF THE ODD
By Edgar Allan Poe (1809-1849)

[From *The Columbian Magazine*, October, 1844.]

IT was a chilly November afternoon. I had just consummated an unusually hearty dinner, of which the dyspeptic *truffe* formed not the least important item, and was sitting alone in the dining-room with my feet upon the fender and at my elbow a small table which I had rolled up to the fire, and upon which were some apologies for dessert, with some miscellaneous bottles of wine, spirit, and *liqueur*. In the morning I had been reading Glover's *Leonidas*, Wilkie's *Epigoniad*, Lamartine's *Pilgrimage*, Barlow's *Columbiad*, Tuckerman's *Sicily*, and Griswold's *Curiosities*, I am willing to confess, therefore, that I now felt a little stupid. I made effort to arouse myself by frequent aid of Lafitte, and all failing, I betook myself to a stray newspaper in despair. Having carefully perused the column of "Houses to let," and the column of "Dogs lost," and then the columns of "Wives and apprentices runaway," I attacked with great resolution the editorial matter, and reading it from beginning to end without understanding a syllable, conceived the possibility of its being Chinese, and so re-read it from the end to the beginning, but with no more satisfactory result. I was about throwing away in disgust

> This folio of four pages, happy work
> Which not even critics criticise,

when I felt my attention somewhat aroused by the paragraph which follows:

"The avenues to death are numerous and strange. A London paper mentions the decease of a person from a singular cause. He was playing at 'puff the dart,' which is played with a long needle inserted in some worsted, and blown at a target through a tin tube. He placed the needle at the wrong end of the tube, and drawing his breath strongly to puff the dart forward with force, drew the needle into his throat. It entered the lungs, and in a few days killed him."

Upon seeing this I fell into a great rage, without exactly knowing why. "This thing," I exclaimed, "is a contemptible falsehood—a poor hoax—the lees of the invention of some pitiable penny-a-liner, of some wretched concocter of accidents in Cocaigne. These fellows knowing the extravagant gullibility of the age set their wits to work in the imagination of improbable possibilities, of odd accidents as they term them, but to a reflecting intellect (like mine, I added, in parenthesis, putting my forefinger unconsciously to the side of my nose), to a contemplative understanding such as I myself possess, it seems evident at once that the marvelous increase of late in these 'odd accidents' is by far the oddest accident of all. For my own part, I intend to believe nothing henceforward that has anything of the 'singular' about it."

"Mein Gott, den, vat a vool you bees for dat!" replied one of the most remarkable voices I ever heard. At first I took it for a rumbling in my ears—such as a man sometimes experiences when getting very drunk—but upon second thought, I considered the sound as more nearly resembling that which proceeds from an empty barrel beaten with a big stick; and, in fact, this I should have concluded it to be, but for the articulation of the syllables and words. I am by no means naturally nervous, and the very few glasses of Lafitte which I had sipped served to embolden me a little, so that I felt nothing of trepidation, but merely uplifted my eyes with a leisurely movement and looked carefully around the room for the intruder. I could not, however, perceive any one at all.

"Humph!" resumed the voice as I continued my survey, "you mus pe so dronk as de pig den for not zee me as I zit here at your zide."

Hereupon I bethought me of looking immediately before my nose, and there, sure enough, confronting me at the table sat a personage nondescript, although not altogether indescribable. His body was a wine-pipe or a rum puncheon, or something of that character, and had a truly Falstaffian air. In its nether extremity were inserted two kegs, which seemed to answer all the purposes of legs. For arms there dangled from the upper portion of the carcass two tolerably long bottles with the necks outward for hands. All the head that I saw the monster possessed of was one of those Hessian canteens which resemble a large snuff-box with a hole in the middle of the lid. This canteen (with a funnel on its top like a cavalier cap slouched over the eyes) was set on edge upon the puncheon, with the hole toward myself; and through this hole, which seemed puckered up like the mouth of a very precise old maid, the creature was emitting certain rumbling and grumbling noises which he evidently intended for intelligible talk.

"I zay," said he, "you mos pe dronk as de pig, vor zit dare and not zee me zit ere; and I zay, doo, you mos pe pigger vool as de goose, vor to dispelief vat iz print in de print. 'Tiz de troof—dat it iz—ebery vord ob it."

"Who are you, pray?" said I with much dignity, although somewhat puzzled; "how did you get here? and what is it you are talking about?"

"As vor ow I com'd ere," replied the figure, "dat iz none of your pizziness; and as vor vat I be talking apout, I be talk apout vat I tink proper; and as vor who I be, vy dat is de very ting I com'd here for to let you zee for yourself."

"You are a drunken vagabond," said I, "and I shall ring the bell and order my footman to kick you into the street."

"He! he! he!" said the fellow, "hu! hu! hu! dat you can't do."

"Can't do!" said I, "what do you mean? I can't do what?"

"Ring de pell," he replied, attempting a grin with his little villainous mouth.

Upon this I made an effort to get up in order to put my threat into execution, but the ruffian just reached across the table very deliberately, and hitting me a tap on the forehead with the neck of one of the long bottles, knocked me back into the armchair from which I had half arisen. I was utterly astounded, and for a moment was quite at a loss what to do. In the meantime he continued his talk.

"You zee," said he, "it iz te bess vor zit still; and now you shall know who I pe. Look at me! zee! I am te *Angel ov te Odd*."

"And odd enough, too," I ventured to reply; "but I was always under the impression that an angel had wings."

"Te wing!" he cried, highly incensed, "vat I pe do mit te wing? Mein Gott! do you take me for a shicken?"

"No—oh, no!" I replied, much alarmed; "you are no chicken—certainly not."

"Well, den, zit still and pehabe yourself, or I'll rap you again mid me vist. It iz te shicken ab te wing, und te owl ab te wing, und te imp ab te wing, und te head-teuffel ab te wing. Te angel ab *not* te wing, and I am te *Angel ov te Odd*."

"And your business with me at present is—is——"

"My pizziness!" ejaculated the thing, "vy vat a low-bred puppy you mos pe vor to ask a gentleman und an angel apout his pizziness!"

This language was rather more than I could bear, even from an angel; so, pluck-ing up courage, I seized a salt-cellar which lay within reach, and hurled it at the head of the intruder. Either he dodged, however, or my aim was inaccurate; for all I accomplished was the demolition of the crystal which protected the dial of the clock upon the mantelpiece. As for the Angel, he evinced his sense of my assault by giving me two or three hard, consecutive raps upon the forehead as before. These reduced me at once to submission, and I am almost ashamed to confess that, either through pain or vexation, there came a few tears into my eyes.

"Mein Gott!" said the Angel of the Odd, apparently much softened at my dis-tress; "mein Gott, te man is eder ferry dronk or ferry zorry. You mos not trink it so strong—you mos put te water in te wine. Here, trink dis, like a good veller, and don't gry now—don't!"

Hereupon the Angel of the Odd replenished my goblet (which was about a third full of port) with a colorless fluid that he poured from one of his hand-bottles. I observed that these bottles had labels about their necks, and that these labels were inscribed "Kirschenwaesser."

The considerate kindness of the Angel mollified me in no little measure; and, aided by the water with which he diluted my port more than once, I at length re-gained sufficient temper to listen to his very extraordinary discourse. I cannot pre-tend to recount all that he told me, but I gleaned from what he said that he was a genius who presided over the *contretemps* of mankind, and whose business it was to bring about the *odd accidents* which are continually astonishing the skeptic. Once or twice, upon my venturing to express my total incredulity in respect to his preten-sions, he grew very angry indeed, so that at length I considered it the wiser policy to say nothing at all, and let him have his own way. He talked on, therefore, at great length, while I merely leaned back in my chair with my eyes shut, and amused my-self with munching raisins and filiping the stems about the room. But, by and by, the Angel suddenly construed this behavior of mine into contempt. He arose in a terrible passion, slouched his funnel down over his eyes, swore a vast oath, uttered a threat of some character, which I did not precisely comprehend, and finally made me a low bow and departed, wishing me, in the language of the archbishop in "Gil Bias," *beaucoup de bonheur et un peu plus de bon sens*.

His departure afforded me relief. The *very* few glasses of Lafitte that I had sipped had the effect of rendering me drowsy, and I felt inclined to take a nap of some fifteen or twenty minutes, as is my custom after dinner. At six I had an appointment of consequence, which it was quite indispensable that I should keep. The policy of insurance for my dwelling-house had expired the day before; and some dispute having arisen it was agreed that, at six, I should meet the board of directors of the company and settle the terms of a renewal. Glancing upward at the clock on the mantelpiece (for I felt too drowsy to take out my watch), I had the pleasure to find that I had still twenty-five minutes to spare. It was half-past five; I could easily walk to the insurance office in five minutes; and my usual siestas had never been known to exceed five-and-twenty. I felt sufficiently safe, therefore, and composed myself to my slumbers forthwith.

Having completed them to my satisfaction, I again looked toward the time-piece, and was half inclined to believe in the possibility of odd accidents when I found that, instead of my ordinary fifteen or twenty minutes, I had been dozing only three; for it still wanted seven-and-twenty of the appointed hour. I betook myself again to my nap, and at length a second time awoke, when, to my utter amazement, it still wanted twenty-seven minutes of six. I jumped up to examine the clock, and found that it had ceased running. My watch informed me that it was half-past seven; and, of course, having slept two hours, I was too late for my appointment. "It will make no difference," I said: "I can call at the office in the morning and apologize; in the meantime what can be the matter with the clock?" Upon examining it I discovered that one of the raisin stems which I had been fliping about the room during the discourse of the Angel of the Odd had flown through the fractured crystal, and lodging, singularly enough, in the keyhole, with an end projecting outward, had thus arrested the revolution of the minute hand.

"Ah!" said I, "I see how it is. This thing speaks for itself. A natural accident, such as will happen now and then!"

I gave the matter no further consideration, and at my usual hour retired to bed. Here, having placed a candle upon a reading stand at the bed head, and having made an attempt to peruse some pages of the *Omnipresence of the Deity*, I unfortunately fell asleep in less than twenty seconds, leaving the light burning as it was.

My dreams were terrifically disturbed by visions of the Angel of the Odd. Methought he stood at the foot of the couch, drew aside the curtains, and in the hollow, detestable tones of a rum puncheon, menaced me with the bitterest vengeance for the contempt with which I had treated him. He concluded a long harangue by taking off his funnel-cap, inserting the tube into my gullet, and thus deluging me with an ocean of Kirschenwaesser, which he poured in a continuous flood, from one of the long-necked bottles that stood him instead of an arm. My agony was at length insufferable, and I awoke just in time to perceive that a rat had run off with the lighted candle from the stand, but *not* in season to prevent his making his escape with it through the hole, Very soon a strong, suffocating odor assailed my nostrils; the house, I clearly perceived, was on fire. In a few minutes the blaze broke forth with violence, and in an incredibly brief period the entire building was wrapped in flames. All egress from my chamber, except through a window, was cut off. The crowd, however, quickly procured and raised a long ladder. By means of this I was descending rapidly, and in apparent safety, when a huge hog, about whose rotund stomach, and indeed about whose whole air and physiognomy, there was something which reminded me of the Angel of the Odd—when this hog, I say, which hitherto had been quietly slumbering in the mud, took it suddenly into his head that his left shoulder needed scratching, and could find no more convenient rubbing-post than that afforded by the foot of the ladder. In an instant I was precipitated, and had the misfortune to fracture my arm.

This accident, with the loss of my insurance, and with the more serious loss of my hair, the whole of which had been singed off by the fire, predisposed me to serious impressions, so that finally I made up my mind to take a wife. There was a rich widow disconsolate for the loss of her seventh husband, and to her wounded spirit I offered the balm of my vows. She yielded a reluctant consent to my prayers. I knelt at her feet in gratitude and adoration. She blushed and bowed her luxuriant tresses into close contact with those supplied me temporarily by Grandjean. I know not how the entanglement took place but so it was. I arose with a shining pate, wigless; she in disdain and wrath, half-buried in alien hair. Thus ended my hopes of the widow by an accident which could not have been anticipated, to be sure, but which the natural sequence of events had brought about.

Without despairing, however, I undertook the siege of a less implacable heart. The fates were again propitious for a brief period, but again a trivial incident interfered. Meeting my betrothed in an avenue thronged with the elite of the city, I was hastening to greet her with one of my best considered bows, when a small particle of some foreign matter lodging in the corner of my eye rendered me for the moment completely blind. Before I could recover my sight, the lady of my love had disappeared—irreparably affronted at what she chose to consider my premeditated rudeness in passing her by ungreeted. While I stood bewildered at the suddenness of this accident (which might have happened, nevertheless, to any one under the sun), and while I still continued incapable of sight, I was accosted by the Angel of the Odd, who proffered me his aid with a civility which I had no reason to expect. He examined my disordered eye with much gentleness and skill, informed me that I had a drop in it, and (whatever a "drop" was) took it out, and afforded me relief.

I now considered it high time to die (since fortune had so determined to persecute me), and accordingly made my way to the nearest river. Here, divesting myself of my clothes (for there is no reason why we cannot die as we were born), I threw myself headlong into the current; the sole witness of my fate being a solitary crow that had been seduced into the eating of brandy-saturated corn, and so had staggered away from his fellows. No sooner had I entered the water than this bird took it into his head to fly away with the most indispensable portion of my apparel. Postponing, therefore, for the present, my suicidal design, I just slipped my nether extremities into the sleeves of my coat, and betook myself to a pursuit of the felon with all the nimbleness which the case required and its circumstances would admit. But my evil destiny attended me still. As I ran at full speed, with my nose up in the atmosphere, and intent only upon the purloiner of my property, I suddenly perceived that my feet rested no longer upon *terra firma*; the fact is, I had thrown myself over a precipice, and should inevitably have been dashed to pieces but for my good fortune in grasping the end of a long guide-rope, which depended from a passing balloon.

As soon as I sufficiently recovered my senses to comprehend the terrific predicament in which I stood, or rather hung, I exerted all the power of my lungs to make that predicament known to the aeronaut overhead. But for a long time I exerted myself in vain. Either the fool could not, or the villain would not perceive me. Meanwhile the machine rapidly soared, while my strength even more rapidly failed. I was soon upon the point of resigning myself to my fate, and dropping quietly into the sea, when my spirits were suddenly revived by hearing a hollow voice from above, which seemed to be lazily humming an opera air. Looking up, I perceived the Angel of the Odd. He was leaning, with his arms folded, over the rim of the car; and with a pipe in his mouth, at which he puffed leisurely, seemed to be upon excellent terms with himself and the universe. I was too much exhausted to speak, so I merely regarded him with an imploring air.

For several minutes, although he looked me full in the face, he said nothing. At length, removing carefully his meerschaum from the right to the left corner of his mouth, he condescended to speak.

"Who pe you," he asked, "und what der teuffel you pe do dare?"

To this piece of impudence, cruelty, and affectation, I could reply only by ejaculating the monosyllable "Help!"

"Elp!" echoed the ruffian, "not I. Dare iz te pottle—elp yourself, und pe tam'd!"

With these words he let fall a heavy bottle of Kirschenwaesser, which, dropping precisely upon the crown of my head, caused me to imagine that my brains were entirely knocked out. Impressed with this idea I was about to relinquish my hold and give up the ghost with a good grace, when I was arrested by the cry of the Angel, who bade me hold on.

"'Old on!" he said: "don't pe in te 'urry—don't. Will you pe take de odder pottle, or 'ave you pe got zober yet, and come to your zenzes?"

I made haste, hereupon, to nod my head twice—once in the negative, meaning thereby that I would prefer not taking the other bottle at present; and once in the affirmative, intending thus to imply that I *was* sober and *had* positively come to my senses. By these means I somewhat softened the Angel.

"Und you pelief, ten," he inquired, "at te last? You pelief, ten, in te possibility of te odd?"

I again nodded my head in assent.

"Und you ave pelief in *me*, te Angel of te Odd?"

I nodded again.

"Und you acknowledge tat you pe te blind dronk und te vool?"

I nodded once more.

"Put your right hand into your left preeches pocket, ten, in token ov your vull zubmizzion unto te Angel ov te Odd."

This thing, for very obvious reasons, I found it quite impossible to do. In the first place, my left arm had been broken in my fall from the ladder, and therefore, had I let go my hold with the right hand I must have let go altogether. In the second place, I could have no breeches until I came across the crow. I was therefore obliged, much to my regret, to shake my head in the negative, intending thus to give the Angel to understand that I found it inconvenient, just at that moment, to comply with his very reasonable demand! No sooner, however, had I ceased shaking my head than—

"Go to der teuffel, ten!" roared the Angel of the Odd.

In pronouncing these words he drew a sharp knife across the guide-rope by which I was suspended, and as we then happened to be precisely over my own house (which, during my peregrinations, had been handsomely rebuilt), it so occurred that I tumbled headlong down the ample chimney and alit upon the dining-room hearth.

Upon coming to my senses (for the fall had very thoroughly stunned me) I found it about four o'clock in the morning. I lay outstretched where I had fallen from the balloon. My head groveled in the ashes of an extinguished fire, while my feet reposed upon the wreck of a small table, overthrown, and amid the fragments of a miscellaneous dessert, intermingled with a newspaper, some broken glasses and shattered bottles, and an empty jug of the Schiedam Kirschenwaesser. Thus revenged himself the Angel of the Odd.

THE SCHOOLMASTER'S PROGRESS
By Caroline M.S. Kirkland (1801-1864)

[From *The Gift* for 1845, published late in 1844. Republished in the volume, *Western Clearings* (1845), by Caroline M.S. Kirkland.]

MASTER William Horner came to our village to school when he was about eighteen years old: tall, lank, straight-sided, and straight-haired, with a mouth of the most puckered and solemn kind. His figure and movements were those of a puppet cut out of shingle and jerked by a string; and his address corresponded very well with his appearance. Never did that prim mouth give way before a laugh. A faint and misty smile was the widest departure from its propriety, and this unaccustomed disturbance made wrinkles in the flat, skinny cheeks like those in the surface of a lake, after the intrusion of a stone. Master Horner knew well what belonged to the pedagogical character, and that facial solemnity stood high on the list of indispensable qualifications. He had made up his mind before he left his father's house how he would look during the term. He had not planned any smiles (knowing that he must "board round"), and it was not for ordinary occurrences to alter his arrangements; so that when he was betrayed into a relaxation of the muscles, it was "in such a sort" as if he was putting his bread and butter in jeopardy.

Truly he had a grave time that first winter. The rod of power was new to him, and he felt it his "duty" to use it more frequently than might have been thought necessary by those upon whose sense the privilege had palled. Tears and sulky faces, and impotent fists doubled fiercely when his back was turned, were the rewards of his conscientiousness; and the boys—and girls too—were glad when working time came round again, and the master went home to help his father on the farm.

But with the autumn came Master Horner again, dropping among us as quietly as the faded leaves, and awakening at least as much serious reflection. Would he be as self-sacrificing as before, postponing his own ease and comfort to the public good, or would he have become more sedentary, and less fond of circumambulating the school-room with a switch over his shoulder? Many were fain to hope he might have learned to smoke during the summer, an accomplishment which would probably have moderated his energy not a little, and disposed him rather to reverie than to action. But here he was, and all the broader-chested and stouter-armed for his labors in the harvest-field.

Let it not be supposed that Master Horner was of a cruel and ogrish nature—a babe-eater—a Herod—one who delighted in torturing the helpless. Such souls there may be, among those endowed with the awful control of the ferule, but they are rare in the fresh and natural regions we describe. It is, we believe, where young gentlemen are to be crammed for college, that the process of hardening heart and skin together goes on most vigorously. Yet among the uneducated there is so high a respect for bodily strength, that it is necessary for the schoolmaster to show, first of all, that he possesses this inadmissible requisite for his place. The rest is more readily taken for granted. Brains he *may* have—a strong arm he *must* have: so he proves the more important claim first. We must therefore make all due allowance for Master Horner, who could not be expected to overtop his position so far as to discern at once the philosophy of teaching.

He was sadly brow-beaten during his first term of service by a great broad-shouldered lout of some eighteen years or so, who thought he needed a little more "schooling," but at the same time felt quite competent to direct the manner and measure of his attempts.

"You'd ought to begin with large-hand, Joshuay," said Master Horner to this youth.

"What should I want coarse-hand for?" said the disciple, with great contempt; "coarse-hand won't never do me no good. I want a fine-hand copy."

The master looked at the infant giant, and did as he wished, but we say not with what secret resolutions.

At another time, Master Horner, having had a hint from some one more knowing than himself, proposed to his elder scholars to write after dictation, expatiating at the same time quite floridly (the ideas having been supplied by the knowing friend), upon the advantages likely to arise from this practice, and saying, among other things,

"It will help you, when you write letters, to spell the words good."

"Pooh!" said Joshua, "spellin' ain't nothin'; let them that finds the mistakes correct 'em. I'm for every one's havin' a way of their own."

"How dared you be so saucy to the master?" asked one of the little boys, after school.

"Because I could lick him, easy," said the hopeful Joshua, who knew very well why the master did not undertake him on the spot.

Can we wonder that Master Horner determined to make his empire good as far as it went?

A new examination was required on the entrance into a second term, and, with whatever secret trepidation, the master was obliged to submit. Our law prescribes examinations, but forgets to provide for the competency of the examiners; so that few better farces offer than the course of question and answer on these occasions. We know not precisely what were Master Horner's trials; but we have heard of a sharp dispute between the inspectors whether a-n-g-e-l spelt *angle* or *angel*. *Angle* had it, and the school maintained that pronunciation ever after. Master Horner passed, and he was requested to draw up the certificate for the inspectors to sign, as one had left his spectacles at home, and the other had a bad cold, so that it was not convenient for either to write more than his name. Master Homer's exhibition of learning on this occasion did not reach us, but we know that it must have been considerable, since he stood the ordeal.

"What is orthography?" said an inspector once, in our presence.

The candidate writhed a good deal, studied the beams overhead and the chickens out of the window, and then replied,

"It is so long since I learnt the first part of the spelling-book, that I can't justly answer that question. But if I could just look it over, I guess I could."

Our schoolmaster entered upon his second term with new courage and invigorated authority. Twice certified, who should dare doubt his competency? Even Josh-

ua was civil, and lesser louts of course obsequious; though the girls took more liber-
ties, for they feel even at that early age, that influence is stronger than strength.

Could a young schoolmaster think of feruling a girl with her hair in ringlets
and a gold ring on her finger? Impossible—and the immunity extended to all the
little sisters and cousins; and there were enough large girls to protect all the feminine part of the school. With the boys Master Horner still had many a battle, and
whether with a view to this, or as an economical ruse, he never wore his coat in
school, saying it was too warm. Perhaps it was an astute attention to the prejudices
of his employers, who love no man that does not earn his living by the sweat of
his brow. The shirt-sleeves gave the idea of a manual-labor school in one sense at
least. It was evident that the master worked, and that afforded a probability that the
scholars worked too.

Master Horner's success was most triumphant that winter. A year's growth had
improved his outward man exceedingly, filling out the limbs so that they did not
remind you so forcibly of a young colt's, and supplying the cheeks with the flesh
and blood so necessary where mustaches were not worn. Experience had given him
a degree of confidence, and confidence gave him power. In short, people said the
master had waked up; and so he had. He actually set about reading for improve-
ment; and although at the end of the term he could not quite make out from his historical studies which side Hannibal was on, yet this is readily explained by the fact
that he boarded round, and was obliged to read generally by firelight, surrounded
by ungoverned children.

After this, Master Horner made his own bargain. When schooltime came round
with the following autumn, and the teacher presented himself for a third examination, such a test was pronounced no longer necessary; and the district consented to
engage him at the astounding rate of sixteen dollars a month, with the understanding that he was to have a fixed home, provided he was willing to allow a dollar a
week for it. Master Horner bethought him of the successive "killing-times," and
consequent doughnuts of the twenty families in which he had sojourned the years
before, and consented to the exaction.

Behold our friend now as high as district teacher can ever hope to be—his
scholarship established, his home stationary and not revolving, and the good behavior of the community insured by the fact that he, being of age, had now a farm

to retire upon in case of any disgust.

Master Horner was at once the preeminent beau of the neighborhood, spite of the prejudice against learning. He brushed his hair straight up in front, and wore a sky-blue ribbon for a guard to his silver watch, and walked as if the tall heels of his blunt boots were egg-shells and not leather. Yet he was far from neglecting the duties of his place. He was beau only on Sundays and holidays; very schoolmaster the rest of the time.

It was at a "spelling-school" that Master Horner first met the educated eyes of Miss Harriet Bangle, a young lady visiting the Engleharts in our neighborhood. She was from one of the towns in Western New York, and had brought with her a variety of city airs and graces somewhat caricatured, set off with year-old French fashions much travestied. Whether she had been sent out to the new country to try, somewhat late, a rustic chance for an establishment, or whether her company had been found rather trying at home, we cannot say. The view which she was at some pains to make understood was, that her friends had contrived this method of keeping her out of the way of a desperate lover whose addresses were not acceptable to them.

If it should seem surprising that so high-bred a visitor should be sojourning in the wild woods, it must be remembered that more than one celebrated Englishman and not a few distinguished Americans have farmer brothers in the western country, no whit less rustic in their exterior and manner of life than the plainest of their neighbors. When these are visited by their refined kinsfolk, we of the woods catch glimpses of the gay world, or think we do.

> That great medicine hath
> With its tinct gilded—

many a vulgarism to the satisfaction of wiser heads than ours.

Miss Bangle's manner bespoke for her that high consideration which she felt to be her due. Yet she condescended to be amused by the rustics and their awkward attempts at gaiety and elegance; and, to say truth, few of the village merry-makings escaped her, though she wore always the air of great superiority.

The spelling-school is one of the ordinary winter amusements in the country.

It occurs once in a fortnight, or so, and has power to draw out all the young people for miles round, arrayed in their best clothes and their holiday behavior. When all is ready, umpires are elected, and after these have taken the distinguished place usually occupied by the teacher, the young people of the school choose the two best scholars to head the opposing classes. These leaders choose their followers from the mass, each calling a name in turn, until all the spellers are ranked on one side or the other, lining the sides of the room, and all standing. The schoolmaster, standing too, takes his spelling-book, and gives a placid yet awe-inspiring look along the ranks, remarking that he intends to be very impartial, and that he shall give out nothing *that is not in the spelling-book*. For the first half hour or so he chooses common and easy words, that the spirit of the evening may not be damped by the too early thinning of the classes. When a word is missed, the blunderer has to sit down, and be a spectator only for the rest of the evening. At certain intervals, some of the best speakers mount the platform, and "speak a piece," which is generally as declamatory as possible.

The excitement of this scene is equal to that afforded by any city spectacle whatever; and towards the close of the evening, when difficult and unusual words are chosen to confound the small number who still keep the floor, it becomes scarcely less than painful. When perhaps only one or two remain to be puzzled, the master, weary at last of his task, though a favorite one, tries by tricks to put down those whom he cannot overcome in fair fight. If among all the curious, useless, unheard-of words which may be picked out of the spelling-book, he cannot find one which the scholars have not noticed, he gets the last head down by some quip or catch. "Bay" will perhaps be the sound; one scholar spells it "bey," another, "bay," while the master all the time means "ba," which comes within the rule, being *in the spelling-book*.

It was on one of these occasions, as we have said, that Miss Bangle, having come to the spelling-school to get materials for a letter to a female friend, first shone upon Mr. Horner. She was excessively amused by his solemn air and puckered mouth, and set him down at once as fair game. Yet she could not help becoming somewhat interested in the spelling-school, and after it was over found she had not stored up half as many of the schoolmaster's points as she intended, for the benefit of her correspondent.

In the evening's contest a young girl from some few miles' distance, Ellen Kingsbury, the only child of a substantial farmer, had been the very last to sit down, after a prolonged effort on the part of Mr. Horner to puzzle her, for the credit of his own school. She blushed, and smiled, and blushed again, but spelt on, until Mr. Horner's cheeks were crimson with excitement and some touch of shame that he should be baffled at his own weapons. At length, either by accident or design, Ellen missed a word, and sinking into her seat was numbered with the slain.

In the laugh and talk which followed (for with the conclusion of the spelling, all form of a public assembly vanishes), our schoolmaster said so many gallant things to his fair enemy, and appeared so much animated by the excitement of the contest, that Miss Bangle began to look upon him with rather more respect, and to feel somewhat indignant that a little rustic like Ellen should absorb the entire attention of the only beau. She put on, therefore, her most gracious aspect, and mingled in the circle; caused the schoolmaster to be presented to her, and did her best to fascinate him by certain airs and graces which she had found successful elsewhere. What game is too small for the close-woven net of a coquette?

Mr. Horner quitted not the fair Ellen until he had handed her into her father's sleigh; and he then wended his way homewards, never thinking that he ought to have escorted Miss Bangle to her uncle's, though she certainly waited a little while for his return.

We must not follow into particulars the subsequent intercourse of our schoolmaster with the civilized young lady. All that concerns us is the result of Miss Bangle's benevolent designs upon his heart. She tried most sincerely to find its vulnerable spot, meaning no doubt to put Mr. Homer on his guard for the future; and she was unfeignedly surprised to discover that her best efforts were of no avail. She concluded he must have taken a counter-poison, and she was not slow in guessing its source. She had observed the peculiar fire which lighted up his eyes in the presence of Ellen Kingsbury, and she bethought her of a plan which would ensure her some amusement at the expense of these impertinent rustics, though in a manner different somewhat from her original more natural idea of simple coquetry.

A letter was written to Master Horner, purporting to come from Ellen Kingsbury, worded so artfully that the schoolmaster understood at once that it was intended to be a secret communication, though its ostensible object was an inquiry about some ordinary affair. This was laid in Mr. Horner's desk before he came to school, with an intimation that he might leave an answer in a certain spot on the following morning. The bait took at once, for Mr. Horner, honest and true himself, and much smitten with the fair Ellen, was too happy to be circumspect. The answer was duly placed, and as duly carried to Miss Bangle by her accomplice, Joe Engle-hart, an unlucky pickle who "was always for ill, never for good," and who found no difficulty in obtaining the letter unwatched, since the master was obliged to be in school at nine, and Joe could always linger a few minutes later. This answer being opened and laughed at, Miss Bangle had only to contrive a rejoinder, which being rather more particular in its tone than the original communication, led on yet again the happy schoolmaster, who branched out into sentiment, "taffeta phrases, silken terms precise," talked of hills and dales and rivulets, and the pleasures of friendship, and concluded by entreating a continuance of the correspondence.

Another letter and another, every one more flattering and encouraging than the last, almost turned the sober head of our poor master, and warmed up his heart so effectually that he could scarcely attend to his business. The spelling-schools were remembered, however, and Ellen Kingsbury made one of the merry company; but the latest letter had not forgotten to caution Mr. Horner not to betray the inti-macy; so that he was in honor bound to restrict himself to the language of the eyes hard as it was to forbear the single whisper for which he would have given his very dictionary. So, their meeting passed off without the explanation which Miss Bangle began to fear would cut short her benevolent amusement.

The correspondence was resumed with renewed spirit, and carried on un-til Miss Bangle, though not overburdened with sensitiveness, began to be a little alarmed for the consequences of her malicious pleasantry. She perceived that she herself had turned schoolmistress, and that Master Horner, instead of being merely her dupe, had become her pupil too; for the style of his replies had been constantly improving and the earnest and manly tone which he assumed promised any thing but the quiet, sheepish pocketing of injury and insult, upon which she had counted. In truth, there was something deeper than vanity in the feelings with which he regarded Ellen Kingsbury. The encouragement which he supposed himself to have received, threw down the barrier which his extreme bashfulness would have inter-posed between himself and any one who possessed charms enough to attract him;

and we must excuse him if, in such a case, he did not criticise the mode of encouragement, but rather grasped eagerly the proffered good without a scruple, or one which he would own to himself, as to the propriety with which it was tendered. He was as much in love as a man can be, and the seriousness of real attachment gave both grace and dignity to his once awkward diction.

The evident determination of Mr. Horner to come to the point of asking papa brought Miss Bangle to a very awkward pass. She had expected to return home before matters had proceeded so far, but being obliged to remain some time longer, she was equally afraid to go on and to leave off, a *denouement* being almost certain to ensue in either case. Things stood thus when it was time to prepare for the grand exhibition which was to close the winter's term.

This is an affair of too much magnitude to be fully described in the small space yet remaining in which to bring out our veracious history. It must be "slubber'd o'er in haste"—its important preliminaries left to the cold imagination of the reader—its fine spirit perhaps evaporating for want of being embodied in words. We can only say that our master, whose school-life was to close with the term, labored as man never before labored in such a cause, resolute to trail a cloud of glory after him when he left us. Not a candlestick nor a curtain that was attainable, either by coaxing or bribery, was left in the village; even the only piano, that frail treasure, was wiled away and placed in one corner of the rickety stage. The most splendid of all the pieces in the *Columbian Orator*, the *American Speaker*, the——but we must not enumerate—in a word, the most astounding and pathetic specimens of eloquence within ken of either teacher or scholars, had been selected for the occasion; and several young ladies and gentlemen, whose academical course had been happily concluded at an earlier period, either at our own institution or at some other, had consented to lend themselves to the parts, and their choicest decorations for the properties, of the dramatic portion of the entertainment.

Among these last was pretty Ellen Kingsbury, who had agreed to personate the Queen of Scots, in the garden scene from Schiller's tragedy of *Mary Stuart*; and this circumstance accidentally afforded Master Horner the opportunity he had so long desired, of seeing his fascinating correspondent without the presence of peering eyes. A dress-rehearsal occupied the afternoon before the day of days, and the pathetic expostulations of the lovely Mary—

Mine all doth hang—my life—my destiny—
Upon my words—upon the force of tears!—

aided by the long veil, and the emotion which sympathy brought into Ellen's countenance, proved too much for the enforced prudence of Master Horner. When the rehearsal was over, and the heroes and heroines were to return home, it was found that, by a stroke of witty invention not new in the country, the harness of Mr. Kingsbury's horses had been cut in several places, his whip hidden, his buffalo-skins spread on the ground, and the sleigh turned bottom upwards on them. This afforded an excuse for the master's borrowing a horse and sleigh of somebody, and claiming the privilege of taking Miss Ellen home, while her father returned with only Aunt Sally and a great bag of bran from the mill—companions about equally interesting.

Here, then, was the golden opportunity so long wished for! Here was the power of ascertaining at once what is never quite certain until we have heard it from warm, living lips, whose testimony is strengthened by glances in which the whole soul speaks or—seems to speak. The time was short, for the sleighing was but too fine; and Father Kingsbury, having tied up his harness, and collected his scattered equipment, was driving so close behind that there was no possibility of lingering for a moment. Yet many moments were lost before Mr. Horner, very much in earnest, and all unhackneyed in matters of this sort, could find a word in which to clothe his new-found feelings. The horse seemed to fly—the distance was half past—and at length, in absolute despair of anything better, he blurted out at once what he had determined to avoid—a direct reference to the correspondence.

A game at cross-purposes ensued; exclamations and explanations, and denials and apologies filled up the time which was to have made Master Horner so blest. The light from Mr. Kingsbury's windows shone upon the path, and the whole result of this conference so longed for, was a burst of tears from the perplexed and mortified Ellen, who sprang from Mr. Horner's attempts to detain her, rushed into the house without vouchsafing him a word of adieu, and left him standing, no bad personification of Orpheus, after the last hopeless flitting of his Eurydice.

"Won't you 'light, Master?" said Mr. Kingsbury.

"Yes—no—thank you—good evening," stammered poor Master Horner, so stupefied that even Aunt Sally called him "a dummy."

The horse took the sleigh against the fence, going home, and threw out the master, who scarcely recollected the accident; while to Ellen the issue of this unfortunate drive was a sleepless night and so high a fever in the morning that our village doctor was called to Mr. Kingsbury's before breakfast.

Poor Master Horner's distress may hardly be imagined. Disappointed, bewildered, cut to the quick, yet as much in love as ever, he could only in bitter silence turn over in his thoughts the issue of his cherished dream; now persuading himself that Ellen's denial was the effect of a sudden bashfulness, now inveighing against the fickleness of the sex, as all men do when they are angry with any one woman in particular. But his exhibition must go on in spite of wretchedness; and he went about mechanically, talking of curtains and candles, and music, and attitudes, and pauses, and emphasis, looking like a somnambulist whose "eyes are open but their sense is shut," and often surprising those concerned by the utter unfitness of his answers.

It was almost evening when Mr. Kingsbury, having discovered, through the intervention of the Doctor and Aunt Sally the cause of Ellen's distress, made his appearance before the unhappy eyes of Master Horner, angry, solemn and determined; taking the schoolmaster apart, and requiring, an explanation of his treatment of his daughter. In vain did the perplexed lover ask for time to clear himself, declare his respect for Miss Ellen and his willingness to give every explanation which she might require; the father was not to be put off; and though excessively reluctant, Mr. Horner had no resource but to show the letters which alone could account for his strange discourse to Ellen. He unlocked his desk, slowly and unwillingly, while the old man's impatience was such that he could scarcely forbear thrusting in his own hand to snatch at the papers which were to explain this vexatious mystery. What could equal the utter confusion of Master Horner and the contemptuous anger of the father, when no letters were to be found! Mr. Kingsbury was too passionate to listen to reason, or to reflect for one moment upon the irreproachable good name of the schoolmaster. He went away in inexorable wrath; threatening every practicable visitation of public and private justice upon the head of the offender, whom he accused of having attempted to trick his daughter into an entanglement which should result in his favor.

A doleful exhibition was this last one of our thrice approved and most worthy teacher! Stern necessity and the power of habit enabled him to go through with most of his part, but where was the proud fire which had lighted up his eye on similar occasions before? He sat as one of three judges before whom the unfortunate Robert Emmet was dragged in his shirt-sleeves, by two fierce-looking officials; but the chief judge looked far more like a criminal than did the proper representative. He ought to have personated Othello, but was obliged to excuse himself from raving for "the handkerchief! the handkerchief!" on the rather anomalous plea of a bad cold. *Mary Stuart* being "i' the bond," was anxiously expected by the impatient crowd, and it was with distress amounting to agony that the master was obliged to announce, in person, the necessity of omitting that part of the representation, on account of the illness of one of the young ladies.

Scarcely had the words been uttered, and the speaker hidden his burning face behind the curtain, when Mr. Kingsbury started up in his place amid the throng, to give a public recital of his grievance—no uncommon resort in the new country. He dashed at once to the point; and before some friends who saw the utter impropriety of his proceeding could persuade him to defer his vengeance, he had laid before the assembly—some three hundred people, perhaps—his own statement of the case. He was got out at last, half coaxed, half hustled; and the gentle public only half understanding what had been set forth thus unexpectedly, made quite a pretty row of it. Some clamored loudly for the conclusion of the exercises; others gave utterances in no particularly choice terms to a variety of opinions as to the schoolmaster's proceedings, varying the note occasionally by shouting, "The letters! the letters! why don't you bring out the letters?"

At length, by means of much rapping on the desk by the president of the evening, who was fortunately a "popular" character, order was partially restored; and the favorite scene from Miss More's dialogue of David and Goliath was announced as the closing piece. The sight of little David in a white tunic edged with red tape, with a calico scrip and a very primitive-looking sling; and a huge Goliath decorated with a militia belt and sword, and a spear like a weaver's beam indeed, enchained everybody's attention. Even the peccant schoolmaster and his pretended letters were forgotten, while the sapient Goliath, every time that he raised the spear, in the energy of his declamation, to thump upon the stage, picked away fragments of the low ceiling, which fell conspicuously on his great shock of black hair. At last, with the crowning threat, up went the spear for an astounding thump, and down came a large piece of the ceiling, and with it—a shower of letters.

The confusion that ensued beggars all description. A general scramble took place, and in another moment twenty pairs of eyes, at least, were feasting on the choice phrases lavished upon Mr. Horner. Miss Bangle had sat through the whole previous scene, trembling for herself, although she had, as she supposed, guarded cunningly against exposure. She had needed no prophet to tell her what must be the result of a tete-a-tete between Mr. Horner and Ellen; and the moment she saw them drive off together, she induced her imp to seize the opportunity of abstracting the whole parcel of letters from Mr. Horner's desk; which he did by means of a sort of skill which comes by nature to such goblins; picking the lock by the aid of a crooked nail, as neatly as if he had been born within the shadow of the Tombs.

But magicians sometimes suffer severely from the malice with which they have themselves inspired their familiars. Joe Englehart having been a convenient tool thus far thought it quite time to torment Miss Bangle a little; so, having stolen the letters at her bidding, he hid them on his own account, and no persuasions of hers could induce him to reveal this important secret, which he chose to reserve as a rod in case she refused him some intercession with his father, or some other accommodation, rendered necessary by his mischievous habits.

He had concealed the precious parcels in the unfloored loft above the school-room, a place accessible only by means of a small trap-door without staircase or ladder; and here he meant to have kept them while it suited his purposes, but for the untimely intrusion of the weaver's beam.

Miss Bangle had sat through all, as we have said, thinking the letters safe, yet vowing vengeance against her confederate for not allowing her to secure them by a satisfactory conflagration; and it was not until she heard her own name whispered through the crowd, that she was awakened to her true situation. The sagacity of the low creatures whom she had despised showed them at once that the letters must be hers, since her character had been pretty shrewdly guessed, and the handwriting wore a more practised air than is usual among females in the country. This was first taken for granted, and then spoken of as an acknowledged fact.

The assembly moved like the heavings of a troubled sea. Everybody felt that this was everybody's business. "Put her out!" was heard from more than one rough voice near the door, and this was responded to by loud and angry murmurs from within.

Mr. Englehart, not waiting to inquire into the merits of the case in this scene of confusion, hastened to get his family out as quietly and as quickly as possible, but groans and hisses followed his niece as she hung half-fainting on his arm, quailing completely beneath the instinctive indignation of the rustic public. As she passed out, a yell resounded among the rude boys about the door, and she was lifted into a sleigh, insensible from terror. She disappeared from that evening, and no one knew the time of her final departure for "the east."

Mr. Kingsbury, who is a just man when he is not in a passion, made all the reparation in his power for his harsh and ill-considered attack upon the master; and we believe that functionary did not show any traits of implacability of character. At least he was seen, not many days after, sitting peaceably at tea with Mr. Kingsbury, Aunt Sally, and Miss Ellen; and he has since gone home to build a house upon his farm. And people *do* say, that after a few months more, Ellen will not need Miss Bangle's intervention if she should see fit to correspond with the schoolmaster.

THE WATKINSON EVENING
By Eliza Leslie (1787-1858)

[From *Godey's Lady's Book*, December, 1846.]

MRS. Morland, a polished and accomplished woman, was the widow of a distinguished senator from one of the western states, of which, also, her husband had twice filled the office of governor. Her daughter having completed her education at the best boarding-school in Philadelphia, and her son being about to graduate at Princeton, the mother had planned with her children a tour to Niagara and the lakes, returning by way of Boston. On leaving Philadelphia, Mrs. Morland and the delighted Caroline stopped at Princeton to be present at the annual commencement, and had the happiness of seeing their beloved Edward receive his diploma as bachelor of arts; after hearing him deliver, with great applause, an oration on the beauties of the American character. College youths are very prone to treat on subjects that imply great experience of the world. But Edward Morland was full of kind feeling for everything and everybody; and his views of life had hitherto been tinted with a perpetual rose-color.

Mrs. Morland, not depending altogether upon the celebrity of her late husband, and wishing that her children should see specimens of the best society in the northern cities, had left home with numerous letters of introduction. But when they arrived at New York, she found to her great regret, that having unpacked and taken out her small traveling desk, during her short stay in Philadelphia, she had strangely left it behind in the closet of her room at the hotel. In this desk were deposited all her letters, except two which had been offered to her by friends in

Philadelphia. The young people, impatient to see the wonders of Niagara, had entreated her to stay but a day or two in the city of New York, and thought these two letters would be quite sufficient for the present. In the meantime she wrote back to the hotel, requesting that the missing desk should be forwarded to New York as soon as possible.

On the morning after their arrival at the great commercial metropolis of America, the Morland family took a carriage to ride round through the principal parts of the city, and to deliver their two letters at the houses to which they were addressed, and which were both situated in the region that lies between the upper part of Broadway and the North River. In one of the most fashionable streets they found the elegant mansion of Mrs. St. Leonard; but on stopping at the door, were informed that its mistress was not at home. They then left the introductory letter (which they had prepared for this mischance, by enclosing it in an envelope with a card), and proceeding to another street considerably farther up, they arrived at the dwelling of the Watkinson family, to the mistress of which the other Philadelphia letter was directed. It was one of a large block of houses all exactly alike, and all shut up from top to bottom, according to a custom more prevalent in New York than in any other city.

Here they were also unsuccessful; the servant who came to the door telling them that the ladies were particularly engaged and could see no company. So they left their second letter and card and drove off, continuing their ride till they reached the Croton water works, which they quitted the carriage to see and admire. On returning to the hotel, with the intention after an hour or two of rest to go out again, and walk till near dinner-time, they found waiting them a note from Mrs. Watkinson, expressing her regret that she had not been able to see them when they called; and explaining that her family duties always obliged her to deny herself the pleasure of receiving morning visitors, and that her servants had general orders to that effect. But she requested their company for that evening (naming nine o'clock as the hour), and particularly desired an immediate answer.

"I suppose," said Mrs. Morland, "she intends asking some of her friends to meet us, in case we accept the invitation; and therefore is naturally desirous of a reply as soon as possible. Of course we will not keep her in suspense. Mrs. Denham, who volunteered the letter, assured me that Mrs. Watkinson was one of the most estimable women in New York, and a pattern to the circle in which she moved. It seems that Mr. Denham and Mr. Watkinson are connected in business. Shall we go?"

The young people assented, saying they had no doubt of passing a pleasant evening.

The billet of acceptance having been written, it was sent off immediately, entrusted to one of the errand-goers belonging to the hotel, that it might be received in advance of the next hour for the dispatch-post—and Edward Morland desired the man to get into an omnibus with the note that no time might be lost in delivering it. "It is but right"—said he to his mother—"that we should give Mrs. Watkinson an ample opportunity of making her preparations, and sending round to invite her friends."

"How considerate you are, dear Edward"—said Caroline—"always so thoughtful of every one's convenience. Your college friends must have idolized you."

"No"—said Edward—"they called me a prig." Just then a remarkably handsome carriage drove up to the private door of the hotel. From it alighted a very elegant woman, who in a few moments was ushered into the drawing-room by the head waiter, and on his designating Mrs. Morland's family, she advanced and gracefully announced herself as Mrs. St. Leonard. This was the lady at whose house they had left the first letter of introduction. She expressed regret at not having been at home when they called; but said that on finding their letter, she had immediately come down to see them, and to engage them for the evening. "Tonight"—said Mrs. St. Leonard—"I expect as many friends as I can collect for a summer party. The occasion is the recent marriage of my niece, who with her husband has just returned from their bridal excursion, and they will be soon on their way to their residence in Baltimore. I think I can promise you an agreeable evening, as I expect some very delightful people, with whom I shall be most happy to make you acquainted."

Edward and Caroline exchanged glances, and could not refrain from looking wistfully at their mother, on whose countenance a shade of regret was very apparent. After a short pause she replied to Mrs. St. Leonard—"I am truly sorry to say that we have just answered in the affirmative a previous invitation for this very evening."

"I am indeed disappointed"—said Mrs. St. Leonard, who had been looking approvingly at the prepossessing appearance of the two young people. "Is there no way in which you can revoke your compliance with this unfortunate first invitation—at least, I am sure, it is unfortunate for me. What a vexatious *contretemps* that I should have chanced to be out when you called; thus missing the pleasure of seeing you at once, and securing that of your society for this evening? The truth is, I was disappointed in some of the preparations that had been sent home this morning, and I had to go myself and have the things rectified, and was detained away longer than I expected. May I ask to whom you are engaged this evening? Perhaps I know the lady—if so, I should be very much tempted to go and beg you from her."

"The lady is Mrs. John Watkinson"—replied Mrs. Morland—"most probably she will invite some of her friends to meet us."

"That of course"—answered Mrs. St. Leonard—"I am really very sorry—and I regret to say that I do not know her at all."

"We shall have to abide by our first decision," said Mrs. Morland. "By Mrs. Watkinson, mentioning in her note the hour of nine, it is to be presumed she intends asking some other company. I cannot possibly disappoint her. I can speak feelingly as to the annoyance (for I have known it by my own experience) when after inviting a number of my friends to meet some strangers, the strangers have sent an excuse almost at the eleventh hour. I think no inducements, however strong, could tempt me to do so myself."

"I confess that you are perfectly right," said Mrs. St. Leonard. "I see you must go to Mrs. Watkinson. But can you not divide the evening, by passing a part of it with her and then finishing with me?"

At this suggestion the eyes of the young people sparkled, for they had become delighted with Mrs. St. Leonard, and imagined that a party at her house must be every way charming. Also, parties were novelties to both of them.

"If possible we will do so," answered Mrs. Morland, "and with what pleasure I need not assure you. We leave New York to-morrow, but we shall return this way in September, and will then be exceedingly happy to see more of Mrs. St. Leonard."

After a little more conversation Mrs. St. Leonard took her leave, repeating her hope of still seeing her new friends at her house that night; and enjoining them to let her know as soon as they returned to New York on their way home.

Edward Morland handed her to her carriage, and then joined his mother and sister in their commendations of Mrs. St. Leonard, with whose exceeding beauty were united a countenance beaming with intelligence, and a manner that put every one at their ease immediately.

"She is an evidence," said Edward, "how superior our women of fashion are to those of Europe."

"Wait, my dear son," said Mrs. Morland, "till you have been in Europe, and had an opportunity of forming an opinion on that point (as on many others) from actual observation. For my part, I believe that in all civilized countries the upper classes of people are very much alike, at least in their leading characteristics."

"Ah! here comes the man that was sent to Mrs. Watkinson," said Caroline Morland. "I hope he could not find the house and has brought the note back with him. We shall then be able to go at first to Mrs. St. Leonard's, and pass the whole evening there."

The man reported that he *had* found the house, and had delivered the note into Mrs. Watkinson's own hands, as she chanced to be crossing the entry when the door was opened; and that she read it immediately, and said "Very well."

"Are you certain that you made no mistake in the house," said Edward, "and that you really *did* give it to Mrs. Watkinson?"

"And it's quite sure I am, sir," replied the man, "when I first came over from the ould country I lived with them awhile, and though when she saw me to-day, she did not let on that she remembered my doing that same, she could not help calling me James. Yes, the rale words she said when I handed her the billy-dux was, 'Very well, James.'"

"Come, come," said Edward, when they found themselves alone, "let us look on the bright side. If we do not find a large party at Mrs. Watkinson's, we may in all probability meet some very agreeable people there, and enjoy the feast of reason and the flow of soul. We may find the Watkinson house so pleasant as to leave it with regret even for Mrs. St. Leonard's."

"I do not believe Mrs. Watkinson is in fashionable society," said Caroline, "or Mrs. St. Leonard would have known her. I heard some of the ladies here talking last evening of Mrs. St. Leonard, and I found from what they said that she is among the *elite* of the *lite*."

"Even if she is," observed Mrs. Morland, "are polish of manners and cultivation of mind confined exclusively to persons of that class?"

"Certainly not," said Edward, "the most talented and refined youth at our college, and he in whose society I found the greatest pleasure, was the son of a bricklayer."

In the ladies' drawing-room, after dinner, the Morlands heard a conversation between several of the female guests, who all seemed to know Mrs. St. Leonard very well by reputation, and they talked of her party that was to "come off" on this evening.

"I hear," said one lady, "that Mrs. St. Leonard is to have an unusual number of lions."

She then proceeded to name a gallant general, with his elegant wife and accomplished daughter; a celebrated commander in the navy; two highly distinguished members of Congress, and even an ex-president. Also several of the most eminent among the American literati, and two first-rate artists.

Edward Morland felt as if he could say, "Had I three ears I'd hear thee."

"Such a woman as Mrs. St. Leonard can always command the best lions that are to be found," observed another lady.

"And then," said a third, "I have been told that she has such exquisite taste in lighting and embellishing her always elegant rooms. And her supper table, whether for summer or winter parties, is so beautifully arranged; all the viands are so delicious, and the attendance of the servants so perfect—and Mrs. St. Leonard does the honors with so much ease and tact."

"Some friends of mine that visit her," said a fourth lady, "describe her parties as absolute perfection. She always manages to bring together those persons that are best fitted to enjoy each other's conversation. Still no one is overlooked or neglected. Then everything at her reunions is so well proportioned—she has just enough of music, and just enough of whatever amusement may add to the pleasure of her guests; and still there is no appearance of design or management on her part."

"And better than all," said the lady who had spoken firsts "Mrs. St. Leonard is one of the kindest, most generous, and most benevolent of women—she does good in every possible way."

"I can listen no longer," said Caroline to Edward, rising to change her seat. "If I hear any more I shall absolutely hate the Watkinsons. How provoking that they should have sent us the first invitation. If we had only thought of waiting till we could hear from Mrs. St. Leonard!"

"For shame, Caroline," said her brother, "how can you talk so of persons you have never seen, and to whom you ought to feel grateful for the kindness of their invitation; even if it has interfered with another party, that I must confess seems to offer unusual attractions. Now I have a presentiment that we shall find the Watkinson part of the evening very enjoyable."

As soon as tea was over, Mrs. Morland and her daughter repaired to their toilettes. Fortunately, fashion as well as good taste, has decided that, at a summer party, the costume of the ladies should never go beyond an elegant simplicity. Therefore our two ladies in preparing for their intended appearance at Mrs. St. Leonard's, were enabled to attire themselves in a manner that would not seem out of place in the smaller company they expected to meet at the Watkinsons. Over an under-dress of lawn, Caroline Morland put on a white organdy trimmed with lace, and decorated with bows of pink ribbon. At the back of her head was a wreath of fresh and beautiful pink flowers, tied with a similar ribbon. Mrs. Morland wore a black grenadine over a satin, and a lace cap trimmed with white.

It was but a quarter past nine o'clock when their carriage stopped at the Watkinson door. The front of the house looked very dark. Not a ray gleamed through the Venetian shutters, and the glimmer beyond the fan-light over the door was almost imperceptible. After the coachman had rung several times, an Irish girl opened the door, cautiously (as Irish girls always do), and admitted them into the entry, where one light only was burning in a branch lamp. "Shall we go upstairs?" said Mrs. Morland. "And what for would ye go upstairs?" said the girl in a pert tone. "It's all dark there, and there's no preparations. Ye can lave your things here a-hanging on the rack. It is a party ye're expecting? Blessed are them what expects nothing."

The sanguine Edward Morland looked rather blank at this intelligence, and his sister whispered to him, "We'll get off to Mrs. St. Leonard's as soon as we possibly can. When did you tell the coachman to come for us?"

"At half past ten," was the brother's reply.

"Oh! Edward, Edward!" she exclaimed, "And I dare say he will not be punctual. He may keep us here till eleven."

"*Courage, mes enfants*," said their mother, "*et parlez plus doucement*."

The girl then ushered them into the back parlor, saying, "Here's the company."

The room was large and gloomy. A checquered mat covered the floor, and all the furniture was encased in striped calico covers, and the lamps, mirrors, etc. concealed under green gauze. The front parlor was entirely dark, and in the back apartment was no other light than a shaded lamp on a large centre table, round which was assembled a circle of children of all sizes and ages. On a backless, cushionless sofa sat Mrs. Watkinson, and a young lady, whom she introduced as her daughter Jane. And Mrs. Morland in return presented Edward and Caroline.

"Will you take the rocking-chair, ma'am?" inquired Mrs. Watkinson.

Mrs. Morland declining the offer, the hostess took it herself, and see-sawed on it nearly the whole time. It was a very awkward, high-legged, crouch-backed rocking-chair, and shamefully unprovided with anything in the form of a footstool.

"My husband is away, at Boston, on business," said Mrs. Watkinson. "I thought at first, ma'am, I should not be able to ask you here this evening, for it is not our way to have company in his absence; but my daughter Jane over-persuaded me to send for you."

"What a pity," thought Caroline.

"You must take us as you find us, ma'am," continued Mrs. Watkinson. "We use no ceremony with anybody; and our rule is never to put ourselves out of the way. We do not give parties [looking at the dresses of the ladies]. Our first duty is to our children, and we cannot waste our substance on fashion and folly. They'll have cause to thank us for it when we die."

Something like a sob was heard from the centre table, at which the children were sitting, and a boy was seen to hold his handkerchief to his face.

"Joseph, my child," said his mother, "do not cry. You have no idea, ma'am, what an extraordinary boy that is. You see how the bare mention of such a thing as our deaths has overcome him."

There was another sob behind the handkerchief, and the Morlands thought it now sounded very much like a smothered laugh.

"As I was saying, ma'am," continued Mrs. Watkinson, "we never give parties. We leave all sinful things to the vain and foolish. My daughter Jane has been telling me, that she heard this morning of a party that is going on tonight at the widow St.

Leonard's. It is only fifteen years since her husband died. He was carried off with a three days' illness, but two months after they were married. I have had a domestic that lived with them at the time, so I know all about it. And there she is now, living in an elegant house, and riding in her carriage, and dressing and dashing, and giving parties, and enjoying life, as she calls it. Poor creature, how I pity her! Thank heaven, nobody that I know goes to her parties. If they did I would never wish to see them again in my house. It is an encouragement to folly and nonsense—and folly and nonsense are sinful. Do not you think so, ma'am?"

"If carried too far they may certainly become so," replied Mrs. Morland.

"We have heard," said Edward, "that Mrs. St. Leonard, though one of the ornaments of the gay world, has a kind heart, a beneficent spirit and a liberal hand."

"I know very little about her," replied Mrs. Watkinson, drawing up her head, "and I have not the least desire to know any more. It is well she has no children; they'd be lost sheep if brought up in her fold. For my part, ma'am," she continued, turning to Mrs. Morland, "I am quite satisfied with the quiet joys of a happy home. And no mother has the least business with any other pleasures. My innocent babes know nothing about plays, and balls, and parties; and they never shall. Do they look as if they had been accustomed to a life of pleasure?"

They certainly did not! for when the Morlands took a glance at them, they thought they had never seen youthful faces that were less gay, and indeed less prepossessing.

There was not a good feature or a pleasant expression among them all. Edward Morland recollected his having often read "that childhood is always lovely." But he saw that the juvenile Watkinsons were an exception to the rule.

"The first duty of a mother is to her children," repeated Mrs. Watkinson. "Till nine o'clock, my daughter Jane and myself are occupied every evening in hearing the lessons that they have learned for to-morrow's school. Before that hour we can receive no visitors, and we never have company to tea, as that would interfere too much with our duties. We had just finished hearing these lessons when you arrived. Afterwards the children are permitted to indulge themselves in rational play, for I permit no amusement that is not also instructive. My children are so well trained, that even when alone their sports are always serious."

Two of the boys glanced slyly at each other, with what Edward Morland comprehended as an expression of pitch-penny and marbles.

"They are now engaged at their game of astronomy," continued Mrs. Watkinson. "They have also a sort of geography cards, and a set of mathematical cards. It is a blessed discovery, the invention of these educational games; so that even the play-time of children can be turned to account. And you have no idea, ma'am, how they enjoy them."

Just then the boy Joseph rose from the table, and stalking up to Mrs. Watkinson, said to her, "Mamma, please to whip me."

At this unusual request the visitors looked much amazed, and Mrs. Watkinson replied to him, "Whip you, my best Joseph—for what cause? I have not seen you do anything wrong this evening, and you know my anxiety induces me to watch my children all the time."

"You could not see me," answered Joseph, "for I have not *done* anything very wrong. But I have had a bad thought, and you know Mr. Ironrule says that a fault imagined is just as wicked as a fault committed."

"You see, ma'am, what a good memory he has," said Mrs. Watkinson aside to Mrs. Morland. "But my best Joseph, you make your mother tremble. What fault have you imagined? What was your bad thought?"

"Ay," said another boy, "what's your thought like?"

"My thought," said Joseph, "was 'Confound all astronomy, and I could see the man hanged that made this game.'"

"Oh! my child," exclaimed the mother, stopping her ears, "I am indeed shocked. I am glad you repented so immediately."

"Yes," returned Joseph, "but I am afraid my repentance won't last. If I am not whipped, I may have these bad thoughts whenever I play at astronomy, and worse still at the geography game. Whip me, ma, and punish me as I deserve. There's the rattan in the corner: I'll bring it to you myself."

"Excellent boy!" said his mother. "You know I always pardon my children when they are so candid as to confess their faults."

"So you do," said Joseph, "but a whipping will cure me better."

"I cannot resolve to punish so conscientious a child," said Mrs. Watkinson.

"Shall I take the trouble off your hands?" inquired Edward, losing all patience in his disgust at the sanctimonious hypocrisy of this young Blifil. "It is such a rarity for a boy to request a whipping, that so remarkable a desire ought by all means to be gratified."

Joseph turned round and made a face at him.

"Give me the rattan," said Edward, half laughing, and offering to take it out of his hand. "I'll use it to your full satisfaction."

The boy thought it most prudent to stride off and return to the table, and ensconce himself among his brothers and sisters; some of whom were staring with stupid surprise; others were whispering and giggling in the hope of seeing Joseph get a real flogging.

Mrs. Watkinson having bestowed a bitter look on Edward, hastened to turn the attention of his mother to something else. "Mrs. Morland," said she, "allow me to introduce you to my youngest hope." She pointed to a sleepy boy about five years old, who with head thrown back and mouth wide open, was slumbering in his chair.

Mrs. Watkinson's children were of that uncomfortable species who never go to bed; at least never without all manner of resistance. All her boasted authority was inadequate to compel them; they never would confess themselves sleepy; always wanted to "sit up," and there was a nightly scene of scolding, coaxing, threatening and manoeuvring to get them off.

"I declare," said Mrs. Watkinson, "dear Benny is almost asleep. Shake him up, Christopher. I want him to speak a speech. His school-mistress takes great pains in teaching her little pupils to speak, and stands up herself and shows them how."

The child having been shaken up hard (two or three others helping Christopher), rubbed his eyes and began to whine. His mother went to him, took him on her lap, hushed him up, and began to coax him. This done, she stood him on his feet before Mrs. Morland, and desired him to speak a speech for the company. The child put his thumb into his mouth, and remained silent.

"Ma," said Jane Watkinson, "you had better tell him what speech to speak."

"Speak Cato or Plato," said his mother. "Which do you call it? Come now, Benny—how does it begin? 'You are quite right and reasonable, Plato.' That's it."

"Speak Lucius," said his sister Jane. "Come now, Benny—say 'your thoughts are turned on peace.'"

The little boy looked very much as if they were *not*, and as if meditating an outbreak.

"No, no!" exclaimed Christopher, "let him say Hamlet. Come now, Benny—'To be or not to be.'"

"It ain't to be at all," cried Benny, "and I won't speak the least bit of it for any of you. I hate that speech!"

"Only see his obstinacy," said the solemn Joseph. "And is he to be given up to?"

"Speak anything, Benny," said Mrs. Watkinson, "anything so that it is only a speech."

All the Watkinson voices now began to clamor violently at the obstinate child—"Speak a speech! speak a speech! speak a speech!" But they had no more effect than the reiterated exhortations with which nurses confuse the poor heads of babies, when they require them to "shake a day-day—shake a day-day!"

Mrs. Morland now interfered, and begged that the sleepy little boy might be excused; on which he screamed out that "he wasn't sleepy at all, and would not go to bed ever."

"I never knew any of my children behave so before," said Mrs. Watkinson. "They are always models of obedience, ma'am. A look is sufficient for them. And I must say that they have in every way profited by the education we are giving them. It is not our way, ma'am, to waste our money in parties and fooleries, and fine furniture and fine clothes, and rich food, and all such abominations. Our first duty is to our children, and to make them learn everything that is taught in the schools. If they go wrong, it will not be for want of education. Hester, my dear, come and talk to Miss Morland in French."

Hester (unlike her little brother that would not speak a speech) stepped boldly forward, and addressed Caroline Morland with: "*Parlez-vous Francais, mademoiselle? Comment se va madame votre mere? Aimez-vous la musique? Aimez-vous la danse? Bon jour—bon soir—bon repos. Comprenez-vous?*"

To this tirade, uttered with great volubility, Miss Morland made no other reply than, "*Oui—je comprens.*"

"Very well, Hester—very well indeed," said Mrs. Watkinson. "You see, ma'am," turning to Mrs. Morland, "how very fluent she is in French; and she has only been learning eleven quarters."

After considerable whispering between Jane and her mother, the former withdrew, and sent in by the Irish girl a waiter with a basket of soda biscuit, a pitcher of water, and some glasses. Mrs. Watkinson invited her guests to consider themselves at home and help themselves freely, saying: "We never let cakes, sweetmeats, confectionery, or any such things enter the house, as they would be very unwholesome for the children, and it would be sinful to put temptation in their way. I am sure, ma'am, you will agree with me that the plainest food is the best for everybody. People that want nice things may go to parties for them; but they will never get any with me."

When the collation was over, and every child provided with a biscuit, Mrs. Watkinson said to Mrs. Morland: "Now, ma'am, you shall have some music from my daughter Jane, who is one of Mr. Bangwhanger's best scholars."

Jane Watkinson sat down to the piano and commenced a powerful piece of six mortal pages, which she played out of time and out of tune; but with tremendous force of hands; notwithstanding which, it had, however, the good effect of putting most of the children to sleep.

To the Morlands the evening had seemed already five hours long. Still it was only half past ten when Jane was in the midst of her piece. The guests had all tacitly determined that it would be best not to let Mrs. Watkinson know their intention to go directly from her house to Mrs. St. Leonard's party; and the arrival of their carriage would have been the signal of departure, even if Jane's piece had not reached its termination. They stole glances at the clock on the mantel. It wanted but a quarter of eleven, when Jane rose from the piano, and was congratulated by her mother on the excellence of her music. Still no carriage was heard to stop; no doorbell was heard to ring. Mrs. Morland expressed her fears that the coachman had forgotten to come for them.

"Has he been paid for bringing you here?" asked Mrs. Watkinson.

"I paid him when we came to the door," said Edward. "I thought perhaps he might want the money for some purpose before he came for us."

"That was very kind in you, sir," said Mrs. Watkinson, "but not very wise. There's no dependence on any coachman; and perhaps as he may be sure of business enough this rainy night he may never come at all—being already paid for bringing you here."

Now, the truth was that the coachman *had* come at the appointed time, but the noise of Jane's piano had prevented his arrival being heard in the back parlor. The Irish girl had gone to the door when he rang the bell, and recognized in him what she called "an ould friend." Just then a lady and gentleman who had been caught in the rain came running along, and seeing a carriage drawing up at a door, the gentleman inquired of the driver if he could not take them to Rutgers Place. The driver replied that he had just come for two ladies and a gentleman whom he had brought from the Astor House.

"Indeed and Patrick," said the girl who stood at the door, "if I was you I'd be after making another penny to-night. Miss Jane is pounding away at one of her long music pieces, and it won't be over before you have time to get to Rutgers and back again. And if you do make them wait awhile, where's the harm? They've a dry roof over their heads, and I warrant it's not the first waiting they've ever had in their lives; and it won't be the last neither."

"Exactly so," said the gentleman; and regardless of the propriety of first sending to consult the persons who had engaged the carriage, he told his wife to step in, and following her instantly himself, they drove away to Rutgers Place.

Reader, if you were ever detained in a strange house by the non-arrival of your carriage, you will easily understand the excessive annoyance of finding that you are keeping a family out of their beds beyond their usual hour. And in this case, there was a double grievance; the guests being all impatience to get off to a better place. The children, all crying when wakened from their sleep, were finally taken to bed by two servant maids, and Jane Watkinson, who never came back again. None were left but Hester, the great French scholar, who, being one of those young imps that seem to have the faculty of living without sleep, sat bolt upright with her eyes wide open, watching the uncomfortable visitors.

The Morlands felt as if they could bear it no longer, and Edward proposed sending for another carriage to the nearest livery stable.

"We don't keep a man now," said Mrs. Watkinson, who sat nodding in the rocking-chair, attempting now and then a snatch of conversation, and saying "ma'am" still more frequently than usual. "Men servants are dreadful trials, ma'am, and we gave them up three years ago. And I don't know how Mary or Katy are to go out this stormy night in search of a livery stable."

"On no consideration could I allow the women to do so," replied Edward. "If you will oblige me by the loan of an umbrella, I will go myself."

Accordingly he set out on this business, but was unsuccessful at two livery stables, the carriages being all out. At last he found one, and was driven in it to Mr. Watkinson's house, where his mother and sister were awaiting him, all quite ready, with their calashes and shawls on. They gladly took their leave; Mrs. Watkinson rousing herself to hope they had spent a pleasant evening, and that they would come and pass another with her on their return to New York. In such cases how difficult it is to reply even with what are called "words of course."

A kitchen lamp was brought to light them to the door, the entry lamp having long since been extinguished. Fortunately the rain had ceased; the stars began to re-appear, and the Morlands, when they found themselves in the carriage and on their way to Mrs. St. Leonard's, felt as if they could breathe again. As may be supposed, they freely discussed the annoyances of the evening; but now those troubles were over they felt rather inclined to be merry about them.

"Dear mother," said Edward, "how I pitied you for having to endure Mrs. Watkinson's perpetual 'ma'aming' and 'ma'aming'; for I know you dislike the word."

"I wish," said Caroline, "I was not so prone to be taken with ridiculous recollections. But really to-night I could not get that old foolish child's play out of my head—

> Here come three knights out of Spain
> A-courting of your daughter Jane."

"*I* shall certainly never be one of those Spanish knights," said Edward. "Her daughter Jane is in no danger of being ruled by any 'flattering tongue' of mine. But what a shame for us to be talking of them in this manner."

They drove to Mrs. St. Leonard's, hoping to be yet in time to pass half an hour there; though it was now near twelve o'clock and summer parties never continue to a very late hour. But as they came into the street in which she lived they were met by a number of coaches on their way home, and on reaching the door of her brilliantly lighted mansion, they saw the last of the guests driving off in the last of the carriages, and several musicians coming down the steps with their instruments in their hands.

"So there *has* been a dance, then!" sighed Caroline. "Oh, what we have missed! It is really too provoking."

"So it is," said Edward; "but remember that to-morrow morning we set off for Niagara."

"I will leave a note for Mrs. St. Leonard," said his mother, "explaining that we were detained at Mrs. Watkinson's by our coachman disappointing us. Let us console ourselves with the hope of seeing more of this lady on our return. And now, dear Caroline, you must draw a moral from the untoward events of to-day. When you are mistress of a house, and wish to show civility to strangers, let the invitation be always accompanied with a frank disclosure of what they are to expect. And if you cannot conveniently invite company to meet them, tell them at once that you will not insist on their keeping their engagement with *you* if anything offers afterwards that they think they would prefer; provided only that they apprize you in time of the change in their plan."

"Oh, mamma," replied Caroline, "you may be sure I shall always take care not to betray my visitors into an engagement which they may have cause to regret, particularly if they are strangers whose time is limited. I shall certainly, as you say, tell them not to consider themselves bound to me if they afterwards receive an invitation which promises them more enjoyment. It will be a long while before I forget, the Watkinson evening."

TITBOTTOM'S SPECTACLES
By George William Curtis (1824-1892)

[From *Putnam's Monthly*, December, 1854. Republished in the volume, *Prue and I* (1856), by George William Curtis (Harper & Brothers).]

IN my mind's eye, Horatio.

Prue and I do not entertain much; our means forbid it. In truth, other people entertain for us. We enjoy that hospitality of which no account is made. We see the show, and hear the music, and smell the flowers of great festivities, tasting as it were the drippings from rich dishes. Our own dinner service is remarkably plain, our dinners, even on state occasions, are strictly in keeping, and almost our only guest is Titbottom. I buy a handful of roses as I come up from the office, perhaps, and Prue arranges them so prettily in a glass dish for the centre of the table that even when I have hurried out to see Aurelia step into her carriage to go out to dine, I have thought that the bouquet she carried was not more beautiful because it was more costly. I grant that it was more harmonious with her superb beauty and her rich attire. And I have no doubt that if Aurelia knew the old man, whom she must have seen so often watching her, and his wife, who ornaments her sex with as much sweetness, although with less splendor, than Aurelia herself, she would also acknowledge that the nosegay of roses was as fine and fit upon their table as her own sumptuous bouquet is for herself. I have that faith in the perception of that lovely lady. It is at least my habit—I hope I may say, my nature, to believe the best of people, rather than the worst. If I thought that all this sparkling setting of beauty—this fine fashion—these blazing jewels and lustrous silks and airy gauzes, embellished with gold-threaded embroidery and wrought in a thousand exquisite elaborations, so that I cannot see one of those lovely girls pass me by without thanking God for the vision—if I thought that this was all, and that underneath her lace flounces and diamond bracelets Aurelia was a sullen, selfish woman, then I should turn sadly homewards, for I should see that her jewels were flashing scorn upon the object they adorned, and that her laces were of a more exquisite loveliness than the woman whom they merely touched with a superficial grace. It would be like a gaily decorated mausoleum—bright to see, but silent and dark within.

"Great excellences, my dear Prue," I sometimes allow myself to say, "lie concealed in the depths of character, like pearls at the bottom of the sea. Under the laughing, glancing surface, how little they are suspected! Perhaps love is nothing else than the sight of them by one person. Hence every man's mistress is apt to be an enigma to everybody else. I have no doubt that when Aurelia is engaged, people will say that she is a most admirable girl, certainly; but they cannot understand why any man should be in love with her. As if it were at all necessary that they should! And her lover, like a boy who finds a pearl in the public street, and wonders as much that others did not see it as that he did, will tremble until he knows his passion is returned; feeling, of course, that the whole world must be in love with this paragon who cannot possibly smile upon anything so unworthy as he."

"I hope, therefore, my dear Mrs. Prue," I continue to say to my wife, who looks up from her work regarding me with pleased pride, as if I were such an irresistible humorist, "you will allow me to believe that the depth may be calm although the surface is dancing. If you tell me that Aurelia is but a giddy girl, I shall believe that you think so. But I shall know, all the while, what profound dignity, and sweetness, and peace lie at the foundation of her character."

I say such things to Titbottom during the dull season at the office. And I have known him sometimes to reply with a kind of dry, sad humor, not as if he enjoyed the joke, but as if the joke must be made, that he saw no reason why I should be dull because the season was so.

"And what do I know of Aurelia or any other girl?" he says to me with that abstracted air. "I, whose Aurelias were of another century and another zone."

Then he falls into a silence which it seems quite profane to interrupt. But as we sit upon our high stools at the desk opposite each other, I leaning upon my elbows and looking at him; he, with sidelong face, glancing out of the window, as if it commanded a boundless landscape, instead of a dim, dingy office court, I cannot refrain from saying:

"Well!"

He turns slowly, and I go chatting on—a little too loquacious, perhaps, about those young girls. But I know that Titbottom regards such an excess as venial, for his sadness is so sweet that you could believe it the reflection of a smile from long, long years ago.

One day, after I had been talking for a long time, and we had put up our books, and were preparing to leave, he stood for some time by the window, gazing with a drooping intentness, as if he really saw something more than the dark court, and said slowly:

"Perhaps you would have different impressions of things if you saw them through my spectacles."

There was no change in his expression. He still looked from the window, and I said:

"Titbottom, I did not know that you used glasses. I have never seen you wearing spectacles."

"No, I don't often wear them. I am not very fond of looking through them. But sometimes an irresistible necessity compels me to put them on, and I cannot help seeing." Titbottom sighed.

"Is it so grievous a fate, to see?" inquired I.

"Yes; through my spectacles," he said, turning slowly and looking at me with wan solemnity.

It grew dark as we stood in the office talking, and taking our hats we went out together. The narrow street of business was deserted. The heavy iron shutters were gloomily closed over the windows. From one or two offices struggled the dim gleam of an early candle, by whose light some perplexed accountant sat belated, and hunting for his error. A careless clerk passed, whistling. But the great tide of life had ebbed. We heard its roar far away, and the sound stole into that silent street like the murmur of the ocean into an inland dell.

"You will come and dine with us, Titbottom?"

He assented by continuing to walk with me, and I think we were both glad when we reached the house, and Prue came to meet us, saying:

"Do you know I hoped you would bring Mr. Titbottom to dine?"

Titbottom smiled gently, and answered:

"He might have brought his spectacles with him, and I have been a happier man for it."

Prue looked a little puzzled.

"My dear," I said, "you must know that our friend, Mr. Titbottom, is the happy possessor of a pair of wonderful spectacles. I have never seen them, indeed; and, from what he says, I should be rather afraid of being seen by them. Most short-sighted persons are very glad to have the help of glasses; but Mr. Titbottom seems to find very little pleasure in his."

"It is because they make him too far-sighted, perhaps," interrupted Prue quietly, as she took the silver soup-ladle from the sideboard.

We sipped our wine after dinner, and Prue took her work. Can a man be too far-sighted? I did not ask the question aloud. The very tone in which Prue had spoken convinced me that he might.

"At least," I said, "Mr. Titbottom will not refuse to tell us the history of his mysterious spectacles. I have known plenty of magic in eyes"—and I glanced at the tender blue eyes of Prue—"but I have not heard of any enchanted glasses."

"Yet you must have seen the glass in which your wife looks every morning, and I take it that glass must be daily enchanted." said Titbottom, with a bow of quaint respect to my wife.

I do not think I have seen such a blush upon Prue's cheek since—well, since a great many years ago.

"I will gladly tell you the history of my spectacles," began Titbottom. "It is very simple; and I am not at all sure that a great many other people have not a pair of the same kind. I have never, indeed, heard of them by the gross, like those of our young friend, Moses, the son of the Vicar of Wakefield. In fact, I think a gross would be quite enough to supply the world. It is a kind of article for which the demand does not increase with use. If we should all wear spectacles like mine, we should never smile any more. Oh—I am not quite sure—we should all be very happy."

"A very important difference," said Prue, counting her stitches.

"You know my grandfather Titbottom was a West Indian. A large proprietor, and an easy man, he basked in the tropical sun, leading his quiet, luxurious life. He lived much alone, and was what people call eccentric, by which I understand that he was very much himself, and, refusing the influence of other people, they had their little revenges, and called him names. It is a habit not exclusively tropical. I think I have seen the same thing even in this city. But he was greatly beloved—my bland and bountiful grandfather. He was so large-hearted and open-handed. He was so friendly, and thoughtful, and genial, that even his jokes had the air of graceful benedictions. He did not seem to grow old, and he was one of those who never appear to have been very young. He flourished in a perennial maturity, an immortal middle-age.

"My grandfather lived upon one of the small islands, St. Kit's, perhaps, and his domain extended to the sea. His house, a rambling West Indian mansion, was surrounded with deep, spacious piazzas, covered with luxurious lounges, among which one capacious chair was his peculiar seat. They tell me he used sometimes to sit there for the whole day, his great, soft, brown eyes fastened upon the sea, watching the specks of sails that flashed upon the horizon, while the evanescent expressions chased each other over his placid face, as if it reflected the calm and changing sea before him. His morning costume was an ample dressing-gown of gorgeously flowered silk, and his morning was very apt to last all day.

"He rarely read, but he would pace the great piazza for hours, with his hands sunken in the pockets of his dressing-gown, and an air of sweet reverie, which any author might be very happy to produce.

"Society, of course, he saw little. There was some slight apprehension that if he were bidden to social entertainments he might forget his coat, or arrive without some other essential part of his dress; and there is a sly tradition in the Titbottom family that, having been invited to a ball in honor of the new governor of the island, my grandfather Titbottom sauntered into the hall towards midnight, wrapped in the gorgeous flowers of his dressing-gown, and with his hands buried in the pockets, as usual. There was great excitement, and immense deprecation of gubernatorial ire. But it happened that the governor and my grandfather were old friends, and there was no offense. But as they were conversing together, one of the distressed managers cast indignant glances at the brilliant costume of my grandfather, who summoned him, and asked courteously:

"'Did you invite me or my coat?'

"'You, in a proper coat,' replied the manager.

"The governor smiled approvingly, and looked at my grandfather.

"'My friend," said he to the manager, 'I beg your pardon, I forgot.'

"The next day my grandfather was seen promenading in full ball dress along the streets of the little town.

"'They ought to know,' said he, 'that I have a proper coat, and that not contempt nor poverty, but forgetfulness, sent me to a ball in my dressing-gown.'

"He did not much frequent social festivals after this failure, but he always told the story with satisfaction and a quiet smile.

"To a stranger, life upon those little islands is uniform even to weariness. But the old native dons like my grandfather ripen in the prolonged sunshine, like the turtle upon the Bahama banks, nor know of existence more desirable. Life in the tropics I take to be a placid torpidity. During the long, warm mornings of nearly half a century, my grandfather Titbottom had sat in his dressing-gown and gazed at the sea. But one calm June day, as he slowly paced the piazza after breakfast, his dreamy glance was arrested by a little vessel, evidently nearing the shore. He called for his spyglass, and surveying the craft, saw that she came from the neighboring island. She glided smoothly, slowly, over the summer sea. The warm morning air was sweet with perfumes, and silent with heat. The sea sparkled languidly, and the brilliant blue hung cloudlessly over. Scores of little island vessels had my grandfather seen come over the horizon, and cast anchor in the port. Hundreds of summer mornings had the white sails flashed and faded, like vague faces through forgotten dreams. But this time he laid down the spyglass, and leaned against a column of the piazza, and watched the vessel with an intentness that he could not explain. She came nearer and nearer, a graceful spectre in the dazzling morning.

"'Decidedly I must step down and see about that vessel,' said my grandfather Titbottom.

"He gathered his ample dressing-gown about him, and stepped from the piazza with no other protection from the sun than the little smoking cap upon his head. His face wore a calm, beaming smile, as if he approved of all the world. He was not an old man, but there was almost a patriarchal pathos in his expression as he sauntered along in the sunshine towards the shore. A group of idle gazers was collected to watch the arrival. The little vessel furled her sails and drifted slowly landward, and as she was of very light draft, she came close to the shelving shore. A long plank was put out from her side, and the debarkation commenced. My grandfather Titbottom stood looking on to see the passengers descend. There were but a few of them, and mostly traders from the neighboring island. But suddenly the face of a young girl appeared over the side of the vessel, and she stepped upon the plank to descend. My grandfather Titbottom instantly advanced, and moving briskly reached the top of the plank at the same moment, and with the old tassel of his cap flashing in the sun, and one hand in the pocket of his dressing gown, with the other he handed the young lady carefully down the plank. That young lady was afterwards my grandmother Titbottom.

"And so, over the gleaming sea which he had watched so long, and which seemed thus to reward his patient gaze, came his bride that sunny morning.

"'Of course we are happy,' he used to say: 'For you are the gift of the sun I have loved so long and so well.' And my grandfather Titbottom would lay his hand so tenderly upon the golden hair of his young bride, that you could fancy him a devout Parsee caressing sunbeams.

"There were endless festivities upon occasion of the marriage; and my grandfather did not go to one of them in his dressing-gown. The gentle sweetness of his wife melted every heart into love and sympathy. He was much older than she, without doubt. But age, as he used to say with a smile of immortal youth, is a matter of feeling, not of years. And if, sometimes, as she sat by his side upon the piazza, her fancy looked through her eyes upon that summer sea and saw a younger lover, perhaps some one of those graceful and glowing heroes who occupy the foreground of all young maidens' visions by the sea, yet she could not find one more generous and gracious, nor fancy one more worthy and loving than my grandfather Titbottom. And if in the moonlit midnight, while he lay calmly sleeping, she leaned out of the window and sank into vague reveries of sweet possibility, and watched the gleaming path of the moonlight upon the water, until the dawn glided over it—it was only that mood of nameless regret and longing, which underlies all human happiness,—or it was the vision of that life of society, which she had never seen, but of which she had often read, and which looked very fair and alluring across the sea to a girlish imagination which knew that it should never know that reality.

"These West Indian years were the great days of the family," said Titbottom, with an air of majestic and regal regret, pausing and musing in our little parlor, like a late Stuart in exile, remembering England. Prue raised her eyes from her work, and looked at him with a subdued admiration; for I have observed that, like the rest of her sex, she has a singular sympathy with the representative of a reduced family. Perhaps it is their finer perception which leads these tender-hearted women to recognize the divine right of social superiority so much more readily than we; and yet, much as Titbottom was enhanced in my wife's admiration by the discovery that his dusky sadness of nature and expression was, as it were, the expiring gleam and late twilight of ancestral splendors, I doubt if Mr. Bourne would have preferred him for bookkeeper a moment sooner upon that account. In truth, I have observed, down town, that the fact of your ancestors doing nothing is not considered good proof that you can do anything. But Prue and her sex regard sentiment more than action, and I understand easily enough why she is never tired of hearing me read of Prince Charlie. If Titbottom had been only a little younger, a little handsomer, a little more gallantly dressed—in fact, a little more of the Prince Charlie, I am sure her eyes would not have fallen again upon her work so tranquilly, as he resumed his story.

"I can remember my grandfather Titbottom, although I was a very young child, and he was a very old man. My young mother and my young grandmother are very distinct figures in my memory, ministering to the old gentleman, wrapped in his dressing-gown, and seated upon the piazza. I remember his white hair and his calm smile, and how, not long before he died, he called me to him, and laying his hand upon my head, said to me:

"My child, the world is not this great sunny piazza, nor life the fairy stories which the women tell you here as you sit in their laps. I shall soon be gone, but I want to leave with you some memento of my love for you, and I know nothing more valuable than these spectacles, which your grandmother brought from her native island, when she arrived here one fine summer morning, long ago. I cannot quite tell whether, when you grow older, you will regard it as a gift of the greatest value or as something that you had been happier never to have possessed.'

"'But grandpapa, I am not short-sighted.'

"'My son, are you not human?' said the old gentleman; and how shall I ever forget the thoughtful sadness with which, at the same time he handed me the spectacles.

"Instinctively I put them on, and looked at my grandfather. But I saw no grand-father, no piazza, no flowered dressing-gown: I saw only a luxuriant palm-tree, wav-ing broadly over a tranquil landscape. Pleasant homes clustered around it. Gardens teeming with fruit and flowers; flocks quietly feeding; birds wheeling and chirp-ing. I heard children's voices, and the low lullaby of happy mothers. The sound of cheerful singing came wafted from distant fields upon the light breeze. Golden harvests glistened out of sight, and I caught their rustling whisper of prosperity. A warm, mellow atmosphere bathed the whole. I have seen copies of the landscapes of the Italian painter Claude which seemed to me faint reminiscences of that calm and happy vision. But all this peace and prosperity seemed to flow from the spreading palm as from a fountain.

"I do not know how long I looked, but I had, apparently, no power, as I had no will, to remove the spectacles. What a wonderful island must Nevis be, thought I, if people carry such pictures in their pockets, only by buying a pair of spectacles! What wonder that my dear grandmother Titbottom has lived such a placid life, and has blessed us all with her sunny temper, when she has lived surrounded by such images of peace.

"My grandfather died. But still, in the warm morning sunshine upon the pi-azza, I felt his placid presence, and as I crawled into his great chair, and drifted on in reverie through the still, tropical day, it was as if his soft, dreamy eye had passed into my soul. My grandmother cherished his memory with tender regret. A violent passion of grief for his loss was no more possible than for the pensive decay of the year. We have no portrait of him, but I see always, when I remember him, that peaceful and luxuriant palm. And I think that to have known one good old man— one man who, through the chances and rubs of a long life, has carried his heart in his hand, like a palm branch, waving all discords into peace, helps our faith in God, in ourselves, and in each other, more than many sermons. I hardly know whether to be grateful to my grandfather for the spectacles; and yet when I remember that it is to them I owe the pleasant image of him which I cherish, I seem to myself sadly ungrateful.

"Madam," said Titbottom to Prue, solemnly, "my memory is a long and gloomy gallery, and only remotely, at its further end, do I see the glimmer of soft sunshine, and only there are the pleasant pictures hung. They seem to me very happy along whose gallery the sunlight streams to their very feet, striking all the pictured walls into unfading splendor."

Prue had laid her work in her lap, and as Titbottom paused a moment, and I turned towards her, I found her mild eyes fastened upon my face, and glistening with happy tears.

"Misfortunes of many kinds came heavily upon the family after the head was gone. The great house was relinquished. My parents were both dead, and my grandmother had entire charge of me. But from the moment that I received the gift of the spectacles, I could not resist their fascination, and I withdrew into myself, and became a solitary boy. There were not many companions for me of my own age, and they gradually left me, or, at least, had not a hearty sympathy with me; for if they teased me I pulled out my spectacles and surveyed them so seriously that they acquired a kind of awe of me, and evidently regarded my grandfather's gift as a concealed magical weapon which might be dangerously drawn upon them at any moment. Whenever, in our games, there were quarrels and high words, and I began to feel about my dress and to wear a grave look, they all took the alarm, and shouted, 'Look out for Titbottom's spectacles,' and scattered like a flock of scared sheep.

"Nor could I wonder at it. For, at first, before they took the alarm, I saw strange sights when I looked at them through the glasses. If two were quarrelling about a marble or a ball, I had only to go behind a tree where I was concealed and look at them leisurely. Then the scene changed, and no longer a green meadow with boys playing, but a spot which I did not recognize, and forms that made me shudder or smile. It was not a big boy bullying a little one, but a young wolf with glistening teeth and a lamb cowering before him; or, it was a dog faithful and famishing—or a star going slowly into eclipse—or a rainbow fading—or a flower blooming—or a sun rising—or a waning moon. The revelations of the spectacles determined my feeling for the boys, and for all whom I saw through them. No shyness, nor awkwardness, nor silence, could separate me from those who looked lovely as lilies to my illuminated eyes. If I felt myself warmly drawn to any one I struggled with the fierce desire of seeing him through the spectacles. I longed to enjoy the luxury of ignorant feeling, to love without knowing, to float like a leaf upon the eddies of life, drifted now to a sunny point, now to a solemn shade—now over glittering ripples, now over gleaming calms,—and not to determined ports, a trim vessel with an inexorable rudder.

"But, sometimes, mastered after long struggles, I seized my spectacles and sauntered into the little town. Putting them to my eyes I peered into the houses and at the people who passed me. Here sat a family at breakfast, and I stood at the window looking in. O motley meal! fantastic vision! The good mother saw her lord sitting opposite, a grave, respectable being, eating muffins. But I saw only a bank-bill, more or less crumpled and tattered, marked with a larger or lesser figure. If a sharp wind blew suddenly, I saw it tremble and flutter; it was thin, flat, impalpable. I removed my glasses, and looked with my eyes at the wife. I could have smiled to see the humid tenderness with which she regarded her strange *vis-a-vis*. Is life only a game of blind-man's-buff? of droll cross-purposes?

"Or I put them on again, and looked at the wife. How many stout trees I saw,—how many tender flowers,—how many placid pools; yes, and how many little streams winding out of sight, shrinking before the large, hard, round eyes opposite, and slipping off into solitude and shade, with a low, inner song for their own solace. And in many houses I thought to see angels, nymphs, or at least, women, and could only find broomsticks, mops, or kettles, hurrying about, rattling, tinkling, in a state of shrill activity. I made calls upon elegant ladies, and after I had enjoyed the gloss of silk and the delicacy of lace, and the flash of jewels, I slipped on my spectacles, and saw a peacock's feather, flounced and furbelowed and fluttering; or an iron rod, thin, sharp, and hard; nor could I possibly mistake the movement of the drapery for any flexibility of the thing draped,—or, mysteriously chilled, I saw a statue of perfect form, or flowing movement, it might be alabaster, or bronze, or marble,—but sadly often it was ice; and I knew that after it had shone a little, and frozen a few eyes with its despairing perfection, it could not be put away in the niches of palaces for ornament and proud family tradition, like the alabaster, or bronze, or marble statues, but would melt, and shrink, and fall coldly away in colorless and useless water, be absorbed in the earth and utterly forgotten.

"But the true sadness was rather in seeing those who, not having the spectacles, thought that the iron rod was flexible, and the ice statue warm. I saw many a gallant heart, which seemed to me brave and loyal as the crusaders sent by genuine and noble faith to Syria and the sepulchre, pursuing, through days and nights, and a long life of devotion, the hope of lighting at least a smile in the cold eyes, if not a fire in the icy heart. I watched the earnest, enthusiastic sacrifice. I saw the pure resolve, the generous faith, the fine scorn of doubt, the impatience of suspicion. I watched the grace, the ardor, the glory of devotion. Through those strange spectacles how often I saw the noblest heart renouncing all other hope, all other ambition, all other life, than the possible love of some one of those statues. Ah! me, it was terrible, but they had not the love to give. The Parian face was so polished and smooth, because there was no sorrow upon the heart,—and, drearily often, no heart to be touched. I could not wonder that the noble heart of devotion was broken, for it had dashed itself against a stone. I wept, until my spectacles were dimmed for that hopeless sorrow; but there was a pang beyond tears for those icy statues.

"Still a boy, I was thus too much a man in knowledge,—I did not comprehend the sights I was compelled to see. I used to tear my glasses away from my eyes, and, frightened at myself, run to escape my own consciousness. Reaching the small house where we then lived, I plunged into my grandmother's room and, throwing myself upon the floor, buried my face in her lap; and sobbed myself to sleep with premature grief. But when I awakened, and felt her cool hand upon my hot forehead, and heard the low, sweet song, or the gentle story, or the tenderly told parable from the Bible, with which she tried to soothe me, I could not resist the mystic fascination that lured me, as I lay in her lap, to steal a glance at her through the spectacles.

"Pictures of the Madonna have not her rare and pensive beauty. Upon the tranquil little islands her life had been eventless, and all the fine possibilities of her nature were like flowers that never bloomed. Placid were all her years; yet I have read of no heroine, of no woman great in sudden crises, that it did not seem to me she might have been. The wife and widow of a man who loved his own home better than the homes of others, I have yet heard of no queen, no belle, no imperial beauty, whom in grace, and brilliancy, and persuasive courtesy, she might not have surpassed.

"Madam," said Titbottom to my wife, whose heart hung upon his story; "your husband's young friend, Aurelia, wears sometimes a camelia in her hair, and no diamond in the ball-room seems so costly as that perfect flower, which women envy, and for whose least and withered petal men sigh; yet, in the tropical solitudes of Brazil, how many a camelia bud drops from a bush that no eye has ever seen, which, had it flowered and been noticed, would have gilded all hearts with its memory.

"When I stole these furtive glances at my grandmother, half fearing that they were wrong, I saw only a calm lake, whose shores were low, and over which the sky hung unbroken, so that the least star was clearly reflected. It had an atmosphere of solemn twilight tranquillity, and so completely did its unruffled surface blend with the cloudless, star-studded sky, that, when I looked through my spectacles at my grandmother, the vision seemed to me all heaven and stars. Yet, as I gazed and gazed, I felt what stately cities might well have been built upon those shores, and have flashed prosperity over the calm, like coruscations of pearls.

"I dreamed of gorgeous fleets, silken sailed and blown by perfumed winds, drifting over those depthless waters and through those spacious skies. I gazed upon the twilight, the inscrutable silence, like a God-fearing discoverer upon a new, and vast, and dim sea, bursting upon him through forest glooms, and in the fervor of whose impassioned gaze, a millennial and poetic world arises, and man need no longer die to be happy.

"My companions naturally deserted me, for I had grown wearily grave and abstracted: and, unable to resist the allurement of my spectacles, I was constantly lost in a world, of which those companions were part, yet of which they knew nothing. I grew cold and hard, almost morose; people seemed to me blind and unreasonable. They did the wrong thing. They called green, yellow; and black, white. Young men said of a girl, 'What a lovely, simple creature!' I looked, and there was only a glistening wisp of straw, dry and hollow. Or they said, 'What a cold, proud beauty!' I looked, and lo! a Madonna, whose heart held the world. Or they said, 'What a wild, giddy girl!' and I saw a glancing, dancing mountain stream, pure as the virgin snows whence it flowed, singing through sun and shade, over pearls and gold dust, slipping along unstained by weed, or rain, or heavy foot of cattle, touching the flowers with a dewy kiss,—a beam of grace, a happy song, a line of light, in the dim and troubled landscape.

"My grandmother sent me to school, but I looked at the master, and saw that he was a smooth, round ferule—or an improper noun—or a vulgar fraction, and refused to obey him. Or he was a piece of string, a rag, a willow-wand, and I had a contemptuous pity. But one was a well of cool, deep water, and looking suddenly in, one day, I saw the stars. He gave me all my schooling. With him I used to walk by the sea, and, as we strolled and the waves plunged in long legions before us, I looked at him through the spectacles, and as his eye dilated with the boundless view, and his chest heaved with an impossible desire, I saw Xerxes and his army tossing and glittering, rank upon rank, multitude upon multitude, out of sight, but ever regularly advancing and with the confused roar of ceaseless music, prostrating themselves in abject homage. Or, as with arms outstretched and hair streaming on the wind, he chanted full lines of the resounding Iliad, I saw Homer pacing the AEgean sands in the Greek sunsets of forgotten times.

"My grandmother died, and I was thrown into the world without resources, and with no capital but my spectacles. I tried to find employment, but men were shy of me. There was a vague suspicion that I was either a little crazed, or a good deal in league with the Prince of Darkness. My companions who would persist in calling a piece of painted muslin a fair and fragrant flower had no difficulty; success waited for them around every corner, and arrived in every ship. I tried to teach, for I loved children. But if anything excited my suspicion, and, putting on my spectacles, I saw that I was fondling a snake, or smelling at a bud with a worm in it, I sprang up in horror and ran away; or, if it seemed to me through the glasses that a cherub smiled upon me, or a rose was blooming in my buttonhole, then I felt myself imperfect and impure, not fit to be leading and training what was so essentially superior in quality to myself, and I kissed the children and left them weeping and wondering.

"In despair I went to a great merchant on the island, and asked him to employ me.

"'My young friend,' said he, 'I understand that you have some singular secret, some charm, or spell, or gift, or something, I don't know what, of which people are afraid. Now, you know, my dear,' said the merchant, swelling up, and apparently prouder of his great stomach than of his large fortune, 'I am not of that kind. I am not easily frightened. You may spare yourself the pain of trying to impose upon me. People who propose to come to time before I arrive, are accustomed to arise very early in the morning,' said he, thrusting his thumbs in the armholes of his waistcoat, and spreading the fingers, like two fans, upon his bosom. 'I think I have heard something of your secret. You have a pair of spectacles, I believe, that you value very much, because your grandmother brought them as a marriage portion to your grandfather. Now, if you think fit to sell me those spectacles, I will pay you the largest market price for glasses. What do you say?'

"I told him that I had not the slightest idea of selling my spectacles.

"'My young friend means to eat them, I suppose,' said he with a contemptuous smile.

"I made no reply, but was turning to leave the office, when the merchant called after me—

"'My young friend, poor people should never suffer themselves to get into pets. Anger is an expensive luxury, in which only men of a certain income can indulge. A pair of spectacles and a hot temper are not the most promising capital for success in life, Master Titbottom.'

"I said nothing, but put my hand upon the door to go out, when the merchant said more respectfully,—

"'Well, you foolish boy, if you will not sell your spectacles, perhaps you will agree to sell the use of them to me. That is, you shall only put them on when I direct you, and for my purposes. Hallo! you little fool!' cried he impatiently, as he saw that I intended to make no reply.

"But I had pulled out my spectacles, and put them on for my own purpose, and against his direction and desire. I looked at him, and saw a huge bald-headed wild boar, with gross chops and a leering eye—only the more ridiculous for the high-arched, gold-bowed spectacles, that straddled his nose. One of his fore hoofs was thrust into the safe, where his bills payable were hived, and the other into his pocket, among the loose change and bills there. His ears were pricked forward with a brisk, sensitive smartness. In a world where prize pork was the best excellence, he would have carried off all the premiums.

"I stepped into the next office in the street, and a mild-faced, genial man, also a large and opulent merchant, asked me my business in such a tone, that I instantly looked through my spectacles, and saw a land flowing with milk and honey. There I pitched my tent, and stayed till the good man died, and his business was discontinued.

"But while there," said Titbottom, and his voice trembled away into a sigh, "I first saw Preciosa. Spite of the spectacles, I saw Preciosa. For days, for weeks, for months, I did not take my spectacles with me. I ran away from them, I threw them up on high shelves, I tried to make up my mind to throw them into the sea, or down the well. I could not, I would not, I dared not look at Preciosa through the spectacles. It was not possible for me deliberately to destroy them; but I awoke in the night, and could almost have cursed my dear old grandfather for his gift. I escaped from the office, and sat for whole days with Preciosa. I told her the strange things I had seen with my mystic glasses. The hours were not enough for the wild romances which I raved in her ear. She listened, astonished and appalled. Her blue eyes turned upon me with a sweet deprecation. She clung to me, and then withdrew, and fled fearfully from the room. But she could not stay away. She could not resist my voice, in whose tones burned all the love that filled my heart and brain. The very effort to resist the desire of seeing her as I saw everybody else, gave a frenzy and an unnatural tension to my feeling and my manner. I sat by her side, looking into her eyes, smoothing her hair, folding her to my heart, which was sunken and deep—why not forever?—in that dream of peace. I ran from her presence, and shouted, and leaped with joy, and sat the whole night through, thrilled into happiness by the thought of her love and loveliness, like a wind-harp, tightly strung, and answering the airiest sigh of the breeze with music. Then came calmer days—the conviction of deep love settled upon our lives—as after the hurrying, heaving days of spring, comes the bland and benignant summer.

"'It is no dream, then, after all, and we are happy,' I said to her, one day; and there came no answer, for happiness is speechless.

"We are happy then," I said to myself, "there is no excitement now. How glad I am that I can now look at her through my spectacles."

"I feared lest some instinct should warn me to beware. I escaped from her arms, and ran home and seized the glasses and bounded back again to Preciosa. As I entered the room I was heated, my head was swimming with confused apprehension, my eyes must have glared. Preciosa was frightened, and rising from her seat, stood with an inquiring glance of surprise in her eyes. But I was bent with frenzy upon my purpose. I was merely aware that she was in the room. I saw nothing else. I heard nothing. I cared for nothing, but to see her through that magic glass, and feel at once, all the fulness of blissful perfection which that would reveal. Preciosa stood before the mirror, but alarmed at my wild and eager movements, unable to distinguish what I had in my hands, and seeing me raise them suddenly to my face, she shrieked with terror, and fell fainting upon the floor, at the very moment that

I placed the glasses before my eyes, and beheld—myself, reflected in the mirror, before which she had been standing.

"Dear madam," cried Titbottom, to my wife, springing up and falling back again in his chair, pale and trembling, while Prue ran to him and took his hand, and I poured out a glass of water—"I saw myself."

There was silence for many minutes. Prue laid her hand gently upon the head of our guest, whose eyes were closed, and who breathed softly, like an infant in sleeping. Perhaps, in all the long years of anguish since that hour, no tender hand had touched his brow, nor wiped away the damps of a bitter sorrow. Perhaps the tender, maternal fingers of my wife soothed his weary head with the conviction that he felt the hand of his mother playing with the long hair of her boy in the soft West Indian morning. Perhaps it was only the natural relief of expressing a pent-up sorrow. When he spoke again, it was with the old, subdued tone, and the air of quaint solemnity.

"These things were matters of long, long ago, and I came to this country soon after. I brought with me, premature age, a past of melancholy memories, and the magic spectacles. I had become their slave. I had nothing more to fear. Having seen myself, I was compelled to see others, properly to understand my relations to them. The lights that cheer the future of other men had gone out for me. My eyes were those of an exile turned backwards upon the receding shore, and not forwards with hope upon the ocean. I mingled with men, but with little pleasure. There are but many varieties of a few types. I did not find those I came to clearer sighted than those I had left behind. I heard men called shrewd and wise, and report said they were highly intelligent and successful. But when I looked at them through my glasses, I found no halo of real manliness. My finest sense detected no aroma of purity and principle; but I saw only a fungus that had fattened and spread in a night. They all went to the theater to see actors upon the stage. I went to see actors in the boxes, so consummately cunning, that the others did not know they were acting, and they did not suspect it themselves.

"Perhaps you wonder it did not make me misanthropical. My dear friends, do not forget that I had seen myself. It made me compassionate, not cynical. Of course I could not value highly the ordinary standards of success and excellence. When I went to church and saw a thin, blue, artificial flower, or a great sleepy cushion expounding the beauty of holiness to pews full of eagles, half-eagles, and threepences, however adroitly concealed in broadcloth and boots: or saw an onion in an Easter bonnet weeping over the sins of Magdalen, I did not feel as they felt who saw in all this, not only propriety, but piety. Or when at public meetings an eel stood up on end, and wriggled and squirmed lithely in every direction, and declared that, for his part, he went in for rainbows and hot water—how could I help seeing that he was still black and loved a slimy pool?

"I could not grow misanthropical when I saw in the eyes of so many who were called old, the gushing fountains of eternal youth, and the light of an immortal dawn, or when I saw those who were esteemed unsuccessful and aimless, ruling a fair realm of peace and plenty, either in themselves, or more perfectly in another—a realm and princely possession for which they had well renounced a hopeless search and a belated triumph. I knew one man who had been for years a by-word for having sought the philosopher's stone. But I looked at him through the spectacles and saw a satisfaction in concentrated energies, and a tenacity arising from devotion to a noble dream, which was not apparent in the youths who pitied him in the aimless effeminacy of clubs, nor in the clever gentlemen who cracked their thin jokes upon him over a gossiping dinner.

"And there was your neighbor over the way, who passes for a woman who has failed in her career, because she is an old maid. People wag solemn heads of pity, and say that she made so great a mistake in not marrying the brilliant and famous man who was for long years her suitor. It is clear that no orange flower will ever bloom for her. The young people make tender romances about her as they watch her, and think of her solitary hours of bitter regret, and wasting longing, never to be satisfied. When I first came to town I shared this sympathy, and pleased my imagination with fancying her hard struggle with the conviction that she had lost all that made life beautiful. I supposed that if I looked at her through my spectacles, I should see that it was only her radiant temper which so illuminated her dress, that we did not see it to be heavy sables. But when, one day, I did raise my glasses and glanced at her, I did not see the old maid whom we all pitied for a secret sorrow, but a woman whose nature was a tropic, in which the sun shone, and birds sang, and flowers bloomed forever. There were no regrets, no doubts and half wishes, but a calm sweetness, a transparent peace. I saw her blush when that old lover passed by, or paused to speak to her, but it was only the sign of delicate feminine consciousness. She knew his love, and honored it, although she could not understand it nor return it. I looked closely at her, and I saw that although all the world had exclaimed at her indifference to such homage, and had declared it was astonishing she should lose so fine a match, she would only say simply and quietly—

"'If Shakespeare loved me and I did not love him, how could I marry him?'

"Could I be misanthropical when I saw such fidelity, and dignity, and simplicity?

"You may believe that I was especially curious to look at that old lover of hers, through my glasses. He was no longer young, you know, when I came, and his fame and fortune were secure. Certainly I have heard of few men more beloved, and of none more worthy to be loved. He had the easy manner of a man of the world, the sensitive grace of a poet, and the charitable judgment of a wide traveller. He was accounted the most successful and most unspoiled of men. Handsome, brilliant, wise, tender, graceful, accomplished, rich, and famous, I looked at him, without the spectacles, in surprise, and admiration, and wondered how your neighbor over the way had been so entirely untouched by his homage. I watched their intercourse in society, I saw her gay smile, her cordial greeting; I marked his frank address, his lofty courtesy. Their manner told no tales. The eager world was balked, and I pulled out my spectacles.

"I had seen her, already, and now I saw him. He lived only in memory, and his memory was a spacious and stately palace. But he did not oftenest frequent the banqueting hall, where were endless hospitality and feasting—nor did he loiter much in reception rooms, where a throng of new visitors was forever swarming—nor did he feed his vanity by haunting the apartment in which were stored the trophies of his varied triumphs—nor dream much in the great gallery hung with pictures of his travels. But from all these lofty halls of memory he constantly escaped to a remote and solitary chamber, into which no one had ever penetrated. But my fatal eyes, behind the glasses, followed and entered with him, and saw that the chamber was a chapel. It was dim, and silent, and sweet with perpetual incense that burned upon an altar before a picture forever veiled. There, whenever I chanced to look, I saw him kneel and pray; and there, by day and by night, a funeral hymn was chanted.

"I do not believe you will be surprised that I have been content to remain deputy bookkeeper. My spectacles regulated my ambition, and I early learned that there were better gods than Plutus. The glasses have lost much of their fascination now, and I do not often use them. Sometimes the desire is irresistible. Whenever I am greatly interested, I am compelled to take them out and see what it is that I admire.

"And yet—and yet," said Titbottom, after a pause, "I am not sure that I thank my grandfather."

Prue had long since laid away her work, and had heard every word of the story. I saw that the dear woman had yet one question to ask, and had been earnestly hoping to hear something that would spare her the necessity of asking. But Titbottom had resumed his usual tone, after the momentary excitement, and made no further allusion to himself. We all sat silently; Titbottom's eyes fastened musingly upon the carpet: Prue looking wistfully at him, and I regarding both.

It was past midnight, and our guest arose to go. He shook hands quietly, made his grave Spanish bow to Prue, and taking his hat, went towards the front door. Prue and I accompanied him. I saw in her eyes that she would ask her question. And as Titbottom opened the door, I heard the low words:

"And Preciosa?"

Titbottom paused. He had just opened the door and the moonlight streamed over him as he stood, turning back to us.

"I have seen her but once since. It was in church, and she was kneeling with her eyes closed, so that she did not see me. But I rubbed the glasses well, and looked at her, and saw a white lily, whose stem was broken, but which was fresh; and luminous, and fragrant, still."

"That was a miracle," interrupted Prue.

"Madam, it was a miracle," replied Titbottom, "and for that one sight I am devoutly grateful for my grandfather's gift. I saw, that although a flower may have lost its hold upon earthly moisture, it may still bloom as sweetly, fed by the dews of heaven."

The door closed, and he was gone. But as Prue put her arm in mine and we went upstairs together, she whispered in my ear:

"How glad I am that you don't wear spectacles."

MY DOUBLE; AND HOW HE UNDID ME
By Edward Everett Hale (1822-1909)

[From *The Atlantic Monthly*, September, 1859. Republished in the volume, *The Man Without a Country, and Other Tales* (1868), by Edward Everett Hale (Little, Brown & Co.).]

IT is not often that I trouble the readers of *The Atlantic Monthly*. I should not trouble them now, but for the importunities of my wife, who "feels to insist" that a duty to society is unfulfilled, till I have told why I had to have a double, and how he undid me. She is sure, she says, that intelligent persons cannot understand that pressure upon public servants which alone drives any man into the employment of a double. And while I fear she thinks, at the bottom of her heart, that my fortunes will never be re-made, she has a faint hope, that, as another Rasselas, I may teach a lesson to future publics, from which they may profit, though we die. Owing to the behavior of my double, or, if you please, to that public pressure which compelled me to employ him, I have plenty of leisure to write this communication.

I am, or rather was, a minister, of the Sandemanian connection. I was settled in the active, wide-awake town of Naguadavick, on one of the finest water-powers in Maine. We used to call it a Western town in the heart of the civilization of New England. A charming place it was and is. A spirited, brave young parish had I; and it seemed as if we might have all "the joy of eventful living" to our hearts' content.

Alas! how little we knew on the day of my ordination, and in those halcyon moments of our first housekeeping! To be the confidential friend in a hundred families in the town—cutting the social trifle, as my friend Haliburton says, "from the top of the whipped-syllabub to the bottom of the sponge-cake, which is the foundation"—to keep abreast of the thought of the age in one's study, and to do one's best on Sunday to interweave that thought with the active life of an active town, and to inspirit both and make both infinite by glimpses of the Eternal Glory, seemed such an exquisite forelook into one's life! Enough to do, and all so real and so grand! If this vision could only have lasted.

The truth is, that this vision was not in itself a delusion, nor, indeed, half bright enough. If one could only have been left to do his own business, the vision would have accomplished itself and brought out new paraheliacal visions, each as bright as the original. The misery was and is, as we found out, I and Polly, before long, that, besides the vision, and besides the usual human and finite failures in life (such as breaking the old pitcher that came over in the Mayflower, and putting into the fire the alpenstock with which her father climbed Mont Blanc)—besides, these, I say (imitating the style of Robinson Crusoe), there were pitchforked in on us a great rowen-heap of humbugs, handed down from some unknown seed-time, in which we were expected, and I chiefly, to fulfil certain public functions before the community, of the character of those fulfilled by the third row of supernumeraries who stand behind the Sepoys in the spectacle of the *Cataract of the Ganges*. They were the duties, in a word, which one performs as member of one or another social class or subdivision, wholly distinct from what one does as A. by himself A. What invisible power put these functions on me, it would be very hard to tell. But such power there was and is. And I had not been at work a year before I found I was living two lives, one real and one merely functional—for two sets of people, one my parish, whom I loved, and the other a vague public, for whom I did not care two straws. All this was in a vague notion, which everybody had and has, that this second life would eventually bring out some great results, unknown at present, to somebody somewhere.

Crazed by this duality of life, I first read Dr. Wigan on the *Duality of the Brain*, hoping that I could train one side of my head to do these outside jobs, and the other to do my intimate and real duties. For Richard Greenough once told me that, in studying for the statue of Franklin, he found that the left side of the great man's face was philosophic and reflective, and the right side funny and smiling. If you will go and look at the bronze statue, you will find he has repeated this observation there for posterity. The eastern profile is the portrait of the statesman Franklin, the western of Poor Richard. But Dr. Wigan does not go into these niceties of this subject, and I failed. It was then that, on my wife's suggestion, I resolved to look out for a Double.

I was, at first, singularly successful. We happened to be recreating at Stafford Springs that summer. We rode out one day, for one of the relaxations of that watering-place, to the great Monsonpon House. We were passing through one of the large halls, when my destiny was fulfilled! I saw my man!

He was not shaven. He had on no spectacles. He was dressed in a green baize roundabout and faded blue overalls, worn sadly at the knee. But I saw at once that he was of my height, five feet four and a half. He had black hair, worn off by his hat. So have and have not I. He stooped in walking. So do I. His hands were large, and mine. And—choicest gift of Fate in all—he had, not "a strawberry-mark on his left arm," but a cut from a juvenile brickbat over his right eye, slightly affecting the play of that eyebrow. Reader, so have I!—My fate was sealed!

A word with Mr. Holley, one of the inspectors, settled the whole thing. It proved that this Dennis Shea was a harmless, amiable fellow, of the class known as shiftless, who had sealed his fate by marrying a dumb wife, who was at that moment ironing in the laundry. Before I left Stafford, I had hired both for five years. We had applied to Judge Pynchon, then the probate judge at Springfield, to change the name of Dennis Shea to Frederic Ingham. We had explained to the Judge, what was the precise truth, that an eccentric gentleman wished to adopt Dennis under this new name into his family. It never occurred to him that Dennis might be more than fourteen years old. And thus, to shorten this preface, when we returned at night to my parsonage at Naguadavick, there entered Mrs. Ingham, her new dumb laundress, myself, who am Mr. Frederic Ingham, and my double, who was Mr. Frederic Ingham by as good right as I.

Oh, the fun we had the next morning in shaving his beard to my pattern, cutting his hair to match mine, and teaching him how to wear and how to take off gold-bowed spectacles! Really, they were electroplate, and the glass was plain (for the poor fellow's eyes were excellent). Then in four successive afternoons I taught him four speeches. I had found these would be quite enough for the supernumerary-Sepoy line of life, and it was well for me they were. For though he was good-natured, he was very shiftless, and it was, as our national proverb says, "like pulling teeth" to teach him. But at the end of the next week he could say, with quite my easy and frisky air:

1. "Very well, thank you. And you?" This for an answer to casual salutations.

2. "I am very glad you liked it."

3. "There has been so much said, and, on the whole, so well said, that I will not occupy the time."

4. "I agree, in general, with my friend on the other side of the room."

At first I had a feeling that I was going to be at great cost for clothing him. But it proved, of course, at once, that, whenever he was out, I should be at home. And I went, during the bright period of his success, to so few of those awful pageants which require a black dress-coat and what the ungodly call, after Mr. Dickens, a white choker, that in the happy retreat of my own dressing-gowns and jackets my days went by as happily and cheaply as those of another Thalaba. And Polly declares there was never a year when the tailoring cost so little. He lived (Dennis, not Thalaba) in his wife's room over the kitchen. He had orders never to show himself at that window. When he appeared in the front of the house, I retired to my sanctissimum and my dressing-gown. In short, the Dutchman and, his wife, in the old weather-box, had not less to do with, each other than he and I. He made the furnace-fire and split the wood before daylight; then he went to sleep again, and slept late; then came for orders, with a red silk bandanna tied round his head, with his overalls on, and his dress-coat and spectacles off. If we happened to be interrupted, no one guessed that he was Frederic Ingham as well as I; and, in the neighborhood, there grew up an impression that the minister's Irishman worked day-times in the factory village at New Coventry. After I had given him his orders, I never saw him till the next day.

I launched him by sending him to a meeting of the Enlightenment Board. The Enlightenment Board consists of seventy-four members, of whom sixty-seven are necessary to form a quorum. One becomes a member under the regulations laid down in old Judge Dudley's will. I became one by being ordained pastor of a church in Naguadavick. You see you cannot help yourself, if you would. At this particular time we had had four successive meetings, averaging four hours each—wholly occupied in whipping in a quorum. At the first only eleven men were present; at the next, by force of three circulars, twenty-seven; at the third, thanks to two days' canvassing by Auchmuty and myself, begging men to come, we had sixty. Half the others were in Europe. But without a quorum we could do nothing. All the rest of us waited grimly for our four hours, and adjourned without any action. At the fourth meeting we had flagged, and only got fifty-nine together. But on the first appearance of my double—whom I sent on this fatal Monday to the fifth meeting— he was the *sixty-seventh* man who entered the room. He was greeted with a storm of applause! The poor fellow had missed his way—read the street signs ill through his spectacles (very ill, in fact, without them)—and had not dared to inquire. He entered the room—finding the president and secretary holding to their chairs two judges of the Supreme Court, who were also members *ex officio*, and were begging leave to go away. On his entrance all was changed. *Presto*, the by-laws were amended, and the Western property was given away. Nobody stopped to converse with him. He voted, as I had charged him to do, in every instance, with the minority. I won new laurels as a man of sense, though a little unpunctual—and Dennis, *alias* Ingham, returned to the parsonage, astonished to see with how little wisdom the world is governed. He cut a few of my parishioners in the street; but he had his glasses off, and I am known to be nearsighted. Eventually he recognized them more readily than I.

I "set him again" at the exhibition of the New Coventry Academy; and here he undertook a "speaking part"—as, in my boyish, worldly days, I remember the bills used to say of Mlle. Celeste. We are all trustees of the New Coventry Academy; and there has lately been "a good deal of feeling" because the Sandemanian trustees did not regularly attend the exhibitions. It has been intimated, indeed, that the San-demanians are leaning towards Free-Will, and that we have, therefore, neglected these semi-annual exhibitions, while there is no doubt that Auchmuty last year went to Commencement at Waterville. Now the head master at New Coventry is a real good fellow, who knows a Sanskrit root when he sees it, and often cracks etymologies with me—so that, in strictness, I ought to go to their exhibitions. But think, reader, of sitting through three long July days in that Academy chapel, fol-lowing the program from

Tuesday Morning. English Composition. Sunshine. Miss Jones,

round to

Trio on Three Pianos. Duel from opera of Midshipman Easy. Marryatt.

coming in at nine, Thursday evening! Think of this, reader, for men who know the world is trying to go backward, and who would give their lives if they could help it on! Well! The double had succeeded so well at the Board, that I sent him to the Academy. (Shade of Plato, pardon!) He arrived early on Tuesday, when, indeed, few but mothers and clergymen are generally expected, and returned in the evening to us, covered with honors. He had dined at the right hand of the chairman, and he spoke in high terms of the repast. The chairman had expressed his interest in the French conversation. "I am very glad you liked it," said Dennis; and the poor chairman, abashed, supposed the accent had been wrong. At the end of the day, the gentlemen present had been called upon for speeches—the Rev. Frederic Ingham first, as it happened; upon which Dennis had risen, and had said, "There has been so much said, and, on the whole, so well said, that I will not occupy the time." The girls were delighted, because Dr. Dabney, the year before, had given them at this occasion a scolding on impropriety of behavior at lyceum lectures. They all declared Mr. Ingham was a love—and *so* handsome! (Dennis is good-looking.) Three of them, with arms behind the others' waists, followed him up to the wagon he rode home in; and a little girl with a blue sash had been sent to give him a rosebud. After this debut in speaking, he went to the exhibition for two days more, to the mutual satisfaction of all concerned. Indeed, Polly reported that he had pronounced the trustees' dinners of a higher grade than those of the parsonage. When the next term began, I found six of the Academy girls had obtained permission to come across the river and attend our church. But this arrangement did not long continue.

After this he went to several Commencements for me, and ate the dinners provided; he sat through three of our Quarterly Conventions for me—always voting judiciously, by the simple rule mentioned above, of siding with the minority. And I, meanwhile, who had before been losing caste among my friends, as holding myself aloof from the associations of the body, began to rise in everybody's favor. "Ingham's a good fellow—always on hand"; "never talks much—but does the right thing at the right time"; "is not as unpunctual as he used to be—he comes early, and sits through to the end." "He has got over his old talkative habit, too. I spoke to a friend of his about it once; and I think Ingham took it kindly," etc., etc.

This voting power of Dennis was particularly valuable at the quarterly meetings of the Proprietors of the Naguadavick Ferry. My wife inherited from her father some shares in that enterprise, which is not yet fully developed, though it doubtless will become a very valuable property. The law of Maine then forbade stockholders to appear by proxy at such meetings. Polly disliked to go, not being, in fact, a "hens'-rights hen," and transferred her stock to me. I, after going once, disliked it more than she. But Dennis went to the next meeting, and liked it very much. He said the armchairs were good, the collation good, and the free rides to stockholders pleasant. He was a little frightened when they first took him upon one of the ferry-boats, but after two or three quarterly meetings he became quite brave.

Thus far I never had any difficulty with him. Indeed, being of that type which is called shiftless, he was only too happy to be told daily what to do, and to be charged not to be forthputting or in any way original in his discharge of that duty. He learned, however, to discriminate between the lines of his life, and very much preferred these stockholders' meetings and trustees' dinners and commencement collations to another set of occasions, from which he used to beg off most piteously. Our excellent brother, Dr. Fillmore, had taken a notion at this time that our Sandemanian churches needed more expression of mutual sympathy. He insisted upon it that we were remiss. He said, that, if the Bishop came to preach at Naguadavick, all the Episcopal clergy of the neighborhood were present; if Dr. Pond came, all the Congregational clergymen turned out to hear him; if Dr. Nichols, all the Unitarians; and he thought we owed it to each other that, whenever there was an occasional service at a Sandemanian church, the other brethren should all, if possible, attend. "It looked well," if nothing more. Now this really meant that I had not been to hear one of Dr. Fillmore's lectures on the Ethnology of Religion. He forgot that he did not hear one of my course on the Sandemanianism of Anselm. But I felt badly when he said it; and afterwards I always made Dennis go to hear all the brethren preach, when I was not preaching myself. This was what he took exceptions to—the only thing, as I said, which he ever did except to. Now came the advantage of his long morning-nap, and of the green tea with which Polly supplied the kitchen. But he would plead, so humbly, to be let off, only from one or two! I never excepted him, however. I knew the lectures were of value, and I thought it best he should be able to keep the connection.

Polly is more rash than I am, as the reader has observed in the outset of this memoir. She risked Dennis one night under the eyes of her own sex. Governor Gorges had always been very kind to us; and when he gave his great annual party to the town, asked us. I confess I hated to go. I was deep in the new volume of Pfeiffer's *Mystics*, which Haliburton had just sent me from Boston. "But how rude," said Polly, "not to return the Governor's civility and Mrs. Gorges's, when they will be sure to ask why you are away!" Still I demurred, and at last she, with the wit of Eve and of Semiramis conjoined, let me off by saying that, if I would go in with her, and sustain the initial conversations with the Governor and the ladies staying there, she would risk Dennis for the rest of the evening. And that was just what we did. She took Dennis in training all that afternoon, instructed him in fashionable conversation, cautioned him against the temptations of the supper-table—and at nine in the evening he drove us all down in the carryall. I made the grand star-entree with Polly and the pretty Walton girls, who were staying with us. We had put Dennis into a great rough top-coat, without his glasses—and the girls never dreamed, in the darkness, of looking at him. He sat in the carriage, at the door, while we entered. I did the agreeable to Mrs. Gorges, was introduced to her niece. Miss Fernanda—I complimented Judge Jeffries on his decision in the great case of D'Aulnay *vs.* Laconia Mining Co.—I stepped into the dressing-room for a moment—stepped out for another—walked home, after a nod with Dennis, and tying the horse to a pump— and while I walked home, Mr. Frederic Ingham, my double, stepped in through the library into the Gorges's grand saloon.

Oh! Polly died of laughing as she told me of it at midnight! And even here, where I have to teach my hands to hew the beech for stakes to fence our cave, she dies of laughing as she recalls it—and says that single occasion was worth all we have paid for it. Gallant Eve that she is! She joined Dennis at the library door, and in an instant presented him to Dr. Ochterlong, from Baltimore, who was on a visit in town, and was talking with her, as Dennis came in. "Mr. Ingham would like to hear what you were telling us about your success among the German population." And Dennis bowed and said, in spite of a scowl from Polly, "I'm very glad you liked it." But Dr. Ochterlong did not observe, and plunged into the tide of explanation, Dennis listening like a prime-minister, and bowing like a mandarin—which is, I suppose, the same thing. Polly declared it was just like Haliburton's Latin conversation with the Hungarian minister, of which he is very fond of telling. "*Quoene sit historia Reformationis in Ungaria?*" quoth Haliburton, after some thought. And his *confrere* replied gallantly, "*In seculo decimo tertio,*" etc., etc., etc.; and from *decimo tertio* [Which means, "In the thirteenth century," my dear little bell-and-coral reader. You have rightly guessed that the question means, "What is the history of the Reformation in Hungary?"] to the nineteenth century and a half lasted till the oysters came. So was it that before Dr. Ochterlong came to the "success," or near it, Governor Gorges came to Dennis and asked him to hand Mrs. Jeffries down to supper, a request which he heard with great joy.

Polly was skipping round the room, I guess, gay as a lark. Auchmuty came to her "in pity for poor Ingham," who was so bored by the stupid pundit—and Auchmuty could not understand why I stood it so long. But when Dennis took Mrs. Jeffries down, Polly could not resist standing near them. He was a little flustered, till the sight of the eatables and drinkables gave him the same Mercian courage which it gave Diggory. A little excited then, he attempted one or two of his speeches to the Judge's lady. But little he knew how hard it was to get in even a *promptu* there edgewise. "Very well, I thank you," said he, after the eating elements were adjusted; "and you?" And then did not he have to hear about the mumps, and the measles, and arnica, and belladonna, and chamomile-flower, and dodecathem, till she changed oysters for salad—and then about the old practice and the new, and what her sister said, and what her sister's friend said, and what the physician to her sister's friend said, and then what was said by the brother of the sister of the physician of the friend of her sister, exactly as if it had been in Ollendorff? There was a moment's pause, as she declined champagne. "I am very glad you liked it," said Dennis again, which he never should have said, but to one who complimented a sermon. "Oh! you are so sharp, Mr. Ingham! No! I never drink any wine at all—except sometimes in summer a little currant spirits—from our own currants, you know. My own mother—that is, I call her my own mother, because, you know, I do not remember," etc., etc., etc.; till they came to the candied orange at the end of the feast—when Dennis, rather confused, thought he must say something, and tried No. 4—"I agree, in general, with my friend the other side of the room"—which he never should have said but at a public meeting. But Mrs. Jeffries, who never listens expecting to understand, caught him up instantly with, "Well, I'm sure my husband returns the compliment; he always agrees with you—though we do worship with the Methodists—but you know, Mr. Ingham," etc., etc., etc., till the move was made upstairs; and as Dennis led her through the hall, he was scarcely understood by any but Polly, as he said, "There has been so much said, and, on the whole, so well said, that I will not occupy the time."

His great resource the rest of the evening was standing in the library, carrying on animated conversations with one and another in much the same way. Polly had initiated him in the mysteries of a discovery of mine, that it is not necessary to finish your sentence in a crowd, but by a sort of mumble, omitting sibilants and dentals. This, indeed, if your words fail you, answers even in public extempore speech—but better where other talking is going on. Thus: "We missed you at the Natural History Society, Ingham." Ingham replies: "I am very glighloglum, that is, that you were m-m-m-m-m-m." By gradually dropping the voice, the interlocutor is compelled to supply the answer. "Mrs. Ingham, I hope your friend Augusta is better." Augusta has not been ill. Polly cannot think of explaining, however, and answers: "Thank you, ma'am; she is very rearason wewahwewob," in lower and lower tones. And Mrs. Throckmorton, who forgot the subject of which she spoke, as soon as she asked the question, is quite satisfied. Dennis could see into the card-room, and came to Polly to ask if he might not go and play all-fours. But, of course, she sternly refused. At midnight they came home delightedly: Polly, as I said, wild to tell me the story of victory; only both the pretty Walton girls said: "Cousin Frederic, you did not come near me all the evening."

We always called him Dennis at home, for convenience, though his real name was Frederic Ingham, as I have explained. When the election day came round, however, I found that by some accident there was only one Frederic Ingham's name on the voting-list; and, as I was quite busy that day in writing some foreign letters to Halle, I thought I would forego my privilege of suffrage, and stay quietly at home, telling Dennis that he might use the record on the voting-list and vote. I gave him a ticket, which I told him he might use, if he liked to. That was that very sharp election in Maine which the readers of *The Atlantic* so well remember, and it had been intimated in public that the ministers would do well not to appear at the polls. Of course, after that, we had to appear by self or proxy. Still, Naguadavick was not then a city, and this standing in a double queue at townmeeting several hours to vote was a bore of the first water; and so, when I found that there was but one Frederic Ingham on the list, and that one of us must give up, I stayed at home and finished the letters (which, indeed, procured for Fothergill his coveted appointment of Professor of Astronomy at Leavenworth), and I gave Dennis, as we called him, the chance. Something in the matter gave a good deal of popularity to the Frederic Ingham name; and at the adjourned election, next week, Frederic Ingham was chosen to the legislature. Whether this was I or Dennis, I never really knew. My friends seemed to think it was I; but I felt, that, as Dennis had done the popular thing, he was entitled to the honor; so I sent him to Augusta when the time came, and he took the oaths. And a very valuable member he made. They appointed him on the Committee on Parishes; but I wrote a letter for him, resigning, on the ground that he took an interest in our claim to the stumpage in the minister's sixteenths of Gore A, next No. 7, in the 10th Range. He never made any speeches, and always voted with the minority, which was what he was sent to do. He made me and himself a great many good friends, some of whom I did not afterwards recognize as quickly as Dennis did my parishioners. On one or two occasions, when there was wood to saw at home, I kept him at home; but I took those occasions to go to Augusta myself. Finding myself often in his vacant seat at these times, I watched the proceedings with a good deal of care; and once was so much excited that I delivered my somewhat celebrated speech on the Central School District question, a speech of which the State of Maine printed some extra copies. I believe there is no formal rule permitting strangers to speak; but no one objected.

Dennis himself, as I said, never spoke at all. But our experience this session led me to think, that if, by some such "general understanding" as the reports speak of in legislation daily, every member of Congress might leave a double to sit through those deadly sessions and answer to roll-calls and do the legitimate party-voting, which appears stereotyped in the regular list of Ashe, Bocock, Black, etc., we should gain decidedly in working power. As things stand, the saddest state prison I ever visit is that Representatives' Chamber in Washington. If a man leaves for an hour, twenty "correspondents" may be howling, "Where was Mr. Prendergast when the Oregon bill passed?" And if poor Prendergast stays there! Certainly, the worst use you can make of a man is to put him in prison!

I know, indeed, that public men of the highest rank have resorted to this expedient long ago. Dumas's novel of *The Iron Mask* turns on the brutal imprisonment of Louis the Fourteenth's double. There seems little doubt, in our own history, that it was the real General Pierce who shed tears when the delegate from Lawrence explained to him the sufferings of the people there—and only General Pierce's double who had given the orders for the assault on that town, which was invaded the next day. My charming friend, George Withers, has, I am almost sure, a double, who preaches his afternoon sermons for him. This is the reason that the theology often varies so from that of the forenoon. But that double is almost as charming as the original. Some of the most well-defined men, who stand out most prominently on the background of history, are in this way stereoscopic men; who owe their distinct relief to the slight differences between the doubles. All this I know. My present suggestion is simply the great extension of the system, so that all public machine-work may be done by it.

But I see I loiter on my story, which is rushing to the plunge. Let me stop an instant more, however, to recall, were it only to myself, that charming year while all was yet well. After the double had become a matter of course, for nearly twelve months before he undid me, what a year it was! Full of active life, full of happy love, of the hardest work, of the sweetest sleep, and the fulfilment of so many of the fresh aspirations and dreams of boyhood! Dennis went to every school-committee meeting, and sat through all those late wranglings which used to keep me up till midnight and awake till morning. He attended all the lectures to which foreign exiles sent me tickets begging me to come for the love of Heaven and of Bohemia. He accepted and used all the tickets for charity concerts which were sent to me. He appeared everywhere where it was specially desirable that "our denomination," or "our party," or "our class," or "our family," or "our street," or "our town," or "our country," or "our state," should be fully represented. And I fell back to that charming life which in boyhood one dreams of, when he supposes he shall do his own duty and make his own sacrifices, without being tied up with those of other people. My rusty Sanskrit, Arabic, Hebrew, Greek, Latin, French, Italian, Spanish, German and English began to take polish. Heavens! how little I had done with them while I attended to my *public* duties! My calls on my parishioners became the friendly, frequent, homelike sociabilities they were meant to be, instead of the hard work of a man goaded to desperation by the sight of his lists of arrears. And preaching! what a luxury preaching was when I had on Sunday the whole result of an individual, personal week, from which to speak to a people whom all that week I had been meeting as hand-to-hand friend! I never tired on Sunday, and was in condition to leave the sermon at home, if I chose, and preach it extempore, as all men should do always. Indeed, I wonder, when I think that a sensible people like ours—really more attached to their clergy than they were in the lost days, when the Mathers and Nortons were noblemen—should choose to neutralize so much of their ministers' lives, and destroy so much of their early training, by this undefined passion for seeing them in public. It springs from our balancing of sects. If a spirited Episcopalian takes an interest in the almshouse, and is put on the Poor Board, every other denomination must have a minister there, lest the poorhouse be changed into St. Paul's Cathedral. If a Sandemanian is chosen president of the Young Men's Library, there must be a Methodist vice-president and a Baptist secretary. And if a Universalist Sunday-School Convention collects five hundred delegates, the next Congregationalist Sabbath-School Conference must be as large, "lest 'they'—whoever *they* may be—should think 'we'—whoever *we* may be—are going down."

Freed from these necessities, that happy year, I began to know my wife by sight. We saw each other sometimes. In those long mornings, when Dennis was in the study explaining to map-peddlers that I had eleven maps of Jerusalem already, and to school-book agents that I would see them hanged before I would be bribed to introduce their textbooks into the schools—she and I were at work together, as in those old dreamy days—and in these of our log-cabin again. But all this could not last—and at length poor Dennis, my double, overtasked in turn, undid me.

It was thus it happened. There is an excellent fellow—once a minister—I will call him Isaacs—who deserves well of the world till he dies, and after—because he once, in a real exigency, did the right thing, in the right way, at the right time, as no other man could do it. In the world's great football match, the ball by chance found him loitering on the outside of the field; he closed with it, "camped" it, charged, it home—yes, right through the other side—not disturbed, not frightened by his own success—and breathless found himself a great man—as the Great Delta rang applause. But he did not find himself a rich man; and the football has never come in his way again. From that moment to this moment he has been of no use, that one can see, at all. Still, for that great act we speak of Isaacs gratefully and remember him kindly; and he forges on, hoping to meet the football somewhere again. In that vague hope, he had arranged a "movement" for a general organization of the human family into Debating Clubs, County Societies, State Unions, etc., etc., with a view of inducing all children to take hold of the handles of their knives and forks, instead of the metal. Children have bad habits in that way. The movement, of course, was absurd; but we all did our best to forward, not it, but him. It came time for the annual county-meeting on this subject to be held at Naguadavick. Isaacs came round, good fellow! to arrange for it—got the townhall, got the Governor to preside (the saint!—he ought to have triplet doubles provided him by law), and then came to get me to speak. "No," I said, "I would not speak, if ten Governors presided. I do not believe in the enterprise. If I spoke, it should be to say children should take hold of the prongs of the forks and the blades of the knives. I would subscribe ten dollars, but I would not speak a mill." So poor Isaacs went his way, sadly, to coax Auchmuty to speak, and Delafield. I went out. Not long after, he came back, and told Polly that they had promised to speak—the Governor would speak—and he himself would close with the quarterly report, and some interesting anecdotes regarding. Miss Biffin's way of handling her knife and Mr. Nellis's way of footing his fork. "Now if Mr. Ingham will only come and sit on the platform, he need not say one word; but it will show well in the paper—it will show that the Sandemanians take as much interest in the movement as the Armenians or the Mesopotamians, and will be a great favor to me." Polly, good soul! was tempted, and she promised. She knew Mrs. Isaacs was starving, and the babies—she knew Dennis was at home—and she promised! Night came, and I returned. I heard her story. I was sorry. I doubted. But Polly had promised to beg me, and I dared all! I told Dennis to hold his peace, under all circumstances, and sent him down.

It was not half an hour more before he returned, wild with excitement—in a perfect Irish fury—which it was long before I understood. But I knew at once that he had undone me!

What happened was this: The audience got together, attracted by Governor Gorges's name. There were a thousand people. Poor Gorges was late from Augusta. They became impatient. He came in direct from the train at last, really ignorant of the object of the meeting. He opened it in the fewest possible words, and said other gentlemen were present who would entertain them better than he. The audience were disappointed, but waited. The Governor, prompted by Isaacs, said, "The Honorable Mr. Delafield will address you." Delafield had forgotten the knives and forks, and was playing the Ruy Lopez opening at the chess club. "The Rev. Mr. Auchmuty will address you." Auchmuty had promised to speak late, and was at the school committee. "I see Dr. Stearns in the hall; perhaps he will say a word." Dr. Stearns said he had come to listen and not to speak. The Governor and Isaacs whispered. The Governor looked at Dennis, who was resplendent on the platform; but Isaacs, to give him his due, shook his head. But the look was enough. A miserable lad, ill-bred, who had once been in Boston, thought it would sound well to call for me, and peeped out, "Ingham!" A few more wretches cried, "Ingham! Ingham!" Still Isaacs was firm; but the Governor, anxious, indeed, to prevent a row, knew I would say something, and said, "Our friend Mr. Ingham is always prepared—and though we had not relied upon him, he will say a word, perhaps." Applause followed, which turned Dennis's head. He rose, flattered, and tried No. 3: "There has been so much said, and, on the whole, so well said, that I will not longer occupy the time!" and sat down, looking for his hat; for things seemed squally. But the people cried, "Go on! go on!" and some applauded. Dennis, still confused, but flattered by the applause, to which neither he nor I are used, rose again, and this time tried No. 2: "I am very glad you liked it!" in a sonorous, clear delivery. My best friends stared. All the people who did not know me personally yelled with delight at the aspect of the evening; the Governor was beside himself, and poor Isaacs thought he was undone! Alas, it was I! A boy in the gallery cried in a loud tone, "It's all an infernal humbug," just as Dennis, waving his hand, commanded silence, and tried No. 4: "I agree, in general, with my friend the other side of the room." The poor Governor doubted his senses, and crossed to stop him—not in time, however. The same gallery-boy shouted, "How's your mother?"—and Dennis, now completely lost, tried, as his last shot, No. 1, vainly: "Very well, thank you; and you?"

I think I must have been undone already. But Dennis, like another Lockhard chose "to make sicker." The audience rose in a whirl of amazement, rage, and sorrow. Some other impertinence, aimed at Dennis, broke all restraint, and, in pure Irish, he delivered himself of an address to the gallery, inviting any person who wished to fight to come down and do so—stating, that they were all dogs and cowards—that he would take any five of them single-handed, "Shure, I have said all his Riverence and the Misthress bade me say," cried he, in defiance; and, seizing the Governor's cane from his hand, brandished it, quarter-staff fashion, above his head. He was, indeed, got from the hall only with the greatest difficulty by the Governor, the City Marshal, who had been called in, and the Superintendent of my Sunday School.

The universal impression, of course, was, that the Rev. Frederic Ingham had lost all command of himself in some of those haunts of intoxication which for fifteen years I have been laboring to destroy. Till this moment, indeed, that is the impression in Naguadavick. This number of *The Atlantic* will relieve from it a hundred friends of mine who have been sadly wounded by that notion now for years—but I shall not be likely ever to show my head there again.

No! My double has undone me.

We left town at seven the next morning. I came to No. 9, in the Third Range, and settled on the Minister's Lot, In the new towns in Maine, the first settled minister has a gift of a hundred acres of land. I am the first settled minister in No. 9. My wife and little Paulina are my parish. We raise corn enough to live on in summer. We kill bear's meat enough to carbonize it in winter. I work on steadily on my *Traces of Sandemanianism in the Sixth and Seventh Centuries*, which I hope to persuade Phillips, Sampson & Co. to publish next year. We are very happy, but the world thinks we are undone.

A VISIT TO THE ASYLUM FOR AGED AND DECAYED PUNSTERS
By Oliver Wendell Holmes (1809-1894)

[From *The Atlantic Monthly*, January, 1861. Republished in *Soundings from the Atlantic* (1864), by Oliver Wendell Holmes, whose authorized publishers are the Houghton Mifflin Company.]

HAVING just returned from a visit to this admirable Institution in company with a friend who is one of the Directors, we propose giving a short account of what we saw and heard. The great success of the Asylum for Idiots and Feeble-minded Youth, several of the scholars from which have reached considerable distinction, one of them being connected with a leading Daily Paper in this city, and others having served in the State and National Legislatures, was the motive which led to the foundation of this excellent charity. Our late distinguished townsman, Noah Dow, Esquire, as is well known, bequeathed a large portion of his fortune to this establishment— "being thereto moved," as his will expressed it, "by the desire of *N. Dowing* some public Institution for the benefit of Mankind." Being consulted as to the Rules of the Institution and the selection of a Superintendent, he replied, that "all Boards must construct their own Platforms of operation. Let them select *anyhow* and he should be pleased." N.E. Howe, Esq., was chosen in compliance with this delicate suggestion.

The Charter provides for the support of "One hundred aged and decayed Gentlemen-Punsters." On inquiry if there way no provision for *females*, my friend called my attention to this remarkable psychological fact, namely:

THERE IS NO SUCH THING AS A FEMALE PUNSTER.

This remark struck me forcibly, and on reflection I found that *I never knew nor heard of one*, though I have once or twice heard a woman make a *single detached* pun, as I have known a hen to crow.

On arriving at the south gate of the Asylum grounds, I was about to ring, but my friend held my arm and begged me to rap with my stick, which I did. An old man with a very comical face presently opened the gate and put out his head.

"So you prefer *Cane* to *A bell*, do you?" he said—and began chuckling and coughing at a great rate.

My friend winked at me.

"You're here still, Old Joe, I see," he said to the old man.

"Yes, yes—and it's very odd, considering how often I've *bolted*, nights."

He then threw open the double gates for us to ride through.

"Now," said the old man, as he pulled the gates after us, "you've had a long journey."

"Why, how is that, Old Joe?" said my friend.

"Don't you see?" he answered; "there's the *East hinges* on the one side of the gate, and there's the *West hinges* on t'other side—haw! haw! haw!"

We had no sooner got into the yard than a feeble little gentleman, with a re-markably bright eye, came up to us, looking very serious, as if something had hap-pened.

"The town has entered a complaint against the Asylum as a gambling establish-ment," he said to my friend, the Director.

"What do you mean?" said my friend.

"Why, they complain that there's a *lot o' rye* on the premises," he answered, pointing to a field of that grain—and hobbled away, his shoulders shaking with laughter, as he went.

On entering the main building, we saw the Rules and Regulations for the Asy-lum conspicuously posted up. I made a few extracts which may be interesting:

SECT. I. OF VERBAL EXERCISES.

5. Each Inmate shall be permitted to make Puns freely from eight in the morn-ing until ten at night, except during Service in the Chapel and Grace before Meals.

6. At ten o'clock the gas will be turned off, and no further Puns, Conundrums,

or other play on words will be allowed to be uttered, or to be uttered aloud.

9. Inmates who have lost their faculties and cannot any longer make Puns shall be permitted to repeat such as may be selected for them by the Chaplain out of the work of *Mr. Joseph Miller*.

10. Violent and unmanageable Punsters, who interrupt others when engaged in conversation, with Puns or attempts at the same, shall be deprived of their *Joseph Millers*, and, if necessary, placed in solitary confinement.

SECT. III. OF DEPORTMENT AT MEALS.

4. No Inmate shall make any Pun, or attempt at the same, until the Blessing has been asked and the company are decently seated.

7. Certain Puns having been placed on the *Index Expurgatorius* of the Institution, no Inmate shall be allowed to utter them, on pain of being debarred the perusal of *Punch* and *Vanity Fair*, and, if repeated, deprived of his *Joseph Miller*.

Among these are the following:

Allusions to *Attic salt*, when asked to pass the salt-cellar.

Remarks on the Inmates being *mustered*, etc., etc.

Associating baked beans with the *bene*-factors of the Institution.

Saying that beef-eating is *befitting*, etc., etc.

The following are also prohibited, excepting to such Inmates as may have lost their faculties and cannot any longer make Puns of their own:

"——your own *hair* or a wig"; "it will be *long enough*," etc., etc.; "little of its age," etc., etc.; also, playing upon the following words: *hos*pital; *mayor*; *pun*; *pit-ied*; *bread*; *sauce*, etc., etc., etc. *See* INDEX EXPURGATORIUS, *printed for use of Inmates*.

The subjoined Conundrum is not allowed: Why is Hasty Pudding like the Prince? Because it comes attended by its *sweet*; nor this variation to it, *to wit*: Because the *'lasses runs after it*.

The Superintendent, who went round with us, had been a noted punster in his time, and well known in the business world, but lost his customers by making too free with their names—as in the famous story he set afloat in '29 *of four Jer-ries* attaching to the names of a noted Judge, an eminent Lawyer, the Secretary of the Board of Foreign Missions, and the well-known Landlord at Springfield. One of the *four Jerries*, he added, was of gigantic magnitude. The play on words was brought out by an accidental remark of Solomons, the well-known Banker. "*Capital punishment!*" the Jew was overheard saying, with reference to the guilty parties. He was understood, as saying, *A capital pun is meant*, which led to an investigation and the relief of the greatly excited public mind.

The Superintendent showed some of his old tendencies, as he went round with us.

"Do you know"—he broke out all at once—"why they don't take steppes in Tartary for establishing Insane Hospitals?"

We both confessed ignorance.

"Because there are *nomad* people to be found there," he said, with a dignified smile.

He proceeded to introduce us to different Inmates. The first was a middle-aged, scholarly man, who was seated at a table with a *Webster's Dictionary* and a sheet of paper before him.

"Well, what luck to-day, Mr. Mowzer?" said the Superintendent.

"Three or four only," said Mr. Mowzer. "Will you hear 'em now—now I'm here?"

We all nodded.

"Don't you see Webster *ers* in the words cent *er* and theat *er*?

"If he spells leather *lether*, and feather *fether*, isn't there danger that he'll give us a *bad spell of weather*?

"Besides, Webster is a resurrectionist; he does not allow *u* to rest quietly in the *mould*.

"And again, because Mr. Worcester inserts an illustration in his text, is that any reason why Mr. Webster's publishers should hitch one on in their appendix? It's what I call a *Connect-a-cut* trick.

"Why is his way of spelling like the floor of an oven? Because it is *under bread*."

"Mowzer!" said the Superintendent, "that word is on the Index!"

"I forgot," said Mr. Mowzer; "please don't deprive me of *Vanity Fair* this one time, sir."

"These are all, this morning. Good day, gentlemen." Then to the Superintendent: "Add you, sir!"

The next Inmate was a semi-idiotic-looking old man. He had a heap of block-letters before him, and, as we came up, he pointed, without saying a word, to the arrangements he had made with them on the table. They were evidently anagrams, and had the merit of transposing the letters of the words employed without addition or subtraction. Here are a few of them:

TIMES.	SMITE!
POST.	STOP!
TRIBUNE.	TRUE NIB.
WORLD.	DR. OWL.
ADVERTISER.	{ RES VERI DAT.
	{ IS TRUE. READ!
ALLOPATHY.	ALL O' TH' PAY.
HOMOEOPATHY.	O, THE ——! O! O, MY! PAH!

The mention of several New York papers led to two or three questions. Thus: Whether the Editor of *The Tribune* was *H.G. really*? If the complexion of his politics were not accounted for by his being *an eager* person himself? Whether Wendell *Fillips* were not a reduced copy of John *Knocks*? Whether a New York *Feuilletoniste* is not the same thing as a *Fellow down East*?

At this time a plausible-looking, bald-headed man joined us, evidently waiting to take a part in the conversation.

"Good morning, Mr. Riggles," said the Superintendent, "Anything fresh this morning? Any Conundrum?"

"I haven't looked at the cattle," he answered, dryly.

"Cattle? Why cattle?"

"Why, to see if there's any *corn under 'em*!" he said; and immediately asked, "Why is Douglas like the earth?"

We tried, but couldn't guess.

"Because he was *flattened out at the polls*!" said Mr. Riggles.

"A famous politician, formerly," said the Superintendent. "His grandfather was a *seize-Hessian-ist* in the Revolutionary War. By the way, I hear the *freeze-oil* doctrines don't go down at New Bedford."

The next Inmate looked as if he might have been a sailor formerly.

"Ask him what his calling was," said the Superintendent.

"Followed the sea," he replied to the question put by one of us. "Went as mate in a fishing-schooner."

"Why did you give it up?"

"Because I didn't like working for *two mast-ers*," he replied.

Presently we came upon a group of elderly persons, gathered about a venerable gentleman with flowing locks, who was propounding questions to a row of Inmates.

"Can any Inmate give me a motto for M. Berger?" he said.

Nobody responded for two or three minutes. At last one old man, whom I at once recognized as a Graduate of our University (Anno 1800) held up his hand.

"Rem *a cue* tetigit."

"Go to the head of the class, Josselyn," said the venerable patriarch.

The successful Inmate did as he was told, but in a very rough way, pushing against two or three of the Class.

"How is this?" said the Patriarch.

"You told me to go up *jostlin'*," he replied.

The old gentlemen who had been shoved about enjoyed the pun too much to be angry.

Presently the Patriarch asked again:

"Why was M. Berger authorized to go to the dances given to the Prince?"

The Class had to give up this, and he answered it himself:

"Because every one of his carroms was a *tick-it* to the ball."

"Who collects the money to defray the expenses of the last campaign in Italy?" asked the Patriarch.

Here again the Class failed.

"The war-cloud's rolling *Dun*," he answered.

"And what is mulled wine made with?"

Three or four voices exclaimed at once:

"*Sizzle-y* Madeira!"

Here a servant entered, and said, "Luncheon-time." The old gentlemen, who have excellent appetites, dispersed at once, one of them politely asking us if we would not stop and have a bit of bread and a little mite of cheese.

"There is one thing I have forgotten to show you," said the Superintendent, "the cell for the confinement of violent and unmanageable Punsters."

We were very curious to see it, particularly with reference to the alleged absence of every object upon which a play of words could possibly be made.

The Superintendent led us up some dark stairs to a corridor, then along a narrow passage, then down a broad flight of steps into another passageway, and opened a large door which looked out on the main entrance.

"We have not seen the cell for the confinement of 'violent and unmanageable' Punsters," we both exclaimed.

"This is the *sell!*" he exclaimed, pointing to the outside prospect.

My friend, the Director, looked me in the face so good-naturedly that I had to laugh.

"We like to humor the Inmates," he said. "It has a bad effect, we find, on their health and spirits to disappoint them of their little pleasantries. Some of the jests to which we have listened are not new to me, though I dare say you may not have heard them often before. The same thing happens in general society, with this additional disadvantage, that there is no punishment provided for 'violent and unmanageable' Punsters, as in our Institution."

We made our bow to the Superintendent and walked to the place where our carriage was waiting for us. On our way, an exceedingly decrepit old man moved slowly toward us, with a perfectly blank look on his face, but still appearing as if he wished to speak.

"Look!" said the Director—"that is our Centenarian."

The ancient man crawled toward us, cocked one eye, with which he seemed to see a little, up at us, and said:

"Sarvant, young Gentlemen. Why is a—a—a—like a—a—a—? Give it up? Because it's a—a—a—a—."

He smiled a pleasant smile, as if it were all plain enough.

"One hundred and seven last Christmas," said the Director. "Of late years he puts his whole Conundrums in blank—but they please him just as well."

We took our departure, much gratified and instructed by our visit, hoping to have some future opportunity of inspecting the Records of this excellent Charity and making extracts for the benefit of our Readers.

THE CELEBRATED JUMPING FROG OF CALAVERAS COUNTY
By Mark Twain (1835-1910)

[From *The Saturday Press*, Nov. 18, 1865. Republished in *The Celebrated Jumping Frog of Calaveras County, and Other Sketches* (1867), by Mark Twain, all of whose works are published by Harper & Brothers.]

IN compliance with the request of a friend of mine, who wrote me from the East, I called on good-natured, garrulous old Simon Wheeler, and inquired after my friend's friend, Leonidas W. Smiley, as requested to do, and I hereunto append the result. I have a lurking suspicion that *Leonidas W.* Smiley is a myth; and that my friend never knew such a personage; and that he only conjectured that if I asked old Wheeler about him, it would remind him of his infamous *Jim Smiley*, and he would go to work and bore me to death with some exasperating reminiscence of him as long and as tedious as it should be useless to me. If that was the design, it succeeded.

I found Simon Wheeler dozing comfortably by the barroom stove of the dilapidated tavern in the decayed mining camp of Angel's, and I noticed that he was fat and bald-headed, and had an expression of winning gentleness and simplicity upon his tranquil countenance. He roused up, and gave me good-day. I told him a friend had commissioned me to make some inquiries about a cherished companion of his boyhood named *Leonidas W.* Smiley—*Rev. Leonidas W.* Smiley, a young minister of the Gospel, who he had heard was at one time a resident of Angel's Camp. I added that if Mr. Wheeler could tell me anything about this Rev. Leonidas W. Smiley, I would feel under many obligations to him.

Simon Wheeler backed me into a corner and blockaded me there with his chair, and then sat down and reeled off the monotonous narrative which follows this paragraph. He never smiled, he never frowned, he never changed his voice from the gentle-flowing key to which he tuned his initial sentence, he never betrayed the slightest suspicion of enthusiasm; but all through the interminable narrative there ran a vein of impressive earnestness and sincerity, which showed me plainly that, so far from his imagining that there was anything ridiculous or funny about his story, he regarded it as a really important matter, and admired its two heroes as men of transcendent genius in *finesse*. I let him go on in his own way, and never interrupted him once.

"Rev. Leonidas W. H'm, Reverend Le—well, there was a feller here once by the name of *Jim* Smiley, in the winter of '49—or may be it was the spring of '50—I don't recollect exactly, somehow, though what makes me think it was one or the other is because I remember the big flume warn't finished when he first came to the camp; but any way, he was the curiousest man about always betting on anything that turned up you ever see, if he could get anybody to bet on the other side; and if he couldn't he'd change sides. Any way that suited the other man would suit *him*—any way just so's he got a bet, *he* was satisfied. But still he was lucky, uncommon lucky; he most always come out winner. He was always ready and laying for a chance; there couldn't be no solit'ry thing mentioned but that feller'd offer to bet on it, and take any side you please, as I was just telling you. If there was a horse-race, you'd find him flush or you'd find him busted at the end of it; if there was a dog-fight, he'd bet on it; if there was a cat-fight, he'd bet on it; if there was a chicken-fight, he'd bet on it; why, if there was two birds setting on a fence, he would bet you which one would fly first; or if there was a camp-meeting, he would be there reg'lar to bet on Parson Walker, which he judged to be the best exhorter about here, and he was, too, and a good man. If he even see a straddle-bug start to go anywheres, he would bet you how long it would take him to get to—to wherever he *was* going to, and if you took him up, he would foller that straddle-bug to Mexico but what he would find out where he was bound for and how long he was on the road. Lots of the boys here has seen that Smiley and can tell you about him. Why, it never made no difference to *him*—he'd bet on *any* thing—the dang-est feller. Parson Walker's wife laid very sick once, for a good while, and it seemed as if they warn't going to save her; but one morning he come in, and Smiley up and asked him how she was, and he said she was considerable better—thank the Lord for his inf'nit' mercy—and coming on so smart that with the blessing of Prov'dence she'd get well yet; and Smiley, before he thought, says, 'Well, I'll risk two-and-a-half she don't anyway.'"

Thish-yer Smiley had a mare—the boys called her the fifteen-minute nag, but that was only in fun, you know, because, of course, she was faster than that—and he used to win money on that horse, for all she was so slow and always had the asthma, or the distemper, or the consumption, or something of that kind. They used to give her two or three hundred yards start, and then pass her under way; but always at the fag-end of the race she'd get excited and desperate-like, and come cavorting and straddling up, and scattering her legs around limber, sometimes in the air, and sometimes out to one side amongst the fences, and kicking up m-o-r-e dust and raising m-o-r-e racket with her coughing and sneezing and blowing her nose—and always fetch up at the stand just about a neck ahead, as near as you could cipher it down.

And he had a little small bull-pup, that to look at him you'd think he warn't worth a cent but to set around and look ornery and lay for a chance to steal some-thing. But as soon as money was up on him he was a different dog; his under-jaw'd begin to stick out like the fo'-castle of a steamboat, and his teeth would uncover and shine like the furnaces. And a dog might tackle him and bully-rag him, and bite him, and throw him over his shoulder two or three times, and Andrew Jackson—which was the name of the pup—Andrew Jackson would never let on but what *he* was satisfied, and hadn't expected nothing else—and the bets being doubled and doubled on the other side all the time, till the money was all up; and then all of a sudden he would grab that other dog jest by the j'int of his hind leg and freeze to it—not chaw, you understand, but only just grip and hang on till they throwed up the sponge, if it was a year. Smiley always come out winner on that pup, till he har-nessed a dog once that didn't have no hind legs, because they'd been sawed off in a circular saw, and when the thing had gone along far enough, and the money was all up, and he come to make a snatch for his pet holt, he see in a minute how he'd been imposed on, and how the other dog had him in the door, so to speak, and he 'peared surprised, and then he looked sorter discouraged-like, and didn't try no more to win the fight, and so he got shucked out bad. He gave Smiley a look, as much as to say his heart was broke, and it was *his* fault, for putting up a dog that hadn't no hind legs for him to take holt of, which was his main dependence in a fight, and then he limped off a piece and laid down and died. It was a good pup, was that Andrew Jackson, and would have made a name for hisself if he'd lived, for the stuff was in him and he had genius—I know it, because he hadn't no opportunities to speak of, and it don't stand to reason that a dog could make such a fight as he could under them circumstances if he hadn't no talent. It always makes me feel sorry when I think of that last fight of his'n, and the way it turned out.

Well, thish-yer Smiley had rat-tarriers, and chicken cocks, and tom-cats and all of them kind of things, till you couldn't rest, and you couldn't fetch nothing for him to bet on but he'd match you. He ketched a frog one day, and took him home, and said he cal'lated to educate him; and so he never done nothing for three months but set in his back yard and learn that frog to jump. And you bet you he *did* learn him, too. He'd give him a little punch behind, and the next minute you'd see that frog whirling in the air like a doughnut—see him turn one summerset, or may be a couple, if he got a good start, and come down flat-footed and all right, like a cat. He got him up so in the matter of ketching flies, and kep' him in practice so constant, that he'd nail a fly every time as fur as he could see him. Smiley said all a frog wanted was education, and he could do 'most anything—and I believe him. Why, I've seen him set Dan'l Webster down here on this floor—Dan'l Webster was the name of the frog—and sing out, "Flies, Dan'l, flies!" and quicker'n you could wink he'd spring straight up and snake a fly off'n the counter there, and flop down on the floor ag'in as solid as a gob of mud, and fall to scratching the side of his head with his hind foot as indifferent as if he hadn't no idea he'd been doin' any more'n any frog might do. You never see a frog so modest and straightfor'ard as he was, for all he was so gifted. And when it come to fair and square jumping on a dead level, he could get over more ground at one straddle than any animal of his breed you ever see. Jumping on a dead level was his strong suit, you understand; and when it come to that, Smiley would ante up money on him as long as he had a red. Smiley was monstrous proud of his frog, and well he might be, for fellers that had traveled and been everywheres, all said he laid over any frog that ever *they* see.

Well, Smiley kep' the beast in a little lattice box, and he used to fetch him downtown sometimes and lay for a bet. One day a feller—a stranger in the camp, he was—come acrost him with his box, and says:

"What might be that you've got in the box?"

And Smiley says, sorter indifferent-like, "It might be a parrot, or it might be a canary, maybe, but it ain't—it's only just a frog."

And the feller took it, and looked at it careful, and turned it round this way and that, and says, "H'm—so 'tis. Well, what's *he* good for?"

"Well," Smiley says, easy and careless, "he's good enough for *one* thing, I should judge—he can outjump any frog in Calaveras county."

The feller took the box again, and took another long, particular look, and give it back to Smiley, and says, very deliberate, "Well," he says, "I don't see no p'ints about that frog that's any better'n any other frog."

"Maybe you don't," Smiley says. "Maybe you understand frogs and maybe you don't understand 'em; maybe you've had experience, and maybe you ain't only a amature, as it were. Anyways, I've got *my* opinion and I'll risk forty dollars that he can outjump any frog in Calaveras County."

And the feller studied a minute, and then says, kinder sad like, "Well, I'm only a stranger here, and I ain't got no frog; but if I had a frog, I'd bet you."

And then Smiley says, "That's all right—that's all right—if you'll hold my box a minute, I'll go and get you a frog." And so the feller took the box, and put up his forty dollars along with Smiley's, and set down to wait.

So he set there a good while thinking and thinking to his-self, and then he got the frog out and prized his mouth open and took a teaspoon and filled him full of quail shot—filled! him pretty near up to his chin—and set him on the floor. Smiley he went to the swamp and slopped around in the mud for a long time, and finally he ketched a frog, and fetched him in, and give him to this feller, and says:

"Now, if you're ready, set him alongside of Dan'l, with his forepaws just even with Dan'l's, and I'll give the word." Then he says, "One—two—three—*git!*" and him and the feller touched up the frogs from behind, and the new frog hopped off lively, but Dan'l give a heave, and hysted up his shoulders—so—like a Frenchman, but it warn't no use—he couldn't budge; he was planted as solid as a church, and he couldn't no more stir than if he was anchored out. Smiley was a good deal surprised, and he was disgusted too, but he didn't have no idea what the matter was, of course.

The feller took the money and started away; and when he was going out at the door, he sorter jerked his thumb over his shoulder—so—at Dan'l, and says again, very deliberate, "Well," he says, "*I* don't see no p'ints about that frog that's any better'n any other frog."

Smiley he stood scratching his head and looking down at Dan'l a long time, and at last says, "I do wonder what in the nation that frog throwed off for—I wonder if there ain't something the matter with him—he 'pears to look mighty baggy, somehow." And he ketched Dan'l up by the nap of the neck, and hefted him, and says, "Why blame my cats if he don't weigh five pounds!" and turned him upside down and he belched out a double handful of shot. And then he see how it was, and he was the maddest man—he set the frog down and took out after that feller, but he never ketched him. And——

(Here Simon Wheeler heard his name called from the front yard, and got up to see what was wanted.) And turning to me as he moved away, he said: "Just set where you are, stranger, and rest easy—I ain't going to be gone a second."

But, by your leave, I did not think that a continuation of the history of the enterprising vagabond *Jim* Smiley would be likely to afford me much information concerning the Rev. *Leonidas W.* Smiley, and so I started away.

At the door I met the sociable Wheeler returning, and he buttonholed me and recommenced:

"Well, thish-yer Smiley had a yaller, one-eyed cow that didn't have no tail, only jest a short stump like a bannanner, and——"

However, lacking both time and inclination, I did not wait to hear about the afflicted cow, but took my leave.

ELDER BROWN'S BACKSLIDE
By Harry Stillwell Edwards (1855-)

[From *Harper's Magazine*, August, 1885; copyright, 1885, by Harper & Bros.; republished in the volume, *Two Runaways, and Other Stories* (1889), by Harry Stillwell Edwards (The Century Co.).]

ELDER Brown told his wife good-by at the farmhouse door as mechanically as though his proposed trip to Macon, ten miles away, was an everyday affair, while, as a matter of fact, many years had elapsed since unaccompanied he set foot in the city. He did not kiss her. Many very good men never kiss their wives. But small blame attaches to the elder for his omission on this occasion, since his wife had long ago discouraged all amorous demonstrations on the part of her liege lord, and at this particular moment was filling the parting moments with a rattling list of directions concerning thread, buttons, hooks, needles, and all the many etceteras of an industrious housewife's basket. The elder was laboriously assorting these postscript commissions in his memory, well knowing that to return with any one of them neglected would cause trouble in the family circle.

Elder Brown mounted his patient steed that stood sleepily motionless in the warm sunlight, with his great pointed ears displayed to the right and left, as though their owner had grown tired of the life burden their weight inflicted upon him, and was, old soldier fashion, ready to forego the once rigid alertness of early training for the pleasures of frequent rest on arms.

"And, elder, don't you forgit them caliker scraps, or you'll be wantin' kiver soon an' no kiver will be a-comin'."

Elder Brown did not turn his head, but merely let the whip hand, which had been checked in its backward motion, fall as he answered mechanically. The beast he bestrode responded with a rapid whisking of its tail and a great show of effort, as it ambled off down the sandy road, the rider's long legs seeming now and then to touch the ground.

But as the zigzag panels of the rail fence crept behind him, and he felt the freedom of the morning beginning to act upon his well-trained blood, the mechanical manner of the old man's mind gave place to a mild exuberance. A weight seemed to be lifting from it ounce by ounce as the fence panels, the weedy corners, the persimmon sprouts and sassafras bushes crept away behind him, so that by the time a mile lay between him and the life partner of his joys and sorrows he was in a reasonably contented frame of mind, and still improving.

It was a queer figure that crept along the road that cheery May morning. It was tall and gaunt, and had been for thirty years or more. The long head, bald on top, covered behind with iron-gray hair, and in front with a short tangled growth that curled and kinked in every direction, was surmounted by an old-fashioned stove-pipe hat, worn and stained, but eminently impressive. An old-fashioned Henry Clay cloth coat, stained and threadbare, divided itself impartially over the donkey's back and dangled on his sides. This was all that remained of the elder's wedding suit of forty years ago. Only constant care, and use of late years limited to extra occasions, had preserved it so long. The trousers had soon parted company with their friends. The substitutes were red jeans, which, while they did not well match his court costume, were better able to withstand the old man's abuse, for if, in addition to his frequent religious excursions astride his beast, there ever was a man who was fond of sitting down with his feet higher than his head, it was this selfsame Elder Brown.

The morning expanded, and the old man expanded with it; for while a vigorous leader in his church, the elder at home was, it must be admitted, an uncomplaining slave. To the intense astonishment of the beast he rode, there came new vigor into the whacks which fell upon his flanks; and the beast allowed astonishment to surprise him into real life and decided motion. Somewhere in the elder's expanding soul a tune had begun to ring. Possibly he took up the far, faint tune that came from the straggling gang of negroes away off in the field, as they slowly chopped amid the threadlike rows of cotton plants which lined the level ground, for the melody he hummed softly and then sang strongly, in the quavering, catchy tones of a good old country churchman, was "I'm glad salvation's free."

It was during the singing of this hymn that Elder Brown's regular motion-inspiring strokes were for the first time varied. He began to hold his hickory up at certain pauses in the melody, and beat the changes upon the sides of his astonished steed. The chorus under this arrangement was:

> I'm *glad* salvation's *free*,
> I'm *glad* salvation's *free*,
> I'm *glad* salvation's *free* for *all*,
> I'm *glad* salvation's *free*.

Wherever there is an italic, the hickory descended. It fell about as regularly and after the fashion of the stick beating upon the bass drum during a funeral march. But the beast, although convinced that something serious was impending, did not consider a funeral march appropriate for the occasion. He protested, at first, with vigorous whiskings of his tail and a rapid shifting of his ears. Finding these demonstrations unavailing, and convinced that some urgent cause for hurry had suddenly invaded the elder's serenity, as it had his own, he began to cover the ground with frantic leaps that would have surprised his owner could he have realized what was going on. But Elder Brown's eyes were half closed, and he was singing at the top of his voice. Lost in a trance of divine exaltation, for he felt the effects of the invigorating motion, bent only on making the air ring with the lines which he dimly imagined were drawing upon him the eyes of the whole female congregation, he was supremely unconscious that his beast was hurrying.

And thus the excursion proceeded, until suddenly a shote, surprised in his calm search for roots in a fence corner, darted into the road, and stood for an instant gazing upon the newcomers with that idiotic stare which only a pig can imitate. The sudden appearance of this unlooked-for apparition acted strongly upon the donkey. With one supreme effort he collected himself into a motionless mass of matter, bracing his front legs wide apart; that is to say, he stopped short. There he stood, returning the pig's idiotic stare with an interest which must have led to the presumption that never before in all his varied life had he seen such a singular little creature. End over end went the man of prayer, finally bringing up full length in the sand, striking just as he should have shouted "free" for the fourth time in his glorious chorus.

Fully convinced that his alarm had been well founded, the shote sped out from under the gigantic missile hurled at him by the donkey, and scampered down the road, turning first one ear and then the other to detect any sounds of pursuit. The donkey, also convinced that the object before which he had halted was supernatural, started back violently upon seeing it apparently turn to a man. But seeing that it had turned to nothing but a man, he wandered up into the deserted fence corner, and began to nibble refreshment from a scrub oak.

For a moment the elder gazed up into the sky, half impressed with the idea that the camp-meeting platform had given way. But the truth forced its way to the front in his disordered understanding at last, and with painful dignity he staggered into an upright position, and regained his beaver. He was shocked again. Never before in all the long years it had served him had he seen it in such shape. The truth is, Elder Brown had never before tried to stand on his head in it. As calmly as possible he began to straighten it out, caring but little for the dust upon his garments. The beaver was his special crown of dignity. To lose it was to be reduced to a level with the common woolhat herd. He did his best, pulling, pressing, and pushing, but the hat did not look natural when he had finished. It seemed to have been laid off into counties, sections, and town lots. Like a well-cut jewel, it had a face for him, view it from whatever point he chose, a quality which so impressed him that a lump gathered in his throat, and his eyes winked vigorously.

Elder Brown was not, however, a man for tears. He was a man of action. The sudden vision which met his wandering gaze, the donkey calmly chewing scrub buds, with the green juice already oozing from the corners of his frothy mouth, acted upon him like magic. He was, after all, only human, and when he got hands upon a piece of brush he thrashed the poor beast until it seemed as though even its already half-tanned hide would be eternally ruined. Thoroughly exhausted at last, he wearily straddled his saddle, and with his chin upon his breast resumed the early morning tenor of his way.

II

"Good-mornin', sir."

Elder Brown leaned over the little pine picket which divided the bookkeepers' department of a Macon warehouse from the room in general, and surveyed the well-dressed back of a gentleman who was busily figuring at a desk within. The apartment was carpetless, and the dust of a decade lay deep on the old books, shelves, and the familiar advertisements of guano and fertilizers which decorated the room. An old stove, rusty with the nicotine contributed by farmers during the previous season while waiting by its glowing sides for their cotton to be sold, stood straight up in a bed of sand, and festoons of cobwebs clung to the upper sashes of the murky windows. The lower sash of one window had been raised, and in the yard without, nearly an acre in extent, lay a few bales of cotton, with jagged holes in their ends, just as the sampler had left them. Elder Brown had time to notice all these familiar points, for the figure at the desk kept serenely at its task, and deigned no reply.

"Good-mornin', sir," said Elder Brown again, in his most dignified tones. "Is Mr. Thomas in?"

"Good-morning, sir," said the figure. "I'll wait on you in a minute." The minute passed, and four more joined it. Then the desk man turned.

"Well, sir, what can I do for you?"

The elder was not in the best of humor when he arrived, and his state of mind had not improved. He waited full a minute as he surveyed the man of business.

"I thought I mout be able to make some arrangements with you to git some money, but I reckon I was mistaken." The warehouse man came nearer.

"This is Mr. Brown, I believe. I did not recognize you at once. You are not in often to see us."

"No; my wife usually 'tends to the town bizness, while I run the church and farm. Got a fall from my donkey this morning," he said, noticing a quizzical, interrogating look upon the face before him, "and fell squar' on the hat." He made a pretense of smoothing it. The man of business had already lost interest.

"How much money will you want, Mr. Brown?"

"Well, about seven hundred dollars," said the elder, replacing his hat, and turning a furtive look upon the warehouse man. The other was tapping with his pencil upon the little shelf lying across the rail.

"I can get you five hundred."

"But I oughter have seven."

"Can't arrange for that amount. Wait till later in the season, and come again. Money is very tight now. How much cotton will you raise?"

"Well, I count on a hundr'd bales. An' you can't git the sev'n hundr'd dollars?"

"Like to oblige you, but can't right now; will fix it for you later on."

"Well," said the elder, slowly, "fix up the papers for five, an' I'll make it go as far as possible."

The papers were drawn. A note was made out for $552.50, for the interest was at one and a half per cent. for seven months, and a mortgage on ten mules belonging to the elder was drawn and signed. The elder then promised to send his cotton to the warehouse to be sold in the fall, and with a curt "Anything else?" and a "Thankee, that's all," the two parted.

Elder Brown now made an effort to recall the supplemental commissions shouted to him upon his departure, intending to execute them first, and then take his written list item by item. His mental resolves had just reached this point when a new thought made itself known. Passersby were puzzled to see the old man suddenly snatch his headpiece off and peer with an intent and awestruck air into its irregular caverns. Some of them were shocked when he suddenly and vigorously ejaculated:

"Hannah-Maria-Jemimy! goldarn an' blue blazes!"

He had suddenly remembered having placed his memoranda in that hat, and as he studied its empty depths his mind pictured the important scrap fluttering along the sandy scene of his early-morning tumble. It was this that caused him to graze an oath with less margin that he had allowed himself in twenty years. What would the old lady say?

Alas! Elder Brown knew too well. What she would not say was what puzzled him. But as he stood bareheaded in the sunlight a sense of utter desolation came and dwelt with him. His eye rested upon sleeping Balaam anchored to a post in the street, and so as he recalled the treachery that lay at the base of all his affliction, gloom was added to the desolation.

To turn back and search for the lost paper would have been worse than useless. Only one course was open to him, and at it went the leader of his people. He called at the grocery; he invaded the recesses of the dry-goods establishments; he ransacked the hardware stores; and wherever he went he made life a burden for the clerks, overhauling show-cases and pulling down whole shelves of stock. Occasionally an item of his memoranda would come to light, and thrusting his hand into his capacious pocket, where lay the proceeds of his check, he would pay for it upon the spot, and insist upon having it rolled up. To the suggestion of the slave whom he had in charge for the time being that the articles be laid aside until he had finished, he would not listen.

"Now you look here, sonny," he said, in the dry-goods store, "I'm conducting this revival, an' I don't need no help in my line. Just you tie them stockin's up an' lemme have 'em. Then I *know* I've *got* 'em." As each purchase was promptly paid for, and change had to be secured, the clerk earned his salary for that day at least.

So it was when, near the heat of the day, the good man arrived at the drugstore, the last and only unvisited division of trade, he made his appearance equipped with half a hundred packages, which nestled in his arms and bulged out about the sections of his clothing that boasted of pockets. As he deposited his deck-load upon the counter, great drops of perspiration rolled down his face and over his waterlogged collar to the floor.

There was something exquisitely refreshing in the great glasses of foaming soda that a spruce young man was drawing from a marble fountain, above which half a dozen polar bears in an ambitious print were disporting themselves. There came a break in the run of customers, and the spruce young man, having swept the foam from the marble, dexterously lifted a glass from the revolving rack which had rinsed it with a fierce little stream of water, and asked mechanically, as he caught the intense look of the perspiring elder, "What syrup, sir?"

Now it had not occurred to the elder to drink soda, but the suggestion, coming as it did in his exhausted state, was overpowering. He drew near awkwardly, put on his glasses, and examined the list of syrups with great care. The young man, being for the moment at leisure, surveyed critically the gaunt figure, the faded bandanna, the antique clawhammer coat, and the battered stove-pipe hat, with a gradually relaxing countenance. He even called the prescription clerk's attention by a cough and a quick jerk of the thumb. The prescription clerk smiled freely, and continued his assaults upon a piece of blue mass.

"I reckon," said the elder, resting his hands upon his knees and bending down to the list, "you may gimme sassprilla an' a little strawberry. Sassprilla's good for the blood this time er year, an' strawberry's good any time."

The spruce young man let the syrup stream into the glass as he smiled affably. Thinking, perhaps, to draw out the odd character, he ventured upon a jest himself, repeating a pun invented by the man who made the first soda fountain. With a sweep of his arm he cleared away the swarm of insects as he remarked, "People who like a fly in theirs are easily accommodated."

It was from sheer good-nature only that Elder Brown replied, with his usual broad, social smile, "Well, a fly now an' then don't hurt nobody."

Now if there is anybody in the world who prides himself on knowing a thing or two, it is the spruce young man who presides over a soda fountain. This particular young gentleman did not even deem a reply necessary. He vanished an instant, and when he returned a close observer might have seen that the mixture in the glass he bore had slightly changed color and increased in quantity. But the elder saw only the whizzing stream of water dart into its center, and the rosy foam rise and tremble on the glass's rim. The next instant he was holding his breath and sipping the cooling drink.

As Elder Brown paid his small score he was at peace with the world. I firmly believe that when he had finished his trading, and the little blue-stringed packages had been stored away, could the poor donkey have made his appearance at the door, and gazed with his meek, fawnlike eyes into his master's, he would have obtained full and free forgiveness.

Elder Brown paused at the door as he was about to leave. A rosy-cheeked school-girl was just lifting a creamy mixture to her lips before the fountain. It was a pretty picture, and he turned back, resolved to indulge in one more glass of the delightful beverage before beginning his long ride homeward.

"Fix it up again, sonny," he said, renewing his broad, confiding smile, as the spruce young man poised a glass inquiringly. The living automaton went through the same motions as before, and again Elder Brown quaffed the fatal mixture.

What a singular power is habit! Up to this time Elder Brown had been entirely innocent of transgression, but with the old alcoholic fire in his veins, twenty years dropped from his shoulders, and a feeling came over him familiar to every man who has been "in his cups." As a matter of fact, the elder would have been a confirmed drunkard twenty years before had his wife been less strong-minded. She took the reins into her own hands when she found that his business and strong drink did not mix well, worked him into the church, sustained his resolutions by making it difficult and dangerous for him to get to his toddy. She became the business head of the family, and he the spiritual. Only at rare intervals did he ever "backslide" during the twenty years of the new era, and Mrs. Brown herself used to say that the "sugar in his'n turned to gall before the backslide ended." People who knew her never doubted it.

But Elder Brown's sin during the remainder of the day contained an element of responsibility. As he moved majestically down toward where Balaam slept in the sunlight, he felt no fatigue. There was a glow upon his cheek-bones, and a faint tinge upon his prominent nose. He nodded familiarly to people as he met them, and saw not the look of amusement which succeeded astonishment upon the various faces. When he reached the neighborhood of Balaam it suddenly occurred to him that he might have forgotten some one of his numerous commissions, and he paused to think. Then a brilliant idea rose in his mind. He would forestall blame and disarm anger with kindness—he would purchase Hannah a bonnet.

What woman's heart ever failed to soften at sight of a new bonnet?

As I have stated, the elder was a man of action. He entered a store near at hand.

"Good-morning," said an affable gentleman with a Hebrew countenance, approaching.

"Good-mornin', good-mornin'," said the elder, piling his bundles on the counter. "I hope you are well?" Elder Brown extended his hand fervidly.

"Quite well, I thank you. What—"

"And the little wife?" said Elder Brown, affectionately retaining the Jew's hand.

"Quite well, sir."

"And the little ones—quite well, I hope, too?"

"Yes, sir; all well, thank you. Something I can do for you?"

The affable merchant was trying to recall his customer's name.

"Not now, not now, thankee. If you please to let my bundles stay untell I come back—"

"Can't I show you something? Hat, coat—"

"Not now. Be back bimeby."

Was it chance or fate that brought Elder Brown in front of a bar? The glasses shone bright upon the shelves as the swinging door flapped back to let out a coatless clerk, who passed him with a rush, chewing upon a farewell mouthful of brown bread and bologna. Elder Brown beheld for an instant the familiar scene within. The screws of his resolution had been loosened. At sight of the glistening bar the whole moral structure of twenty years came tumbling down. Mechanically he entered the saloon, and laid a silver quarter upon the bar as he said:

"A little whiskey an' sugar." The arms of the bartender worked like a faker's in a side show as he set out the glass with its little quota of "short sweetening" and a cut-glass decanter, and sent a half-tumbler of water spinning along from the upper end of the bar with a dime in change.

"Whiskey is higher'n used to be," said Elder Brown; but the bartender was taking another order, and did not hear him. Elder Brown stirred away the sugar, and let a steady stream of red liquid flow into the glass. He swallowed the drink as unconcernedly as though his morning tod had never been suspended, and pocketed the change. "But it ain't any better than it was," he concluded, as he passed out. He did not even seem to realize that he had done anything extraordinary.

There was a millinery store up the street, and thither with uncertain step he wended his way, feeling a little more elate, and altogether sociable. A pretty, black-eyed girl, struggling to keep down her mirth, came forward and faced him behind the counter. Elder Brown lifted his faded hat with the politeness, if not the grace, of a Castilian, and made a sweeping bow. Again he was in his element. But he did not speak. A shower of odds and ends, small packages, thread, needles, and buttons, released from their prison, rattled down about him.

The girl laughed. She could not help it. And the elder, leaning his hand on the counter, laughed, too, until several other girls came half-way to the front. Then they, hiding behind counters and suspended cloaks, laughed and snickered until they reconvulsed the elder's vis-a-vis, who had been making desperate efforts to resume her demure appearance.

"Let me help you, sir," she said, coming from behind the counter, upon seeing Elder Brown beginning to adjust his spectacles for a search. He waved her back majestically. "No, my dear, no; can't allow it. You mout sile them purty fingers. No, ma'am. No gen'l'man'll 'low er lady to do such a thing." The elder was gently forcing the girl back to her place. "Leave it to me. I've picked up bigger things 'n them. Picked myself up this mornin'. Balaam—you don't know Balaam; he's my donkey— he tumbled me over his head in the sand this mornin'." And Elder Brown had to resume an upright position until his paroxysm of laughter had passed. "You see this old hat?" extending it, half full of packages; "I fell clear inter it; jes' as clean inter it as them things thar fell out'n it." He laughed again, and so did the girls. "But, my dear, I whaled half the hide off'n him for it."

"Oh, sir! how could you? Indeed, sir. I think you did wrong. The poor brute did not know what he was doing, I dare say, and probably he has been a faithful friend." The girl cast her mischievous eyes towards her companions, who snickered again. The old man was not conscious of the sarcasm. He only saw reproach. His face straightened, and he regarded the girl soberly.

"Mebbe you're right, my dear; mebbe I oughtn't."

"I am sure of it," said the girl. "But now don't you want to buy a bonnet or a cloak to carry home to your wife?"

"Well, you're whistlin' now, birdie; that's my intention; set 'em all out." Again the elder's face shone with delight. "An' I don't want no one-hoss bonnet neither."

"Of course not. Now here is one; pink silk, with delicate pale blue feathers. Just the thing for the season. We have nothing more elegant in stock." Elder Brown held it out, upside down, at arm's-length.

"Well, now, that's suthin' like. Will it soot a sorter redheaded 'ooman?"

A perfectly sober man would have said the girl's corsets must have undergone a terrible strain, but the elder did not notice her dumb convulsion. She answered, heroically:

"Perfectly, sir. It is an exquisite match."

"I think you're whistlin' again. Nancy's head's red, red as a woodpeck's. Sorrel's only half-way to the color of her top-knot, an' it do seem like red oughter to soot red. Nancy's red an' the hat's red; like goes with like, an' birds of a feather flock together." The old man laughed until his cheeks were wet.

The girl, beginning to feel a little uneasy, and seeing a customer entering, rapidly fixed up the bonnet, took fifteen dollars out of a twenty-dollar bill, and calmly asked the elder if he wanted anything else. He thrust his change somewhere into his clothes, and beat a retreat. It had occurred to him that he was nearly drunk.

Elder Brown's step began to lose its buoyancy. He found himself utterly unable to walk straight. There was an uncertain straddle in his gait that carried him from one side of the walk to the other, and caused people whom he met to cheerfully yield him plenty of room.

Balaam saw him coming. Poor Balaam. He had made an early start that day, and for hours he stood in the sun awaiting relief. When he opened his sleepy eyes and raised his expressive ears to a position of attention, the old familiar coat and battered hat of the elder were before him. He lifted up his honest voice and cried aloud for joy.

The effect was electrical for one instant. Elder Brown surveyed the beast with horror, but again in his understanding there rang out the trumpet words.

"Drunk, drunk, drunk, drer-unc, -er-unc, -unc, -unc."

He stooped instinctively for a missile with which to smite his accuser, but brought up suddenly with a jerk and a handful of sand. Straightening himself up with a majestic dignity, he extended his right hand impressively.

"You're a goldarn liar, Balaam, and, blast your old buttons, you kin walk home by yourself, for I'm danged if you sh'll ride me er step."

Surely Coriolanus never turned his back upon Rome with a grander dignity than sat upon the old man's form as he faced about and left the brute to survey with anxious eyes the new departure of his master.

He saw the elder zigzag along the street, and beheld him about to turn a friendly corner. Once more he lifted up his mighty voice:

"Drunk, drunk, drunk, drer-unc, drer-unc, -erunc, -unc, -unc."

Once more the elder turned with lifted hand and shouted back:

"You're a liar, Balaam, goldarn you! You're er iffamous liar." Then he passed from view.

III

Mrs. Brown stood upon the steps anxiously awaiting the return of her liege lord. She knew he had with him a large sum of money, or should have, and she knew also that he was a man without business methods. She had long since repented of the decision which sent him to town. When the old battered hat and flour-covered coat loomed up in the gloaming and confronted her, she stared with terror. The next instant she had seized him.

"For the Lord sakes, Elder Brown, what ails you? As I live, if the man ain't drunk! Elder Brown! Elder Brown! for the life of me can't I make you hear? You crazy old hypocrite! you desavin' old sinner! you black-hearted wretch! where have you ben?"

The elder made an effort to wave her off.

"Woman," he said, with grand dignity, "you forgit yus-sef; shu know ware I've ben 'swell's I do. Ben to town, wife, an' see yer wat I've brought—the fines' hat, ole woman, I could git. Look't the color. Like goes 'ith like; it's red an' you're red, an' it's a dead match. What yer mean? Hey! hole on! ole woman!—you! Hannah!—you." She literally shook him into silence.

"You miserable wretch! you low-down drunken sot! what do you mean by coming home and insulting your wife?" Hannah ceased shaking him from pure exhaustion.

"Where is it, I say? where is it?"

By this time she was turning his pockets wrong side out. From one she got pills, from another change, from another packages.

"The Lord be praised, and this is better luck than I hoped! Oh, elder! elder! elder! what did you do it for? Why, man, where is Balaam?"

Thought of the beast choked off the threatened hysterics.

"Balaam? Balaam?" said the elder, groggily. "He's in town. The infernal ole fool 'sulted me, an' I lef' him to walk home."

His wife surveyed him. Really at that moment she did think his mind was gone; but the leer upon the old man's face enraged her beyond endurance.

"You did, did you? Well, now, I reckon you'll laugh for some cause, you will.

Back you go, sir—straight back; an' don't you come home 'thout that donkey, or you'll rue it, sure as my name is Hannah Brown. Aleck!—you Aleck-k-k!"

A black boy darted round the corner, from behind which, with several others, he had beheld the brief but stirring scene.

"Put a saddle on er mule. The elder's gwine back to town. And don't you be long about it neither."

"Yessum." Aleck's ivories gleamed in the darkness as he disappeared.

Elder Brown was soberer at that moment than he had been for hours.

"Hannah, you don't mean it?"

"Yes, sir, I do. Back you go to town as sure as my name is Hannah Brown."

The elder was silent. He had never known his wife to relent on any occasion after she had affirmed her intention, supplemented with "as sure as my name is Hannah Brown." It was her way of swearing. No affidavit would have had half the claim upon her as that simple enunciation.

So back to town went Elder Brown, not in the order of the early morn, but silently, moodily, despairingly, surrounded by mental and actual gloom.

The old man had turned a last appealing glance upon the angry woman, as he mounted with Aleck's assistance, and sat in the light that streamed from out the kitchen window. She met the glance without a waver.

"She means it, as sure as my name is Elder Brown," he said, thickly. Then he rode on.

IV

To say that Elder Brown suffered on this long journey back to Macon would only mildly outline his experience. His early morning's fall had begun to make itself felt. He was sore and uncomfortable. Besides, his stomach was empty, and called for two meals it had missed for the first time in years.

When, sore and weary, the elder entered the city, the electric lights shone above it like jewels in a crown. The city slept; that is, the better portion of it did. Here and there, however, the lower lights flashed out into the night. Moodily the elder pursued his journey, and as he rode, far off in the night there rose and quivered a plaintive cry. Elder Brown smiled wearily: it was Balaam's appeal, and he recognized it. The animal he rode also recognized it, and replied, until the silence of the city was destroyed. The odd clamor and confusion drew from a saloon near by a group of noisy youngsters, who had been making a night of it. They surrounded Elder Brown as he began to transfer himself to the hungry beast to whose motion he was more accustomed, and in the "hail fellow well met" style of the day began to bandy jests upon his appearance. Now Elder Brown was not in a jesting humor. Positively he was in the worst humor possible. The result was that before many minutes passed the old man was swinging several of the crowd by their collars, and breaking the peace of the city. A policeman approached, and but for the good-humored party, upon whom the elder's pluck had made a favorable impression, would have run the old man into the barracks. The crowd, however, drew him laughingly into the saloon and to the bar. The reaction was too much for his half-rallied senses. He yielded again. The reviving liquor passed his lips. Gloom vanished. He became one of the boys.

The company into which Elder Brown had fallen was what is known as "first-class." To such nothing is so captivating as an adventure out of the common run of accidents. The gaunt countryman, with his battered hat and claw-hammer coat, was a prize of an extraordinary nature. They drew him into a rear room, whose gilded frames and polished tables betrayed the character and purpose of the place, and plied him with wine until ten thousand lights danced about him. The fun increased. One youngster made a political speech from the top of the table; another impersonated Hamlet; and finally Elder Brown was lifted into a chair, and sang a camp-meeting song. This was rendered by him with startling effect. He stood upright, with his hat jauntily knocked to one side, and his coat tails ornamented with a couple of show-bills, kindly pinned on by his admirers. In his left hand he waved the stub of a cigar, and on his back was an admirable representation of Balaam's head, executed by some artist with billiard chalk.

As the elder sang his favorite hymn, "I'm glad salvation's free," his stentorian voice awoke the echoes. Most of the company rolled upon the floor in convulsions of laughter.

The exhibition came to a close by the chair overturning. Again Elder Brown fell into his beloved hat. He arose and shouted: "Whoa, Balaam!" Again he seized the nearest weapon, and sought satisfaction. The young gentleman with political sentiments was knocked under the table, and Hamlet only escaped injury by beating the infuriated elder into the street.

What next? Well, I hardly know. How the elder found Balaam is a mystery yet: not that Balaam was hard to find, but that the old man was in no condition to find anything. Still he did, and climbing laboriously into the saddle, he held on stupidly while the hungry beast struck out for home.

V

Hannah Brown did not sleep that night. Sleep would not come. Hour after hour passed, and her wrath refused to be quelled. She tried every conceivable method, but time hung heavily. It was not quite peep of day, however, when she laid her well-worn family Bible aside. It had been her mother's, and amid all the anxieties and tribulations incident to the life of a woman who had free negroes and a miserable husband to manage, it had been her mainstay and comfort. She had frequently read it in anger, page after page, without knowing what was contained in the lines. But eventually the words became intelligible and took meaning. She wrested consolation from it by mere force of will.

And so on this occasion when she closed the book the fierce anger was gone.

She was not a hard woman naturally. Fate had brought her conditions which covered up the woman heart within her, but though it lay deep, it was there still. As she sat with folded hands her eyes fell upon—what?

The pink bonnet with the blue plume!

It may appear strange to those who do not understand such natures, but to me her next action was perfectly natural. She burst into a convulsive laugh; then, seizing the queer object, bent her face upon it and sobbed hysterically. When the storm was over, very tenderly she laid the gift aside, and bare-headed passed out into the night.

For a half-hour she stood at the end of the lane, and then hungry Balaam and his master hove in sight. Reaching out her hand, she checked the beast.

"William," said she, very gently, "where is the mule?"

The elder had been asleep. He woke and gazed upon her blankly.

"What mule, Hannah?"

"The mule you rode to town."

For one full minute the elder studied her face. Then it burst from his lips:

"Well, bless me! if I didn't bring Balaam and forgit the mule!"

The woman laughed till her eyes ran water.

"William," said she, "you're drunk."

"Hannah," said he, meekly, "I know it. The truth is, Hannah, I—"

"Never mind, now, William," she said, gently. "You are tired and hungry. Come into the house, husband."

Leading Balaam, she disappeared down the lane; and when, a few minutes later, Hannah Brown and her husband entered through the light that streamed out of the open door her arms were around him, and her face upturned to his.

THE HOTEL EXPERIENCE OF MR. PINK FLUKER
By Richard Malcolm Johnston (1822-1898)

[From *The Century Magazine*, June, 1886; copyright, 1886, by The Century Co.; republished in the volume, *Mr. Absalom Billingslea, and Other Georgia Folk* (1888), by Richard Malcolm Johnston (Harper & Brothers).]

I

Mr. Peterson Fluker, generally called Pink, for his fondness for as stylish dressing as he could afford, was one of that sort of men who habitually seem busy and efficient when they are not. He had the bustling activity often noticeable in men of his size, and in one way and another had made up, as he believed, for being so much smaller than most of his adult acquaintance of the male sex. Prominent among his achievements on that line was getting married to a woman who, among other excellent gifts, had that of being twice as big as her husband.

"Fool who?" on the day after his marriage he had asked, with a look at those who had often said that he was too little to have a wife.

They had a little property to begin with, a couple of hundreds of acres, and two or three negroes apiece. Yet, except in the natural increase of the latter, the accretions of worldly estate had been inconsiderable till now, when their oldest child, Marann, was some fifteen years old. These accretions had been saved and taken care of by Mrs. Fluker, who was as staid and silent as he was mobile and voluble.

Mr. Fluker often said that it puzzled him how it was that he made smaller crops than most of his neighbors, when, if not always convincing, he could generally put every one of them to silence in discussions upon agricultural topics. This puzzle had led him to not unfrequent ruminations in his mind as to whether or not his vocation might lie in something higher than the mere tilling of the ground. These ruminations had lately taken a definite direction, and it was after several conversations which he had held with his friend Matt Pike.

Mr. Matt Pike was a bachelor of some thirty summers, a foretime clerk consecutively in each of the two stores of the village, but latterly a trader on a limited scale in horses, wagons, cows, and similar objects of commerce, and at all times a politician. His hopes of holding office had been continually disappointed until Mr. John Sanks became sheriff, and rewarded with a deputyship some important special service rendered by him in the late very close canvass. Now was a chance to rise, Mr. Pike thought. All he wanted, he had often said, was a start. Politics, I would remark, however, had been regarded by Mr. Pike as a means rather than an end. It is doubtful if he hoped to become governor of the state, at least before an advanced period in his career. His main object now was to get money, and he believed that official position would promote him in the line of his ambition faster than was possible to any private station, by leading him into more extensive acquaintance with mankind, their needs, their desires, and their caprices. A deputy sheriff, provided that lawyers were not too indulgent in allowing acknowledgment of service of court processes, in postponing levies and sales, and in settlement of litigated cases, might pick up three hundred dollars, a good sum for those times, a fact which Mr. Pike had known and pondered long.

It happened just about then that the arrears of rent for the village hotel had so accumulated on Mr. Spouter, the last occupant, that the owner, an indulgent man, finally had said, what he had been expected for years and years to say, that he could not wait on Mr. Spouter forever and eternally. It was at this very nick, so to speak, that Mr. Pike made to Mr. Fluker the suggestion to quit a business so far beneath his powers, sell out, or rent out, or tenant out, or do something else with his farm, march into town, plant himself upon the ruins of Jacob Spouter, and begin his upward soar.

Now Mr. Fluker had many and many a time acknowledged that he had ambition; so one night he said to his wife:

"You see how it is here, Nervy. Farmin' somehow don't suit my talons. I need to be flung more 'mong people to fetch out what's in me. Then thar's Marann, which is gittin' to be nigh on to a growd-up woman; an' the child need the s'iety which you 'bleeged to acknowledge is sca'ce about here, six mile from town. Your brer Sam can stay here an' raise butter, chickens, eggs, pigs, an'—an'—an' so forth. Matt Pike say he jes' know they's money in it, an' special with a housekeeper keerful an' equinomical like you."

It is always curious the extent of influence that some men have upon wives who are their superiors. Mrs. Fluker, in spite of accidents, had ever set upon her husband a value that was not recognized outside of his family. In this respect there seems a surprising compensation in human life. But this remark I make only in passing. Mrs. Fluker, admitting in her heart that farming was not her husband's forte, hoped, like a true wife, that it might be found in the new field to which he aspired. Besides, she did not forget that her brother Sam had said to her several times privately that if his brer Pink wouldn't have so many notions and would let him alone in his management, they would all do better. She reflected for a day or two, and then said:

"Maybe it's best, Mr. Fluker. I'm willin' to try it for a year, anyhow. We can't lose much by that. As for Matt Pike, I hain't the confidence in him you has. Still, he bein' a boarder and deputy sheriff, he might accidentally do us some good. I'll try it for a year providin' you'll fetch me the money as it's paid in, for you know I know how to manage that better'n you do, and you know I'll try to manage it and all the rest of the business for the best."

To this provision Mr. Fluker gave consent, qualified by the claim that he was to retain a small margin for indispensable personal exigencies. For he contended, perhaps with justice, that no man in the responsible position he was about to take ought to be expected to go about, or sit about, or even lounge about, without even a continental red in his pocket.

The new house—I say *new* because tongue could not tell the amount of scouring, scalding, and whitewashing that that excellent housekeeper had done before a single stick of her furniture went into it—the new house, I repeat, opened with six eating boarders at ten dollars a month apiece, and two eating and sleeping at eleven, besides Mr. Pike, who made a special contract. Transient custom was hoped to hold its own, and that of the county people under the deputy's patronage and influence to be considerably enlarged.

In words and other encouragement Mr. Pike was pronounced. He could com-mend honestly, and he did so cordially.

"The thing to do, Pink, is to have your prices reg'lar, and make people pay up reg'lar. Ten dollars for eatin', jes' so; eleb'n for eatin' *an'* sleepin'; half a dollar for dinner, jes' so; quarter apiece for breakfast, supper, and bed, is what I call reason'ble bo'd. As for me, I sca'cely know how to rig'late, because, you know, I'm a' officer now, an' in course I natchel *has* to be away sometimes an' on expenses at 'tother places, an' it seem like some 'lowance ought by good rights to be made for that; don't you think so?"

"Why, matter o' course, Matt; what you think? I ain't so powerful good at fig-gers. Nervy is. S'posen you speak to her 'bout it."

"Oh, that's perfec' unuseless, Pink. I'm a' officer o' the law, Pink, an' the law consider women—well, I may say the law, *she* deal 'ith *men*, not women, an' she ex-pect her officers to understan' figgers, an' if I hadn't o' understood figgers Mr. Sanks wouldn't or darsnt' to 'p'int me his dep'ty. Me 'n' you can fix them terms. Now see here, reg'lar bo'd—eatin' bo'd, I mean—is ten dollars, an' sleepin' and singuil meals is 'cordin' to the figgers you've sot for 'em. Ain't that so? Jes' so. Now, Pink, you an' me'll keep a runnin' account, you a-chargin' for reg'lar bo'd, an' I a'lowin' to myself credics for my absentees, accordin' to transion customers an' singuil mealers an' sleepers. Is that fa'r, er is it not fa'r?"

Mr. Fluker turned his head, and after making or thinking he had made a calcu-lation, answered:

"That's—that seem fa'r, Matt."

"Cert'nly 'tis, Pink; I knowed you'd say so, an' you know I'd never wish to be nothin' but fa'r 'ith people I like, like I do you an' your wife. Let that be the under-standin', then, betwix' us. An' Pink, let the understandin' be jes' betwix' *us*, for I've saw enough o' this world to find out that a man never makes nothin' by makin' a blowin' horn o' his business. You make the t'others pay up spuntial, monthly. You 'n' me can settle whensomever it's convenant, say three months from to-day. In course I shall talk up for the house whensomever and wharsomever I go or stay. You know that. An' as for my bed," said Mr. Pike finally, "whensomever I ain't here by bed-time, you welcome to put any transion person in it, an' also an' likewise, when transion custom is pressin', and you cramped for beddin', I'm willin' to give it up for the time bein'; an' rather'n you should be cramped too bad, I'll take my chances somewhars else, even if I has to take a pallet at the head o' the sta'r-steps."

"Nervy," said Mr. Fluker to his wife afterwards, "Matt Pike's a sensibler an' a friendlier an' a 'commodatiner feller'n I thought."

Then, without giving details of the contract, he mentioned merely the willingness of their boarder to resign his bed on occasions of pressing emergency.

"He's talked mighty fine to me and Marann," answered Mrs. Fluker. "We'll see how he holds out. One thing I do not like of his doin', an' that's the talkin' 'bout Sim Marchman to Marann, an' makin' game o' his country ways, as he call 'em. Sech as that ain't right."

It may be as well to explain just here that Simeon Marchman, the person just named by Mrs. Fluker, a stout, industrious young farmer, residing with his parents in the country near by where the Flukers had dwelt before removing to town, had been eying Marann for a year or two, and waiting upon her fast-ripening womanhood with intentions that, he believed to be hidden in his own breast, though he had taken less pains to conceal them from Marann than from the rest of his acquaintance. Not that he had ever told her of them in so many words, but—Oh, I need not stop here in the midst of this narration to explain how such intentions become known, or at least strongly suspected by girls, even those less bright than Marann Fluker. Simeon had not cordially indorsed the movement into town, though, of course, knowing it was none of his business, he had never so much as hinted opposition. I would not be surprised, also, if he reflected that there might be some selfishness in his hostility, or at least that it was heightened by apprehensions personal to himself.

Considering the want of experience in the new tenants, matters went on remarkably well. Mrs. Fluker, accustomed to rise from her couch long before the lark, managed to the satisfaction of all,—regular boarders, single-meal takers, and transient people. Marann went to the village school, her mother dressing her, though with prudent economy, as neatly and almost as tastefully as any of her schoolmates; while, as to study, deportment, and general progress, there was not a girl in the whole school to beat her, I don't care who she was.

II

During a not inconsiderable period Mr. Fluker indulged the honorable conviction that at last he had found the vein in which his best talents lay, and he was
happy in foresight of the prosperity and felicity which that discovery promised to
himself and his family. His native activity found many more objects for its exertion
than before. He rode out to the farm, not often, but sometimes, as a matter of duty,
and was forced to acknowledge that Sam was managing better than could have been
expected in the absence of his own continuous guidance. In town he walked about
the hotel, entertained the guests, carved at the meals, hovered about the stores, the
doctors' offices, the wagon and blacksmith shops, discussed mercantile, medical,
mechanical questions with specialists in all these departments, throwing into them
all more and more of politics as the intimacy between him and his patron and chief
boarder increased.

Now as to that patron and chief boarder. The need of extending his acquaintance seemed to press upon Mr. Pike with ever-increasing weight. He was here
and there, all over the county; at the county-seat, at the county villages, at justices'
courts, at executors' and administrators' sales, at quarterly and protracted religious
meetings, at barbecues of every dimension, on hunting excursions and fishing frolics, at social parties in all neighborhoods. It got to be said of Mr. Pike that a freer
acceptor of hospitable invitations, or a better appreciator of hospitable intentions,
was not and needed not to be found possibly in the whole state. Nor was this admirable deportment confined to the county in which he held so high official position.
He attended, among other occasions less public, the spring sessions of the supreme
and county courts in the four adjoining counties: the guest of acquaintance old and
new over there. When starting upon such travels, he would sometimes breakfast
with his traveling companion in the village, and, if somewhat belated in the return,
sup with him also.

Yet, when at Flukers', no man could have been a more cheerful and otherwise satisfactory boarder than Mr. Matt Pike. He praised every dish set before him,
bragged to their very faces of his host and hostess, and in spite of his absences was
the oftenest to sit and chat with Marann when her mother would let her go into the

parlor. Here and everywhere about the house, in the dining-room, in the passage, at the foot of the stairs, he would joke with Marann about her country beau, as he styled poor Sim Marchman, and he would talk as though he was rather ashamed of Sim, and wanted Marann to string her bow for higher game.

Brer Sam did manage well, not only the fields, but the yard. Every Saturday of the world he sent in something or other to his sister. I don't know whether I ought to tell it or not, but for the sake of what is due to pure veracity I will. On as many as three different occasions Sim Marchman, as if he had lost all self-respect, or had not a particle of tact, brought in himself, instead of sending by a negro, a bucket of butter and a coop of spring chickens as a free gift to Mrs. Fluker. I do think, on my soul, that Mr. Matt Pike was much amused by such degradation—however, he must say that they were all first-rate. As for Marann, she was very sorry for Sim, and wished he had not brought these good things at all.

Nobody knew how it came about; but when the Flukers had been in town somewhere between two and three months, Sim Marchman, who (to use his own words) had never bothered her a great deal with his visits, began to suspect that what few he made were received by Marann lately with less cordiality than before; and so one day, knowing no better, in his awkward, straightforward country manners, he wanted to know the reason why. Then Marann grew distant, and asked Sim the following question:

"You know where Mr. Pike's gone, Mr. Marchman?"

Now the fact was, and she knew it, that Marann Fluker had never before, not since she was born, addressed that boy as *Mister*.

The visitor's face reddened and reddened.

"No," he faltered in answer; "no—no—*ma'am*, I should say. I—I don't know where Mr. Pike's gone."

Then he looked around for his hat, discovered it in time, took it into his hands, turned it around two or three times, then, bidding good-bye without shaking hands, took himself off.

Mrs. Fluker liked all the Marchmans, and she was troubled somewhat when she heard of the quickness and manner of Sim's departure; for he had been fully expected by her to stay to dinner.

"Say he didn't even shake hands, Marann? What for? What you do to him?"

"Not one blessed thing, ma; only he wanted to know why I wasn't gladder to see him." Then Marann looked indignant.

"Say them words, Marann?"

"No, but he hinted 'em."

"What did you say then?"

"I just asked, a-meaning nothing in the wide world, ma—I asked him if he knew where Mr. Pike had gone."

"And that were answer enough to hurt his feelin's. What you want to know where Matt Pike's gone for, Marann?"

"I didn't care about knowing, ma, but I didn't like the way Sim talked."

"Look here, Marann. Look straight at me. You'll be mighty fur off your feet if you let Matt Pike put things in your head that hain't no business a-bein' there, and special if you find yourself a-wantin' to know where he's a-perambulatin' in his everlastin' meanderin's. Not a cent has he paid for his board, and which your pa say he have a' understandin' with him about allowin' for his absentees, which is all right enough, but which it's now goin' on to three mont's, and what is comin' to us I need and I want. He ought, your pa ought to let me bargain with Matt Pike, because he know he don't understan' figgers like Matt Pike. He don't know exactly what the bargain were; for I've asked him, and he always begins with a multiplyin' of words and never answers me."

On his next return from his travels Mr. Pike noticed a coldness in Mrs. Fluker's manner, and this enhanced his praise of the house. The last week of the third month came. Mr. Pike was often noticed, before and after meals, standing at the desk in the hotel office (called in those times the bar-room) engaged in making calculations. The day before the contract expired Mrs. Fluker, who had not indulged herself with a single holiday since they had been in town, left Marann in charge of the house, and rode forth, spending part of the day with Mrs. Marchman, Sim's mother. All were glad to see her, of course, and she returned smartly, freshened by the visit. That night she had a talk with Marann, and oh, how Marann did cry!

The very last day came. Like insurance policies, the contract was to expire at a certain hour. Sim Marchman came just before dinner, to which he was sent for by Mrs. Fluker, who had seen him as he rode into town.

"Hello, Sim," said Mr. Pike as he took his seat opposite him. "You here? What's the news in the country? How's your health? How's crops?"

"Jest mod'rate, Mr. Pike. Got little business with you after dinner, ef you can spare time."

"All right. Got a little matter with Pink here first. 'Twon't take long. See you arfter amejiant, Sim."

Never had the deputy been more gracious and witty. He talked and talked, outtalking even Mr. Fluker; he was the only man in town who could do that. He winked at Marann as he put questions to Sim, some of the words employed in which Sim had never heard before. Yet Sim held up as well as he could, and after dinner followed Marann with some little dignity into the parlor. They had not been there more than ten minutes when Mrs. Fluker was heard to walk rapidly along the passage leading from the dining-room, to enter her own chamber for only a moment, then to come out and rush to the parlor door with the gig-whip in her hand. Such uncommon conduct in a woman like Mrs. Pink Fluker of course needs explanation.

When all the other boarders had left the house, the deputy and Mr. Fluker having repaired to the bar-room, the former said:

"Now, Pink, for our settlement, as you say your wife think we better have one. I'd 'a' been willin' to let accounts keep on a-runnin', knowin' what a straightforrards sort o' man you was. Your count, ef I ain't mistakened, is jes' thirty-three dollars, even money. Is that so, or is it not?"

"That's it, to a dollar, Matt. Three times eleben make thirty-three, don't it?"

"It do, Pink, or eleben times three, jes' which you please. Now here's my count, on which you'll see, Pink, that not nary cent have I charged for infloonce. I has infloonced a consider'ble custom to this house, as you know, bo'din' and transion. But I done that out o' my respects of you an' Missis Fluker, an' your keepin' of a fa'r—I'll say, as I've said freckwent, a *very* fa'r house. I let them infloonces go to friendship, ef you'll take it so. Will you, Pink Fluker?"

"Cert'nly, Matt, an' I'm a thousand times obleeged to you, an'—"

"Say no more, Pink, on that p'int o' view. Ef I like a man, I know how to treat him. Now as to the p'ints o' absentees, my business as dep'ty sheriff has took me away from this inconsider'ble town freckwent, hain't it?"

"It have, Matt, er somethin' else, more'n I were a expectin', an'—"

"Jes' so. But a public officer, Pink, when jooty call on him to go, he got to go; in fack he got to *goth*, as the Scripture say, ain't that so?"

"I s'pose so, Matt, by good rights, a—a official speakin'."

Mr. Fluker felt that he was becoming a little confused.

"Jes' so. Now, Pink, I were to have credics for my absentees 'cordin' to transion an' single-meal bo'ders an' sleepers; ain't that so?"

"I—I—somethin' o' that sort, Matt," he answered vaguely.

"Jes' so. Now look here," drawing from his pocket a paper. "Itom one. Twenty-eight dinners at half a dollar makes fourteen dollars, don't it? Jes' so. Twenty-five breakfasts at a quarter makes six an' a quarter, which make dinners an' breakfasts twenty an' a quarter. Foller me up, as I go up, Pink. Twenty-five suppers at a quarter makes six an' a quarter, an' which them added to the twenty an' a quarter makes them twenty-six an' a half. Foller, Pink, an' if you ketch me in any mistakes in the kyarin' an' addin', p'int it out. Twenty-two an' a half beds—an' I say *half*, Pink, because you 'member one night when them A'gusty lawyers got here 'bout midnight on their way to co't, rather'n have you too bad cramped, I ris to make way for two of 'em; yit as I had one good nap, I didn't think I ought to put that down but for half. Them makes five dollars half an' seb'n pence, an' which kyar'd on to the t'other twenty-six an' a half, fetches the whole cabool to jes' thirty-two dollars an' seb'n pence. But I made up my mind I'd fling out that seb'n pence, an' jes' call it a dollar even money, an' which here's the solid silver."

In spite of the rapidity with which this enumeration of counter-charges was made, Mr. Fluker commenced perspiring at the first item, and when the balance was announced his face was covered with huge drops.

It was at this juncture that Mrs. Fluker, who, well knowing her husband's unfamiliarity with complicated accounts, had felt her duty to be listening near the bar-room door, left, and quickly afterwards appeared before Marann and Sim as I have represented.

"You think Matt Pike ain't tryin' to settle with your pa with a dollar? I'm goin' to make him keep his dollar, an' I'm goin' to give him somethin' to go 'long with it."

"The good Lord have mercy upon us!" exclaimed Marann, springing up and catching hold of her mother's skirts, as she began her advance towards the bar-room. "Oh, ma! for the Lord's sake!—Sim, Sim, Sim, if you care *any*thing for me in this wide world, don't let ma go into that room!"

"Missis Fluker," said Sim, rising instantly, "wait jest two minutes till I see Mr. Pike on some pressin' business; I won't keep you over two minutes a-waitin'."

He took her, set her down in a chair trembling, looked at her a moment as she began to weep, then, going out and closing the door, strode rapidly to the bar-room.

"Let me help you settle your board-bill, Mr. Pike, by payin' you a little one I owe you."

Doubling his fist, he struck out with a blow that felled the deputy to the floor. Then catching him by his heels, he dragged him out of the house into the street. Lifting his foot above his face, he said:

"You stir till I tell you, an' I'll stomp your nose down even with the balance of your mean face. 'Tain't exactly my business how you cheated Mr. Fluker, though, 'pon my soul, I never knowed a trifliner, lowdowner trick. But *I* owed you myself for your talkin' 'bout and your lyin' 'bout me, and now I've paid you; an' ef you only knowed it, I've saved you from a gig-whippin'. Now you may git up."

"Here's his dollar, Sim," said Mr. Fluker, throwing it out of the window. "Nervy say make him take it."

The vanquished, not daring to refuse, pocketed the coin, and slunk away amid the jeers of a score of villagers who had been drawn to the scene.

In all human probability the late omission of the shaking of Sim's and Marann's hands was compensated at their parting that afternoon. I am more confident on this point because at the end of the year those hands were joined inseparably by the preacher. But this was when they had all gone back to their old home; for if Mr. Fluker did not become fully convinced that his mathematical education was not advanced quite enough for all the exigencies of hotel-keeping, his wife declared that she had had enough of it, and that she and Marann were going home. Mr. Fluker may be said, therefore, to have followed, rather than led, his family on the return.

As for the deputy, finding that if he did not leave it voluntarily he would be drummed out of the village, he departed, whither I do not remember if anybody ever knew.

THE NICE PEOPLE
By Henry Cuyler Bunner (1855-1896)

[From *Puck*, July 30, 1890. Republished in the volume, *Short Sixes: Stories to Be Read While the Candle Burns* (1891), by Henry Cuyler Bunner; copyright, 1890, by Alice Larned Bunner; reprinted by permission of the publishers, Charles Scribner'a Sons.]

T HEY certainly are nice people," I assented to my wife's observation, using the colloquial phrase with a consciousness that it was anything but "nice" English, "and I'll bet that their three children are better brought up than most of——"

" *Two* children," corrected my wife.

"Three, he told me."

"My dear, she said there were *two* ."

"He said three."

"You've simply forgotten. I'm *sure* she told me they had only two—a boy and a girl."

"Well, I didn't enter into particulars."

"No, dear, and you couldn't have understood him. Two children."

"All right," I said; but I did not think it was all right. As a near-sighted man learns by enforced observation to recognize persons at a distance when the face is not visible to the normal eye, so the man with a bad memory learns, almost unconsciously, to listen carefully and report accurately. My memory is bad; but I had not had time to forget that Mr. Brewster Brede had told me that afternoon that he had three children, at present left in the care of his mother-in-law, while he and Mrs. Brede took their summer vacation.

"Two children," repeated my wife; "and they are staying with his aunt Jenny."

"He told me with his mother-in-law," I put in. My wife looked at me with a serious expression. Men may not remember much of what they are told about children; but any man knows the difference between an aunt and a mother-in-law.

"But don't you think they're nice people?" asked my wife.

"Oh, certainly," I replied. "Only they seem to be a little mixed up about their children."

"That isn't a nice thing to say," returned my wife. I could not deny it.

*   *   *   *   *

And yet, the next morning, when the Bredes came down and seated themselves opposite us at table, beaming and smiling in their natural, pleasant, well-bred fashion, I knew, to a social certainty, that they were "nice" people. He was a fine-looking fellow in his neat tennis-flannels, slim, graceful, twenty-eight or thirty years old, with a Frenchy pointed beard. She was "nice" in all her pretty clothes, and she herself was pretty with that type of prettiness which outwears most other types—the prettiness that lies in a rounded figure, a dusky skin, plump, rosy cheeks, white teeth and black eyes. She might have been twenty-five; you guessed that she was prettier than she was at twenty, and that she would be prettier still at forty.

And nice people were all we wanted to make us happy in Mr. Jacobus's summer boarding-house on top of Orange Mountain. For a week we had come down to breakfast each morning, wondering why we wasted the precious days of idleness with the company gathered around the Jacobus board. What joy of human companionship was to be had out of Mrs. Tabb and Miss Hoogencamp, the two middle-aged gossips from Scranton, Pa.—out of Mr. and Mrs. Biggle, an indurated head-bookkeeper and his prim and censorious wife—out of old Major Halkit, a retired business man, who, having once sold a few shares on commission, wrote for circulars of every stock company that was started, and tried to induce every one to invest who would listen to him? We looked around at those dull faces, the truthful indices of mean and barren minds, and decided that we would leave that morning.

Then we ate Mrs. Jacobus's biscuit, light as Aurora's cloudlets, drank her honest coffee, inhaled the perfume of the late azaleas with which she decked her table, and decided to postpone our departure one more day. And then we wandered out to take our morning glance at what we called "our view"; and it seemed to us as if Tabb and Hoogencamp and Halkit and the Biggleses could not drive us away in a year.

I was not surprised when, after breakfast, my wife invited the Bredes to walk with us to "our view." The Hoogencamp-Biggle-Tabb-Halkit contingent never stirred off Jacobus's veranda; but we both felt that the Bredes would not profane that sacred scene. We strolled slowly across the fields, passed through the little belt of woods and, as I heard Mrs. Brede's little cry of startled rapture, I motioned to Brede to look up.

"By Jove!" he cried, "heavenly!"

We looked off from the brow of the mountain over fifteen miles of billowing green, to where, far across a far stretch of pale blue lay a dim purple line that we knew was Staten Island. Towns and villages lay before us and under us; there were ridges and hills, uplands and lowlands, woods and plains, all massed and mingled in that great silent sea of sunlit green. For silent it was to us, standing in the silence of a high place—silent with a Sunday stillness that made us listen, without taking thought, for the sound of bells coming up from the spires that rose above the tree-tops—the tree-tops that lay as far beneath us as the light clouds were above us that dropped great shadows upon our heads and faint specks of shade upon the broad sweep of land at the mountain's foot.

"And so that is *your* view?" asked Mrs. Brede, after a moment; "you are very generous to make it ours, too."

Then we lay down on the grass, and Brede began to talk, in a gentle voice, as if he felt the influence of the place. He had paddled a canoe, in his earlier days, he said, and he knew every river and creek in that vast stretch of landscape. He found his landmarks, and pointed out to us where the Passaic and the Hackensack flowed, invisible to us, hidden behind great ridges that in our sight were but combings of the green waves upon which we looked down. And yet, on the further side of those broad ridges and rises were scores of villages—a little world of country life, lying unseen under our eyes.

"A good deal like looking at humanity," he said; "there is such a thing as getting so far above our fellow men that we see only one side of them."

Ah, how much better was this sort of talk than the chatter and gossip of the Tabb and the Hoogencamp—than the Major's dissertations upon his everlasting circulars! My wife and I exchanged glances.

"Now, when I went up the Matterhorn" Mr. Brede began.

"Why, dear," interrupted his wife, "I didn't know you ever went up the Matterhorn."

"It—it was five years ago," said Mr. Brede, hurriedly. "I—I didn't tell you—when I was on the other side, you know—it was rather dangerous—well, as I was saying—it looked—oh, it didn't look at all like this."

A cloud floated overhead, throwing its great shadow over the field where we lay. The shadow passed over the mountain's brow and reappeared far below, a rapidly decreasing blot, flying eastward over the golden green. My wife and I exchanged glances once more.

Somehow, the shadow lingered over us all. As we went home, the Bredes went side by side along the narrow path, and my wife and I walked together.

"*Should you think*," she asked me, "that a man would climb the Matterhorn the very first year he was married?"

"I don't know, my dear," I answered, evasively; "this isn't the first year I have been married, not by a good many, and I wouldn't climb it—for a farm."

"You know what I mean," she said.

I did.

*   *   *   *   *

When we reached the boarding-house, Mr. Jacobus took me aside.

"You know," he began his discourse, "my wife she uset to live in N' York!"

I didn't know, but I said "Yes."

"She says the numbers on the streets runs criss-cross-like. Thirty-four's on one side o' the street an' thirty-five on t'other. How's that?"

"That is the invariable rule, I believe."

"Then—I say—these here new folk that you 'n' your wife seem so mighty taken up with—d'ye know anything about 'em?"

"I know nothing about the character of your boarders, Mr. Jacobus," I replied, conscious of some irritability. "If I choose to associate with any of them——"

"Jess so—jess so!" broke in Jacobus. "I hain't nothin' to say ag'inst yer sosherbil'ty. But do ye *know* them?"

"Why, certainly not," I replied.

"Well—that was all I wuz askin' ye. Ye see, when *he* come here to take the rooms—you wasn't here then—he told my wife that he lived at number thirty-four in his street. An' yistiddy *she* told her that they lived at number thirty-five. He said he lived in an apartment-house. Now there can't be no apartment-house on two sides of the same street, kin they?"

"What street was it?" I inquired, wearily.

"Hundred 'n' twenty-first street."

"May be," I replied, still more wearily. "That's Harlem. Nobody knows what people will do in Harlem."

I went up to my wife's room.

"Don't you think it's queer?" she asked me.

"I think I'll have a talk with that young man to-night," I said, "and see if he can give some account of himself."

"But, my dear," my wife said, gravely, "*she* doesn't know whether they've had the measles or not."

"Why, Great Scott!" I exclaimed, "they must have had them when they were children."

"Please don't be stupid," said my wife. "I meant *their* children."

After dinner that night—or rather, after supper, for we had dinner in the middle of the day at Jacobus's—I walked down the long verandah to ask Brede, who was placidly smoking at the other end, to accompany me on a twilight stroll. Half way down I met Major Halkit.

"That friend of yours," he said, indicating the unconscious figure at the further end of the house, "seems to be a queer sort of a Dick. He told me that he was out of business, and just looking round for a chance to invest his capital. And I've been telling him what an everlasting big show he had to take stock in the Capitoline Trust Company—starts next month—four million capital—I told you all about it. 'Oh, well,' he says, 'let's wait and think about it.' 'Wait!' says I, 'the Capitoline Trust

Company won't wait for *you*, my boy. This is letting you in on the ground floor,' says I, 'and it's now or never.' 'Oh, let it wait,' says he. I don't know what's in- *to* the man."

"I don't know how well he knows his own business, Major," I said as I started again for Brede's end of the veranda. But I was troubled none the less. The Major could not have influenced the sale of one share of stock in the Capitoline Company. But that stock was a great investment; a rare chance for a purchaser with a few thousand dollars. Perhaps it was no more remarkable that Brede should not invest than that I should not—and yet, it seemed to add one circumstance more to the other suspicious circumstances.

*   *   *   *   *

When I went upstairs that evening, I found my wife putting her hair to bed—I don't know how I can better describe an operation familiar to every married man. I waited until the last tress was coiled up, and then I spoke:

"I've talked with Brede," I said, "and I didn't have to catechize him. He seemed to feel that some sort of explanation was looked for, and he was very outspoken. You were right about the children—that is, I must have misunderstood him. There are only two. But the Matterhorn episode was simple enough. He didn't realize how dangerous it was until he had got so far into it that he couldn't back out; and he didn't tell her, because he'd left her here, you see, and under the circumstances——"

"Left her here!" cried my wife. "I've been sitting with her the whole afternoon, sewing, and she told me that he left her at Geneva, and came back and took her to Basle, and the baby was born there—now I'm sure, dear, because I asked her."

"Perhaps I was mistaken when I thought he said she was on this side of the water," I suggested, with bitter, biting irony.

"You poor dear, did I abuse you?" said my wife. "But, do you know, Mrs. Tabb said that *she* didn't know how many lumps of sugar he took in his coffee. Now that seems queer, doesn't it?"

It did. It was a small thing. But it looked queer, Very queer.

*   *   *   *   *

The next morning, it was clear that war was declared against the Bredes. They came down to breakfast somewhat late, and, as soon as they arrived, the Biggleses swooped up the last fragments that remained on their plates, and made a stately march out of the dining-room, Then Miss Hoogencamp arose and departed, leaving a whole fish-ball on her plate. Even as Atalanta might have dropped an apple behind her to tempt her pursuer to check his speed, so Miss Hoogencamp left that fish-ball behind her, and between her maiden self and contamination.

We had finished our breakfast, my wife and I, before the Bredes appeared. We talked it over, and agreed that we were glad that we had not been obliged to take sides upon such insufficient testimony.

After breakfast, it was the custom of the male half of the Jacobus household to go around the corner of the building and smoke their pipes and cigars where they would not annoy the ladies. We sat under a trellis covered with a grapevine that had borne no grapes in the memory of man. This vine, however, bore leaves, and these, on that pleasant summer morning, shielded from us two persons who were in earnest conversation in the straggling, half-dead flower-garden at the side of the house.

"I don't want," we heard Mr. Jacobus say, "to enter in no man's *pry*-vacy; but I do want to know who it may be, like, that I hev in my house. Now what I ask of *you*, and I don't want you to take it as in no ways *personal*, is—hev you your merridge-license with you?"

"No," we heard the voice of Mr. Brede reply. "Have you yours?"

I think it was a chance shot; but it told all the same. The Major (he was a widower) and Mr. Biggle and I looked at each other; and Mr. Jacobus, on the other side of the grape-trellis, looked at—I don't know what—and was as silent as we were.

Where is *your* marriage-license, married reader? Do you know? Four men, not including Mr. Brede, stood or sat on one side or the other of that grape-trellis, and not one of them knew where his marriage-license was. Each of us had had one—the Major had had three. But where were they? Where is *yours?* Tucked in your best-man's pocket; deposited in his desk—or washed to a pulp in his white waistcoat (if white waistcoats be the fashion of the hour), washed out of existence—can you tell where it is? Can you—unless you are one of those people who frame that interesting document and hang it upon their drawing-room walls?

Mr. Brede's voice arose, after an awful stillness of what seemed like five minutes, and was, probably, thirty seconds:

"Mr. Jacobus, will you make out your bill at once, and let me pay it? I shall leave by the six o'clock train. And will you also send the wagon for my trunks?"

"I hain't said I wanted to hev ye leave——" began Mr. Jacobus; but Brede cut him short.

"Bring me your bill."

"But," remonstrated Jacobus, "ef ye ain't——"

"Bring me your bill!" said Mr. Brede.

*   *   *   *   *

My wife and I went out for our morning's walk. But it seemed to us, when we looked at "our view," as if we could only see those invisible villages of which Brede had told us—that other side of the ridges and rises of which we catch no glimpse from lofty hills or from the heights of human self-esteem. We meant to stay out until the Bredes had taken their departure; but we returned just in time to see Pete, the Jacobus darkey, the blacker of boots, the brasher of coats, the general handyman of the house, loading the Brede trunks on the Jacobus wagon.

And, as we stepped upon the verandah, down came Mrs. Brede, leaning on Mr. Brede's arm, as though she were ill; and it was clear that she had been crying. There were heavy rings about her pretty black eyes.

My wife took a step toward her.

"Look at that dress, dear," she whispered; "she never thought anything like this was going to happen when she put *that* on."

It was a pretty, delicate, dainty dress, a graceful, narrow-striped affair. Her hat was trimmed with a narrow-striped silk of the same colors—maroon and white—and in her hand she held a parasol that matched her dress.

"She's had a new dress on twice a day," said my wife, "but that's the prettiest yet. Oh, somehow—I'm *awfully* sorry they're going!"

But going they were. They moved toward the steps. Mrs. Brede looked toward my wife, and my wife moved toward Mrs. Brede. But the ostracized woman, as though she felt the deep humiliation of her position, turned sharply away, and opened her parasol to shield her eyes from the sun. A shower of rice—a half-pound shower of rice—fell down over her pretty hat and her pretty dress, and fell in a spattering circle on the floor, outlining her skirts—and there it lay in a broad, uneven band, bright in the morning sun.

Mrs. Brede was in my wife's arms, sobbing as if her young heart would break.

"Oh, you poor, dear, silly children!" my wife cried, as Mrs. Brede sobbed on her shoulder, "why *didn't* you tell us?"

"W-W-W-We didn't want to be t-t-taken for a b-b-b-b-bridal couple," sobbed Mrs. Brede; "and we d-d-didn't *dream* what awful lies we'd have to tell, and all the aw-awful mixed-up-ness of it. Oh, dear, dear, dear!"

*   *   *   *   *

"Pete!" commanded Mr. Jacobus, "put back them trunks. These folks stays here's long's they wants ter. Mr. Brede"—he held out a large, hard hand—"I'd orter've known better," he said. And my last doubt of Mr. Brede vanished as he shook that grimy hand in manly fashion.

The two women were walking off toward "our view," each with an arm about the other's waist—touched by a sudden sisterhood of sympathy.

"Gentlemen," said Mr. Brede, addressing Jacobus, Biggle, the Major and me, "there is a hostelry down the street where they sell honest New Jersey beer. I recognize the obligations of the situation."

We five men filed down the street. The two women went toward the pleasant slope where the sunlight gilded the forehead of the great hill. On Mr. Jacobus's veranda lay a spattered circle of shining grains of rice. Two of Mr. Jacobus's pigeons flew down and picked up the shining grains, making grateful noises far down in their throats.

THE BULLER-PODINGTON COMPACT
By Frank Richard Stockton (1834-1902)

[From *Scribner's Magazine*, August, 1897. Republished in *Afield and Afloat*, by
Frank Richard Stockton; copyright, 1900, by Charles Scribner's Sons.
Reprinted by permission of the publishers.]

I tell you, William," said Thomas Buller to his friend Mr. Podington, "I am truly
sorry about it, but I cannot arrange for it this year. Now, as to *my* invitation—
that is very different."

"Of course it is different," was the reply, "but I am obliged to say, as I said before,
that I really cannot accept it."

Remarks similar to these had been made by Thomas Buller and William Podington at least once a year for some five years. They were old friends; they had been
schoolboys together and had been associated in business since they were young
men. They had now reached a vigorous middle age; they were each married, and
each had a house in the country in which he resided for a part of the year. They
were warmly attached to each other, and each was the best friend which the other
had in this world. But during all these years neither of them had visited the other
in his country home.

The reason for this avoidance of each other at their respective rural residences
may be briefly stated. Mr. Buller's country house was situated by the sea, and he
was very fond of the water. He had a good cat-boat, which he sailed himself with
much judgment and skill, and it was his greatest pleasure to take his friends and
visitors upon little excursions on the bay. But Mr. Podington was desperately afraid

of the water, and he was particularly afraid of any craft sailed by an amateur. If his friend Buller would have employed a professional mariner, of years and experience, to steer and manage his boat, Podington might have been willing to take an occasional sail; but as Buller always insisted upon sailing his own boat, and took it ill if any of his visitors doubted his ability to do so properly, Podington did not wish to wound the self-love of his friend, and he did not wish to be drowned. Consequently he could not bring himself to consent to go to Buller's house by the sea.

To receive his good friend Buller at his own house in the beautiful upland region in which he lived would have been a great joy to Mr. Podington; but Buller could not be induced to visit him. Podington was very fond of horses and always drove himself, while Buller was more afraid of horses than he was of elephants or lions. To one or more horses driven by a coachman of years and experience he did not always object, but to a horse driven by Podington, who had much experience and knowledge regarding mercantile affairs, but was merely an amateur horseman, he most decidedly and strongly objected. He did not wish to hurt his friend's feelings by refusing to go out to drive with him, but he would not rack his own nervous system by accompanying him. Therefore it was that he had not yet visited the beautiful upland country residence of Mr. Podington.

At last this state of things grew awkward. Mrs. Buller and Mrs. Podington, often with their families, visited each other at their country houses, but the fact that on these occasions they were never accompanied by their husbands caused more and more gossip among their neighbors both in the upland country and by the sea.

One day in spring as the two sat in their city office, where Mr. Podington had just repeated his annual invitation, his friend replied to him thus:

"William, if I come to see you this summer, will you visit me? The thing is beginning to look a little ridiculous, and people are talking about it."

Mr. Podington put his hand to his brow and for a few moments closed his eyes. In his mind he saw a cat-boat upon its side, the sails spread out over the water, and two men, almost entirely immersed in the waves, making efforts to reach the side of the boat. One of these was getting on very well—that was Buller. The other seemed about to sink, his arms were uselessly waving in the air—that was himself. But he opened his eyes and looked bravely out of the window; it was time to conquer all this; it was indeed growing ridiculous. Buller had been sailing many years and had never been upset.

"Yes," said he; "I will do it; I am ready any time you name."

Mr. Buller rose and stretched out his hand.

"Good!" said he; "it is a compact!"

Buller was the first to make the promised country visit. He had not mentioned the subject of horses to his friend, but he knew through Mrs. Buller that Podington still continued to be his own driver. She had informed him, however, that at present he was accustomed to drive a big black horse which, in her opinion, was as gentle and reliable as these animals ever became, and she could not imagine how anybody could be afraid of him. So when, the next morning after his arrival, Mr. Buller was asked by his host if he would like to take a drive, he suppressed a certain rising emotion and said that it would please him very much.

When the good black horse had jogged along a pleasant road for half an hour Mr. Buller began to feel that, perhaps, for all these years he had been laboring under a misconception. It seemed to be possible that there were some horses to which surrounding circumstances in the shape of sights and sounds were so irrelevant that they were to a certain degree entirely safe, even when guided and controlled by an amateur hand. As they passed some meadow-land, somebody behind a hedge fired a gun; Mr. Buller was frightened, but the horse was not.

"William," said Buller, looking cheerfully around him,

"I had no idea that you lived in such a pretty country. In fact, I might almost call it beautiful. You have not any wide stretch of water, such as I like so much, but here is a pretty river, those rolling hills are very charming, and, beyond, you have the blue of the mountains."

"It is lovely," said his friend; "I never get tired of driving through this country. Of course the seaside is very fine, but here we have such a variety of scenery."

Mr. Buller could not help thinking that sometimes the seaside was a little monotonous, and that he had lost a great deal of pleasure by not varying his summers by going up to spend a week or two with Podington.

"William," said he, "how long have you had this horse?"

"About two years," said Mr. Podington; "before I got him, I used to drive a pair."

"Heavens!" thought Buller, "how lucky I was not to come two years ago!" And his regrets for not sooner visiting his friend greatly decreased.

Now they came to a place where the stream, by which the road ran, had been dammed for a mill and had widened into a beautiful pond.

"There now!" cried Mr. Buller. "That's what I like. William, you seem to have everything! This is really a very pretty sheet of water, and the reflections of the trees over there make a charming picture; you can't get that at the seaside, you know."

Mr. Podington was delighted; his face glowed; he was rejoiced at the pleasure of his friend. "I tell you, Thomas," said he, "that——"

"William!" exclaimed Buller, with a sudden squirm in his seat, "what is that I hear? Is that a train?"

"Yes," said Mr. Podington, "that is the ten-forty, up."

"Does it come near here?" asked Mr. Buller, nervously. "Does it go over that bridge?"

"Yes," said Podington, "but it can't hurt us, for our road goes under the bridge; we are perfectly safe; there is no risk of accident."

"But your horse! Your horse!" exclaimed Buller, as the train came nearer and nearer. "What will he do?"

"Do?" said Podington; "he'll do what he is doing now; he doesn't mind trains."

"But look here, William," exclaimed Buller, "it will get there just as we do; no horse could stand a roaring up in the air like that!"

Podington laughed. "He would not mind it in the least," said he.

"Come, come now," cried Buller. "Really, I can't stand this! Just stop a minute, William, and let me get out. It sets all my nerves quivering."

Mr. Podington smiled with a superior smile. "Oh, you needn't get out," said he; "there's not the least danger in the world. But I don't want to make you nervous, and I will turn around and drive the other way."

"But you can't!" screamed Buller. "This road is not wide enough, and that train is nearly here. Please stop!"

The imputation that the road was not wide enough for him to turn was too much for Mr. Podington to bear. He was very proud of his ability to turn a vehicle in a narrow place.

"Turn!" said he; "that's the easiest thing in the world. See; a little to the right, then a back, then a sweep to the left and we will be going the other way." And instantly he began the maneuver in which he was such an adept.

"Oh, Thomas!" cried Buller, half rising in his seat, "that train is almost here!"

"And we are almost——" Mr. Podington was about to say "turned around," but he stopped. Mr. Buller's exclamations had made him a little nervous, and, in his anxiety to turn quickly, he had pulled upon his horse's bit with more energy than was actually necessary, and his nervousness being communicated to the horse, that animal backed with such extraordinary vigor that the hind wheels of the wagon went over a bit of grass by the road and into the water. The sudden jolt gave a new impetus to Mr. Buller's fears.

"You'll upset!" he cried, and not thinking of what he was about, he laid hold of his friend's arm. The horse, startled by this sudden jerk upon his bit, which, combined with the thundering of the train, which was now on the bridge, made him think that something extraordinary was about to happen, gave a sudden and forcible start backward, so that not only the hind wheels of the light wagon, but the fore wheels and his own hind legs went into the water. As the bank at this spot sloped steeply, the wagon continued to go backward, despite the efforts of the agitated horse to find a footing on the crumbling edge of the bank.

"Whoa!" cried Mr. Buller.

"Get up!" exclaimed Mr. Podington, applying his whip upon the plunging beast.

But exclamations and castigations had no effect upon the horse. The original bed of the stream ran close to the road, and the bank was so steep and the earth so soft that it was impossible for the horse to advance or even maintain his footing. Back, back he went, until the whole equipage was in the water and the wagon was afloat.

This vehicle was a road wagon, without a top, and the joints of its box-body were tight enough to prevent the water from immediately entering it; so, somewhat deeply sunken, it rested upon the water. There was a current in this part of the pond and it turned the wagon downstream. The horse was now entirely immersed in the water, with the exception of his head and the upper part of his neck, and, unable to reach the bottom with his feet, he made vigorous efforts to swim.

Mr. Podington, the reins and whip in his hands, sat horrified and pale; the accident was so sudden, he was so startled and so frightened that, for a moment, he could not speak a word. Mr. Buller, on the other hand, was now lively and alert. The wagon had no sooner floated away from the shore than he felt himself at home. He was upon his favorite element; water had no fears for him. He saw that his friend was nearly frightened out of his wits, and that, figuratively speaking, he must step to the helm and take charge of the vessel. He stood up and gazed about him.

"Put her across stream!" he shouted; "she can't make headway against this current. Head her to that clump of trees on the other side; the bank is lower there, and we can beach her. Move a little the other way, we must trim boat. Now then, pull on your starboard rein."

Podington obeyed, and the horse slightly changed his direction.

"You see," said Buller, "it won't do to sail straight across, because the current would carry us down and land us below that spot."

Mr. Podington said not a word; he expected every moment to see the horse sink into a watery grave.

"It isn't so bad after all, is it, Podington? If we had a rudder and a bit of a sail it would be a great help to the horse. This wagon is not a bad boat."

The despairing Podington looked at his feet. "It's coming in," he said in a husky voice. "Thomas, the water is over my shoes!"

"That is so," said Buller. "I am so used to water I didn't notice it. She leaks. Do you carry anything to bail her out with?"

"Bail!" cried Podington, now finding his voice. "Oh, Thomas, we are sinking!"

"That's so," said Buller; "she leaks like a sieve."

The weight of the running-gear and of the two men was entirely too much for the buoyancy of the wagon body. The water rapidly rose toward the top of its sides.

"We are going to drown!" cried Podington, suddenly rising.

"Lick him! Lick him!" exclaimed Buller. "Make him swim faster!"

"There's nothing to lick," cried Podington, vainly lashing at the water, for he could not reach the horse's head. The poor man was dreadfully frightened; he had never even imagined it possible that he should be drowned in his own wagon.

"Whoop!" cried Buller, as the water rose over the sides. "Steady yourself, old boy, or you'll go overboard!" And the next moment the wagon body sunk out of sight.

But it did not go down very far. The deepest part of the channel of the stream had been passed, and with a bump the wheels struck the bottom.

"Heavens!" exclaimed Buller, "we are aground."

"Aground!" exclaimed Podington, "Heaven be praised!"

As the two men stood up in the submerged wagon the water was above their knees, and when Podington looked out over the surface of the pond, now so near his face, it seemed like a sheet of water he had never seen before. It was something horrible, threatening to rise and envelop him. He trembled so that he could scarcely keep his footing.

"William," said his companion, "you must sit down; if you don't, you'll tumble overboard and be drowned. There is nothing for you to hold to."

"Sit down," said Podington, gazing blankly at the water around him, "I can't do that!"

At this moment the horse made a slight movement. Having touched bottom after his efforts in swimming across the main bed of the stream, with a floating wagon in tow, he had stood for a few moments, his head and neck well above water, and his back barely visible beneath the surface. Having recovered his breath, he now thought it was time to move on.

At the first step of the horse Mr. Podington began to totter. Instinctively he clutched Buller.

"Sit down!" cried the latter, "or you'll have us both overboard." There was no help for it; down sat Mr. Podington; and, as with a great splash he came heavily upon the seat, the water rose to his waist.

"Ough!" said he. "Thomas, shout for help."

"No use doing that," replied Buller, still standing on his nautical legs; "I don't see anybody, and I don't see any boat. We'll get out all right. Just you stick tight to the thwart."

"The what?" feebly asked the other.

"Oh, the seat, I mean. We can get to the shore all right if you steer the horse straight. Head him more across the pond."

"I can't head him," cried Podington. "I have dropped the reins!"

"Good gracious!" cried Mr. Buller, "that's bad. Can't you steer him by shouting 'Gee' and 'Haw'?"

"No," said Podington, "he isn't an ox; but perhaps I can stop him." And with as much voice as he could summon, he called out: "Whoa!" and the horse stopped.

"If you can't steer him any other way," said Buller, "we must get the reins. Lend me your whip."

"I have dropped that too," said Podington; "there it floats."

"Oh, dear," said Buller, "I guess I'll have to dive for them; if he were to run away, we should be in an awful fix."

"Don't get out! Don't get out!" exclaimed Podington. "You can reach over the dashboard."

"As that's under water," said Buller, "it will be the same thing as diving; but it's got to be done, and I'll try it. Don't you move now; I am more used to water than you are."

Mr. Buller took off his hat and asked his friend to hold it. He thought of his watch and other contents of his pockets, but there was no place to put them, so he gave them no more consideration. Then bravely getting on his knees in the water, he leaned over the dashboard, almost disappearing from sight. With his disengaged hand Mr. Podington grasped the submerged coat-tails of his friend.

In a few seconds the upper part of Mr. Buller rose from the water. He was dripping and puffing, and Mr. Podington could not but think what a difference it made in the appearance of his friend to have his hair plastered close to his head.

"I got hold of one of them," said the sputtering Buller, "but it was fast to something and I couldn't get it loose."

"Was it thick and wide?" asked Podington.

"Yes," was the answer; "it did seem so."

"Oh, that was a trace," said Podington; "I don't want that; the reins are thinner and lighter."

"Now I remember they are," said Buller. "I'll go down again."

Again Mr. Buller leaned over the dashboard, and this time he remained down longer, and when he came up he puffed and sputtered more than before.

"Is this it?" said he, holding up a strip of wet leather.

"Yes," said Podington, "you've got the reins."

"Well, take them, and steer. I would have found them sooner if his tail had not got into my eyes. That long tail's floating down there and spreading itself out like a fan; it tangled itself all around my head. It would have been much easier if he had been a bob-tailed horse."

"Now then," said Podington, "take your hat, Thomas, and I'll try to drive."

Mr. Buller put on his hat, which was the only dry thing about him, and the nervous Podington started the horse so suddenly that even the sea-legs of Buller were surprised, and he came very near going backward into the water; but recovering himself, he sat down.

"I don't wonder you did not like to do this, William," said he. "Wet as I am, it's ghastly!"

Encouraged by his master's voice, and by the feeling of the familiar hand upon his bit, the horse moved bravely on.

But the bottom was very rough and uneven. Sometimes the wheels struck a large stone, terrifying Mr. Buller, who thought they were going to upset; and sometimes they sank into soft mud, horrifying Mr. Podington, who thought they were going to drown.

Thus proceeding, they presented a strange sight. At first Mr. Podington held his hands above the water as he drove, but he soon found this awkward, and dropped them to their usual position, so that nothing was visible above the water but the head and neck of a horse and the heads and shoulders of two men.

Now the submarine equipage came to a low place in the bottom, and even Mr. Buller shuddered as the water rose to his chin. Podington gave a howl of horror, and the horse, with high, uplifted head, was obliged to swim. At this moment a boy with a gun came strolling along the road, and hearing Mr. Podington's cry, he cast his eyes over the water. Instinctively he raised his weapon to his shoulder, and then, in an instant, perceiving that the objects he beheld were not aquatic birds, he dropped his gun and ran yelling down the road toward the mill.

But the hollow in the bottom was a narrow one, and when it was passed the depth of the water gradually decreased. The back of the horse came into view, the dashboard became visible, and the bodies and the spirits of the two men rapidly rose. Now there was vigorous splashing and tugging, and then a jet black horse, shining as if he had been newly varnished, pulled a dripping wagon containing two well-soaked men upon a shelving shore.

"Oh, I am chilled to the bones!" said Podington.

"I should think so," replied his friend; "if you have got to be wet, it is a great deal pleasanter under the water."

There was a field-road on this side of the pond which Podington well knew, and proceeding along this they came to the bridge and got into the main road.

"Now we must get home as fast as we can," cried Podington, "or we shall both take cold. I wish I hadn't lost my whip. Hi now! Get along!"

Podington was now full of life and energy, his wheels were on the hard road, and he was himself again.

When he found his head was turned toward his home, the horse set off at a great rate.

"Hi there!" cried Podington. "I am so sorry I lost my whip."

"Whip!" said Buller, holding fast to the side of the seat; "surely you don't want him to go any faster than this. And look here, William," he added, "it seems to me we are much more likely to take cold in our wet clothes if we rush through the air in this way. Really, it seems to me that horse is running away."

"Not a bit of it," cried Podington. "He wants to get home, and he wants his dinner. Isn't he a fine horse? Look how he steps out!"

"Steps out!" said Buller, "I think I'd like to step out myself. Don't you think it would be wiser for me to walk home, William? That will warm me up."

"It will take you an hour," said his friend. "Stay where you are, and I'll have you in a dry suit of clothes in less than fifteen minutes."

"I tell you, William," said Mr. Buller, as the two sat smoking after dinner, "what you ought to do; you should never go out driving without a life-preserver and a pair of oars; I always take them. It would make you feel safer."

Mr. Buller went home the next day, because Mr. Podington's clothes did not fit him, and his own outdoor suit was so shrunken as to be uncomfortable. Besides, there was another reason, connected with the desire of horses to reach their homes, which prompted his return. But he had not forgotten his compact with his friend, and in the course of a week he wrote to Podington, inviting him to spend some days with him. Mr. Podington was a man of honor, and in spite of his recent unfortunate water experience he would not break his word. He went to Mr. Buller's seaside home at the time appointed.

Early on the morning after his arrival, before the family were up, Mr. Podington went out and strolled down to the edge of the bay. He went to look at Buller's boat. He was well aware that he would be asked to take a sail, and as Buller had driven with him, it would be impossible for him to decline sailing with Buller; but he must see the boat. There was a train for his home at a quarter past seven; if he were not on the premises he could not be asked to sail. If Buller's boat were a little, flimsy thing, he would take that train—but he would wait and see.

There was only one small boat anchored near the beach, and a man—apparently a fisherman—informed Mr. Podington that it belonged to Mr. Buller. Podington looked at it eagerly; it was not very small and not flimsy.

"Do you consider that a safe boat?" he asked the fisherman.

"Safe?" replied the man. "You could not upset her if you tried. Look at her breadth of beam! You could go anywhere in that boat! Are you thinking of buying her?"

The idea that he would think of buying a boat made Mr. Podington laugh. The information that it would be impossible to upset the little vessel had greatly cheered him, and he could laugh.

Shortly after breakfast Mr. Buller, like a nurse with a dose of medicine, came to Mr. Podington with the expected invitation to take a sail.

"Now, William," said his host, "I understand perfectly your feeling about boats, and what I wish to prove to you is that it is a feeling without any foundation. I don't want to shock you or make you nervous, so I am not going to take you out today on the bay in my boat. You are as safe on the bay as you would be on land—a little safer, perhaps, under certain circumstances, to which we will not allude—but still it is sometimes a little rough, and this, at first, might cause you some uneasiness, and so I am going to let you begin your education in the sailing line on perfectly smooth water. About three miles back of us there is a very pretty lake several miles long. It is part of the canal system which connects the town with the railroad. I have sent my boat to the town, and we can walk up there and go by the canal to the lake; it is only about three miles."

If he had to sail at all, this kind of sailing suited Mr. Podington. A canal, a quiet lake, and a boat which could not be upset. When they reached the town the boat was in the canal, ready for them.

"Now," said Mr. Buller, "you get in and make yourself comfortable. My idea is to hitch on to a canal-boat and be towed to the lake. The boats generally start about this time in the morning, and I will go and see about it."

Mr. Podington, under the direction of his friend, took a seat in the stern of the sailboat, and then he remarked:

"Thomas, have you a life-preserver on board? You know I am not used to any kind of vessel, and I am clumsy. Nothing might happen to the boat, but I might trip and fall overboard, and I can't swim."

"All right," said Buller; "here's a life-preserver, and you can put it on. I want you to feel perfectly safe. Now I will go and see about the tow."

But Mr. Buller found that the canal-boats would not start at their usual time; the loading of one of them was not finished, and he was informed that he might have to wait for an hour or more. This did not suit Mr. Buller at all, and he did not hesitate to show his annoyance.

"I tell you, sir, what you can do," said one of the men in charge of the boats; "if you don't want to wait till we are ready to start, we'll let you have a boy and a horse to tow you up to the lake. That won't cost you much, and they'll be back before we want 'em."

The bargain was made, and Mr. Buller joyfully returned to his boat with the intelligence that they were not to wait for the canal-boats. A long rope, with a horse attached to the other end of it, was speedily made fast to the boat, and with a boy at the head of the horse, they started up the canal.

"Now this is the kind of sailing I like," said Mr. Podington. "If I lived near a canal I believe I would buy a boat and train my horse to tow. I could have a long pair of rope-lines and drive him myself; then when the roads were rough and bad the canal would always be smooth."

"This is all very nice," replied Mr. Buller, who sat by the tiller to keep the boat away from the bank, "and I am glad to see you in a boat under any circumstances. Do you know, William, that although I did not plan it, there could not have been a better way to begin your sailing education. Here we glide along, slowly and gently, with no possible thought of danger, for if the boat should suddenly spring a leak, as if it were the body of a wagon, all we would have to do would be to step on shore, and by the time you get to the end of the canal you will like this gentle motion so much that you will be perfectly ready to begin the second stage of your nautical education."

"Yes," said Mr. Podington. "How long did you say this canal is?"

"About three miles," answered his friend. "Then we will go into the lock and in a few minutes we shall be on the lake."

"So far as I am concerned," said Mr. Podington, "I wish the canal were twelve miles long. I cannot imagine anything pleasanter than this. If I lived anywhere near a canal—a long canal, I mean, this one is too short—I'd—"

"Come, come now," interrupted Buller. "Don't be content to stay in the primary school just because it is easy. When we get on the lake I will show you that in a boat, with a gentle breeze, such as we are likely to have today, you will find the motion quite as pleasing, and ever so much more inspiriting. I should not be a bit surprised, William, if after you have been two or three times on the lake you will ask me—yes, positively ask me—to take you out on the bay!"

Mr. Podington smiled, and leaning backward, he looked up at the beautiful blue sky.

"You can't give me anything better than this, Thomas," said he; "but you needn't think I am weakening; you drove with me, and I will sail with you."

The thought came into Buller's mind that he had done both of these things with Podington, but he did not wish to call up unpleasant memories, and said nothing.

About half a mile from the town there stood a small cottage where house-cleaning was going on, and on a fence, not far from the canal, there hung a carpet gaily adorned with stripes and spots of red and yellow.

When the drowsy tow-horse came abreast of the house, and the carpet caught his eye, he suddenly stopped and gave a start toward the canal. Then, impressed with a horror of the glaring apparition, he gathered himself up, and with a bound dashed along the tow-path. The astounded boy gave a shout, but was speedily left behind. The boat of Mr. Buller shot forward as if she had been struck by a squall.

The terrified horse sped on as if a red and yellow demon were after him. The boat bounded, and plunged, and frequently struck the grassy bank of the canal, as if it would break itself to pieces. Mr. Podington clutched the boom to keep himself from being thrown out, while Mr. Buller, both hands upon the tiller, frantically endeavored to keep the boat from the bank.

"William!" he screamed, "he is running away with us; we shall be dashed to pieces! Can't you get forward and cast off that line?"

"What do you mean?" cried Podington, as the boom gave a great jerk as if it would break its fastenings and drag him overboard.

"I mean untie the tow-line. We'll be smashed if you don't! I can't leave this tiller. Don't try to stand up; hold on to the boom and creep forward. Steady now, or you'll be overboard!"

Mr. Podington stumbled to the bow of the boat, his efforts greatly impeded by the big cork life-preserver tied under his arms, and the motion of the boat was so violent and erratic that he was obliged to hold on to the mast with one arm and to try to loosen the knot with the other; but there was a great strain on the rope, and he could do nothing with one hand.

"Cut it! Cut it!" cried Mr. Buller.

"I haven't a knife," replied Podington.

Mr. Buller was terribly frightened; his boat was cutting through the water as never vessel of her class had sped since sail-boats were invented, and bumping against the bank as if she were a billiard-ball rebounding from the edge of a table. He forgot he was in a boat; he only knew that for the first time in his life he was in a runaway. He let go the tiller. It was of no use to him.

"William," he cried, "let us jump out the next time we are near enough to shore!"

"Don't do that! Don't do that!" replied Podington. "Don't jump out in a runaway; that is the way to get hurt. Stick to your seat, my boy; he can't keep this up much longer. He'll lose his wind!"

Mr. Podington was greatly excited, but he was not frightened, as Buller was. He had been in a runaway before, and he could not help thinking how much better a wagon was than a boat in such a case.

"If he were hitched up shorter and I had a snaffle-bit and a stout pair of reins," thought he, "I could soon bring him up."

But Mr. Buller was rapidly losing his wits. The horse seemed to be going faster than ever. The boat bumped harder against the bank, and at one time Buller thought they could turn over.

Suddenly a thought struck him.

"William," he shouted, "tip that anchor over the side! Throw it in, any way!"

Mr. Podington looked about him, and, almost under his feet, saw the anchor. He did not instantly comprehend why Buller wanted it thrown overboard, but this was not a time to ask questions. The difficulties imposed by the life-preserver, and the necessity of holding on with one hand, interfered very much with his getting at the anchor and throwing it over the side, but at last he succeeded, and just as the boat threw up her bow as if she were about to jump on shore, the anchor went out and its line shot after it. There was an irregular trembling of the boat as the anchor struggled along the bottom of the canal; then there was a great shock; the boat ran into the bank and stopped; the tow-line was tightened like a guitar-string, and the horse, jerked back with great violence, came tumbling in a heap upon the ground.

Instantly Mr. Podington was on the shore and running at the top of his speed toward the horse. The astounded animal had scarcely begun to struggle to his feet when Podington rushed upon him, pressed his head back to the ground, and sat upon it.

"Hurrah!" he cried, waving his hat above his head. "Get out, Buller; he is all right now!"

Presently Mr. Buller approached, very much shaken up.

"All right?" he said. "I don't call a horse flat in a road with a man on his head all right; but hold him down till we get him loose from my boat. That is the thing to do. William, cast him loose from the boat before you let him up! What will he do when he gets up?"

"Oh. he'll be quiet enough when he gets up," said Podington. "But if you've got a knife you can cut his traces—-I mean that rope—but no, you needn't. Here comes the boy. We'll settle this business in very short order now."

When the horse was on his feet, and all connection between the animal and the boat had been severed, Mr. Podington looked at his friend.

"Thomas," said he, "you seem to have had a hard time of it. You have lost your hat and you look as if you had been in a wrestling-match."

"I have," replied the other; "I wrestled with that tiller and I wonder it didn't throw me out."

Now approached the boy. "Shall I hitch him on again, sir?" said he. "He's quiet enough now."

"No," cried Mr. Buller; "I want no more sailing after a horse, and, besides, we can't go on the lake with that boat; she has been battered about so much that she must have opened a dozen seams. The best thing we can do is to walk home."

Mr. Podington agreed with his friend that walking home was the best thing they could do. The boat was examined and found to be leaking, but not very badly, and when her mast had been unshipped and everything had been made tight and right on board, she was pulled out of the way of tow-lines and boats, and made fast until she could be sent for from the town.

Mr. Buller and Mr. Podington walked back toward the town. They had not gone very far when they met a party of boys, who, upon seeing them, burst into unseemly laughter.

"Mister," cried one of them, "you needn't be afraid of tumbling into the canal. Why don't you take off your life-preserver and let that other man put it on his head?"

The two friends looked at each other and could not help joining in the laughter of the boys.

"By George! I forgot all about this," said Podington, as he unfastened the cork jacket. "It does look a little super-timid to wear a life-preserver just because one happens to be walking by the side of a canal."

Mr. Buller tied a handkerchief on his head, and Mr. Podington rolled up his life-preserver and carried it under his arm. Thus they reached the town, where Buller bought a hat, Podington dispensed with his bundle, and arrangements were made to bring back the boat.

"Runaway in a sailboat!" exclaimed one of the canal boatmen when he had heard about the accident. "Upon my word! That beats anything that could happen to a man!"

"No, it doesn't," replied Mr. Buller, quietly. "I have gone to the bottom in a foundered road-wagon."

The man looked at him fixedly.

"Was you ever struck in the mud in a balloon?" he asked.

"Not yet," replied Mr. Buller.

It required ten days to put Mr. Buller's sailboat into proper condition, and for ten days Mr. Podington stayed with his friend, and enjoyed his visit very much. They strolled on the beach, they took long walks in the back country, they fished from the end of a pier, they smoked, they talked, and were happy and content.

"Thomas," said Mr. Podington, on the last evening of his stay, "I have enjoyed myself very much since I have been down here, and now, Thomas, if I were to come down again next summer, would you mind—would you mind, not——"

"I would not mind it a bit," replied Buller, promptly. "I'll never so much as mention it; so you can come along without a thought of it. And since you have alluded to the subject, William," he continued, "I'd like very much to come and see you again; you know my visit was a very short one this year. That is a beautiful country you live in. Such a variety of scenery, such an opportunity for walks and rambles! But, William, if you could only make up your mind not to——"

"Oh, that is all right!" exclaimed Podington. "I do not need to make up my mind. You come to my house and you will never so much as hear of it. Here's my hand upon it!"

"And here's mine!" said Mr. Buller.

And they shook hands over a new compact.

COLONEL STARBOTTLE FOR THE PLAINTIFF
By Bret Harte (1839-1902)

[From *Harper's Magazine*, March, 1901. Republished in the volume, *Openings in the Old Trail* (1902), by Bret Harte; copyright, 1902, by Houghton Mifflin Company, the authorized publishers of Bret Harte's complete works; reprinted by their permission.]

IT had been a day of triumph for Colonel Starbottle. First, for his personality, as it would have been difficult to separate the Colonel's achievements from his individuality; second, for his oratorical abilities as a sympathetic pleader; and third, for his functions as the leading counsel for the Eureka Ditch Company *versus* the State of California. On his strictly legal performances in this issue I prefer not to speak; there were those who denied them, although the jury had accepted them in the face of the ruling of the half-amused, half-cynical Judge himself. For an hour they had laughed with the Colonel, wept with him, been stirred to personal indignation or patriotic exaltation by his passionate and lofty periods—what else could they do than give him their verdict? If it was alleged by some that the American eagle, Thomas Jefferson, and the Resolutions of '98 had nothing whatever to do with the contest of a ditch company over a doubtfully worded legislative document; that wholesale abuse of the State Attorney and his political motives had not the slightest connection with the legal question raised—it was, nevertheless, generally accepted that the losing party would have been only too glad to have the Colonel on their side. And Colonel Starbottle knew this, as, perspiring, florid, and panting, he rebuttoned the lower buttons of his blue frock-coat, which had become loosed in an oratorical spasm, and readjusted his old-fashioned, spotless shirt frill above it as he strutted from the court-room amidst the hand-shakings and acclamations of his friends.

And here an unprecedented thing occurred. The Colonel absolutely declined spirituous refreshment at the neighboring Palmetto Saloon, and declared his intention of proceeding directly to his office in the adjoining square. Nevertheless the Colonel quitted the building alone, and apparently unarmed except for his faithful gold-headed stick, which hung as usual from his forearm. The crowd gazed after him with undisguised admiration of this new evidence of his pluck. It was remembered also that a mysterious note had been handed to him at the conclusion of his speech—evidently a challenge from the State Attorney. It was quite plain that the Colonel—a practised duellist—was hastening home to answer it.

But herein they were wrong. The note was in a female hand, and simply requested the Colonel to accord an interview with the writer at the Colonel's office as soon as he left the court. But it was an engagement that the Colonel—as devoted to the fair sex as he was to the "code"—was no less prompt in accepting. He flicked away the dust from his spotless white trousers and varnished boots with his handkerchief, and settled his black cravat under his Byron collar as he neared his office. He was surprised, however, on opening the door of his private office to find his visitor already there; he was still more startled to find her somewhat past middle age and plainly attired. But the Colonel was brought up in a school of Southern politeness, already antique in the republic, and his bow of courtesy belonged to the epoch of his shirt frill and strapped trousers. No one could have detected his disappointment in his manner, albeit his sentences were short and incomplete. But the Colonel's colloquial speech was apt to be fragmentary incoherencies of his larger oratorical utterances.

"A thousand pardons—for—er—having kept a lady waiting—er! But—er—congratulations of friends—and—er—courtesy due to them—er—interfered with—though perhaps only heightened—by procrastination—pleasure of—ha!" And the Colonel completed his sentence with a gallant wave of his fat but white and well-kept hand.

"Yes! I came to see you along o' that speech of yours. I was in court. When I heard you gettin' it off on that jury, I says to myself that's the kind o' lawyer *I* want.

A man that's flowery and convincin'! Just the man to take up our case."

"Ah! It's a matter of business, I see," said the Colonel, inwardly relieved, but externally careless. "And—er—may I ask the nature of the case?"

"Well! it's a breach-o'-promise suit," said the visitor, calmly.

If the Colonel had been surprised before, he was now really startled, and with an added horror that required all his politeness to conceal. Breach-of-promise cases were his peculiar aversion. He had always held them to be a kind of litigation which could have been obviated by the prompt killing of the masculine offender—in which case he would have gladly defended the killer. But a suit for damages!—*damages!*—with the reading of love-letters before a hilarious jury and court, was against all his instincts. His chivalry was outraged; his sense of humor was small—and in the course of his career he had lost one or two important cases through an unexpected development of this quality in a jury.

The woman had evidently noticed his hesitation, but mistook its cause. "It ain't me—but my darter."

The Colonel recovered his politeness. "Ah! I am relieved, my dear madam! I could hardly conceive a man ignorant enough to—er—er—throw away such evident good fortune—or base enough to deceive the trustfulness of womanhood—matured and experienced only in the chivalry of our sex, ha!"

The woman smiled grimly. "Yes!—it's my darter, Zaidee Hooker—so ye might spare some of them pretty speeches for *her*—before the jury."

The Colonel winced slightly before this doubtful prospect, but smiled. "Ha! Yes!—certainly—the jury. But—er—my dear lady, need we go as far as that? Cannot this affair be settled—er—out of court? Could not this—er—individual—be admonished—told that he must give satisfaction—personal satisfaction—for his dastardly conduct—to —er—near relative—or even valued personal friend? The—er—arrangements necessary for that purpose I myself would undertake."

He was quite sincere; indeed, his small black eyes shone with that fire which a pretty woman or an "affair of honor" could alone kindle. The visitor stared vacantly at him, and said, slowly:

"And what good is that goin' to do *us?*"

"Compel him to—er—perform his promise," said the Colonel, leaning back in his chair.

"Ketch him doin' it!" said the woman, scornfully. "No—that ain't wot we're after. We must make him *pay*! Damages—and nothin' short o' *that*."

The Colonel bit his lip. "I suppose," he said, gloomily, "you have documentary evidence—written promises and protestations—er—er— love-letters, in fact?"

"No—nary a letter! Ye see, that's jest it—and that's where *you* come in. You've got to convince that jury yourself. You've got to show what it is—tell the whole story your own way. Lord! to a man like you that's nothin'."

Startling as this admission might have been to any other lawyer, Starbottle was absolutely relieved by it. The absence of any mirth-provoking correspondence, and the appeal solely to his own powers of persuasion, actually struck his fancy. He lightly put aside the compliment with a wave of his white hand.

"Of course," said the Colonel, confidently, "there is strongly presumptive and corroborative evidence? Perhaps you can give me—er—a brief outline of the affair?"

"Zaidee kin do that straight enough, I reckon," said the woman; "what I want to know first is, kin you take the case?"

The Colonel did not hesitate; his curiosity was piqued. "I certainly can. I have no doubt your daughter will put me in possession of sufficient facts and details—to constitute what we call—er—a brief."

"She kin be brief enough—or long enough—for the matter of that," said the woman, rising. The Colonel accepted this implied witticism with a smile.

"And when may I have the pleasure of seeing her?" he asked, politely.

"Well, I reckon as soon as I can trot out and call her. She's just outside, meanderin' in the road—kinder shy, ye know, at first."

She walked to the door. The astounded Colonel nevertheless gallantly accompanied her as she stepped out into the street and called, shrilly, "You Zaidee!"

A young girl here apparently detached herself from a tree and the ostentatious perusal of an old election poster, and sauntered down towards the office door. Like her mother, she was plainly dressed; unlike her, she had a pale, rather refined face, with a demure mouth and downcast eyes. This was all the Colonel saw as he bowed profoundly and led the way into his office, for she accepted his salutations without lifting her head. He helped her gallantly to a chair, on which she seated herself sideways, somewhat ceremoniously, with her eyes following the point of her parasol as she traced a pattern on the carpet. A second chair offered to the mother that lady, however, declined. "I reckon to leave you and Zaidee together to talk it out," she said; turning to her daughter, she added, "Jest you tell him all, Zaidee," and before the Colonel could rise again, disappeared from the room. In spite of his professional experience, Starbottle was for a moment embarrassed. The young girl, however, broke the silence without looking up.

"Adoniram K. Hotchkiss," she began, in a monotonous voice, as if it were a recitation addressed to the public, "first began to take notice of me a year ago. Arter that—off and on——"

"One moment," interrupted the astounded Colonel; "do you mean Hotchkiss the President of the Ditch Company?" He had recognized the name of a prominent citizen—a rigid ascetic, taciturn, middle-aged man—a deacon—and more than that, the head of the company he had just defended. It seemed inconceivable.

"That's him," she continued, with eyes still fixed on the parasol and without changing her monotonous tone—"off and on ever since. Most of the time at the Free-Will Baptist church—at morning service, prayer-meetings, and such. And at home—outside—er—in the road."

"Is it this gentleman—Mr. Adoniram K. Hotchkiss—who—er—promised marriage?" stammered the Colonel.

"Yes."

The Colonel shifted uneasily in his chair. "Most extraordinary! for—you see—my dear young lady—this becomes—a—er—most delicate affair."

"That's what maw said," returned the young woman, simply, yet with the faintest smile playing around her demure lips and downcast cheek.

"I mean," said the Colonel, with a pained yet courteous smile, "that this—er—gentleman—is in fact—er—one of my clients."

"That's what maw said, too, and of course your knowing him will make it all the easier for you," said the young woman.

A slight flush crossed the Colonel's cheek as he returned quickly and a little stiffly, "On the contrary—er—it may make it impossible for me to—er—act in this matter."

The girl lifted her eyes. The Colonel held his breath as the long lashes were raised to his level. Even to an ordinary observer that sudden revelation of her eyes seemed to transform her face with subtle witchery. They were large, brown, and soft, yet filled with an extraordinary penetration and prescience. They were the eyes of an experienced woman of thirty fixed in the face of a child. What else the Colonel saw there Heaven only knows! He felt his inmost secrets plucked from him—his whole soul laid bare—his vanity, belligerency, gallantry—even his medieval chivalry, penetrated, and yet illuminated, in that single glance. And when the eyelids fell again, he felt that a greater part of himself had been swallowed up in them.

"I beg your pardon," he said, hurriedly. "I mean—this matter may be arranged—er—amicably. My interest with—and as you wisely say—my—er—knowledge of my client—er—Mr. Hotchkiss—may affect—a compromise."

"And *damages*," said the young girl, readdressing her parasol, as if she had never looked up.

The Colonel winced. "And—er—undoubtedly *compensation*—if you do not press a fulfilment of the promise. Unless," he said, with an attempted return to his former easy gallantry, which, however, the recollection of her eyes made difficult, "it is a question of—er—the affections?"

"Which?" said his fair client, softly.

"If you still love him?" explained the Colonel, actually blushing.

Zaidee again looked up; again taking the Colonel's breath away with eyes that expressed not only the fullest perception of what he had *said*, but of what he thought and had not said, and with an added subtle suggestion of what he might have thought. "That's tellin'," she said, dropping her long lashes again. The Colonel laughed vacantly. Then feeling himself growing imbecile, he forced an equally weak gravity. "Pardon me—I understand there are no letters; may I know the way in which he formulated his declaration and promises?"

"Hymn-books," said the girl, briefly.

"I beg your pardon," said the mystified lawyer.

"Hymn-books—marked words in them with pencil—and passed 'em on to me," repeated Zaidee. "Like 'love,' 'dear,' 'precious,' 'sweet,' and 'blessed,'" she added, accenting each word with a push of her parasol on the carpet. "Sometimes a whole line outer Tate and Brady—and *Solomon's Song*, you know, and sich."

"I believe," said the Colonel, loftily, "that the—er—phrases of sacred psalmody lend themselves to the language of the affections. But in regard to the distinct promise of marriage—was there—er—no *other* expression?"

"Marriage Service in the prayer-book—lines and words outer that—all marked," said Zaidee. The Colonel nodded naturally and approvingly. "Very good. Were others cognizant of this? Were there any witnesses?"

"Of course not," said the girl. "Only me and him. It was generally at church-time—or prayer-meeting. Once, in passing the plate, he slipped one o' them peppermint lozenges with the letters stamped on it 'I love you' for me to take."

The Colonel coughed slightly. "And you have the lozenge?"

"I ate it," said the girl, simply.

"Ah," said the Colonel. After a pause he added, delicately: "But were these attentions—er—confined to—er—-sacred precincts? Did he meet you elsewhere?"

"Useter pass our house on the road," returned the girl, dropping into her monotonous recital, "and useter signal."

"Ah, signal?" repeated the Colonel, approvingly.

"Yes! He'd say 'Kerrow,' and I'd say 'Kerree.' Suthing like a bird, you know."

Indeed, as she lifted her voice in imitation of the call the Colonel thought it certainly very sweet and birdlike. At least as *she* gave it. With his remembrance of the grim deacon he had doubts as to the melodiousness of *his* utterance. He gravely made her repeat it.

"And after that signal?" he added, suggestively.

"He'd pass on," said the girl.

The Colonel coughed slightly, and tapped his desk with his pen-holder.

"Were there any endearments—er—caresses—er—such as taking your hand—er—clasping your waist?" he suggested, with a gallant yet respectful sweep of his white hand and bowing of his head;—"er— slight pressure of your fingers in the changes of a dance—I mean," he corrected himself, with an apologetic cough—"in the passing of the plate?"

"No;—he was not what you'd call 'fond,'" returned the girl.

"Ah! Adoniram K. Hotchkiss was not 'fond' in the ordinary acceptance of the word," said the Colonel, with professional gravity.

She lifted her disturbing eyes, and again absorbed his in her own. She also said "Yes," although her eyes in their mysterious prescience of all he was thinking disclaimed the necessity of any answer at all. He smiled vacantly. There was a long pause. On which she slowly disengaged her parasol from the carpet pattern and stood up.

"I reckon that's about all," she said.

"Er—yes—but one moment," said the Colonel, vaguely. He would have liked to keep her longer, but with her strange premonition of him he felt powerless to detain her, or explain his reason for doing so. He instinctively knew she had told him all; his professional judgment told him that a more hopeless case had never come to his knowledge. Yet he was not daunted, only embarrassed. "No matter," he said, vaguely. "Of course I shall have to consult with you again." Her eyes again answered that she expected he would, but she added, simply, "When?"

"In the course of a day or two," said the Colonel, quickly. "I will send you word." She turned to go. In his eagerness to open the door for her he upset his chair, and with some confusion, that was actually youthful, he almost impeded her movements in the hall, and knocked his broad-brimmed Panama hat from his bowing hand in a final gallant sweep. Yet as her small, trim, youthful figure, with its simple Leghorn straw hat confined by a blue bow under her round chin, passed away before him, she looked more like a child than ever.

The Colonel spent that afternoon in making diplomatic inquiries. He found his youthful client was the daughter of a widow who had a small ranch on the cross-roads, near the new Free-Will Baptist church—the evident theatre of this pastoral. They led a secluded life; the girl being little known in the town, and her beauty and fascination apparently not yet being a recognized fact. The Colonel felt a pleasurable relief at this, and a general satisfaction he could not account for. His few inquiries concerning Mr. Hotchkiss only confirmed his own impressions of the alleged lover—a serious-minded, practically abstracted man—abstentive of youthful society, and the last man apparently capable of levity of the affections or serious flirtation. The Colonel was mystified—but determined of purpose—whatever that purpose might have been.

The next day he was at his office at the same hour. He was alone—as usual—the Colonel's office really being his private lodgings, disposed in connecting rooms, a single apartment reserved for consultation. He had no clerk; his papers and briefs being taken by his faithful body-servant and ex-slave "Jim" to another firm who

did his office-work since the death of Major Stryker—the Colonel's only law partner, who fell in a duel some years previous. With a fine constancy the Colonel still
retained his partner's name on his door-plate—and, it was alleged by the super-
stitious, kept a certain invincibility also through the *manes* of that lamented and
somewhat feared man.

The Colonel consulted his watch, whose heavy gold case still showed the marks
of a providential interference with a bullet destined for its owner, and replaced it
with some difficulty and shortness of breath in his fob. At the same moment he
heard a step in the passage, and the door opened to Adoniram K. Hotchkiss. The
Colonel was impressed; he had a duellist's respect for punctuality.

The man entered with a nod and the expectant, inquiring look of a busy man.
As his feet crossed that sacred threshold the Colonel became all courtesy; he placed
a chair for his visitor, and took his hat from his half-reluctant hand. He then opened
a cupboard and brought out a bottle of whiskey and two glasses.

"A—er—slight refreshment, Mr. Hotchkiss," he suggested, politely. "I never
drink," replied Hotchkiss, with the severe attitude of a total abstainer. "Ah—er—
not the finest bourbon whiskey, selected by a Kentucky friend? No? Pardon me! A
cigar, then—the mildest Havana."

"I do not use tobacco nor alcohol in any form," repeated Hotchkiss, ascetically.
"I have no foolish weaknesses."

The Colonel's moist, beady eyes swept silently over his client's sallow face. He
leaned back comfortably in his chair, and half closing his eyes as in dreamy reminiscence, said, slowly: "Your reply, Mr. Hotchkiss, reminds me of—er—sing'lar
circumstances that —er—occurred, in point of fact—at the St. Charles Hotel, New
Orleans. Pinkey Hornblower—personal friend—invited Senator Doolittle to join
him in social glass. Received, sing'larly enough, reply similar to yours. 'Don't drink
nor smoke?' said Pinkey. 'Gad, sir, you must be mighty sweet on the ladies.' Ha!"
The Colonel paused long enough to allow the faint flush to pass from Hotchkiss's
cheek, and went on, half closing his eyes: "'I allow no man, sir, to discuss my personal habits,' said Doolittle, over his shirt collar. 'Then I reckon shootin' must be
one of those habits,' said Pinkey, coolly. Both men drove out on the Shell Road back
of cemetery next morning. Pinkey put bullet at twelve paces through Doolittle's
temple. Poor Doo never spoke again. Left three wives and seven children, they say

—two of 'em black."

"I got a note from you this morning," said Hotchkiss, with badly concealed impatience. "I suppose in reference to our case. You have taken judgment, I believe." The Colonel, without replying, slowly filled a glass of whiskey and water. For a moment he held it dreamily before him, as if still engaged in gentle reminiscences called up by the act. Then tossing it off, he wiped his lips with a large white handkerchief, and leaning back comfortably in his chair, said, with a wave of his hand, "The interview I requested, Mr. Hotchkiss, concerns a subject—which I may say is—er—er—at present *not* of a public or business nature—although *later* it might become—er—er—both. It is an affair of some—er—delicacy."

The Colonel paused, and Mr. Hotchkiss regarded him with increased impatience. The Colonel, however, continued, with unchanged deliberation: "It concerns—er—a young lady—a beautiful, high-souled creature, sir, who, apart from her personal loveliness— er—er—I may say is of one of the first families of Missouri, and— er—not—remotely connected by marriage with one of—er—er—my boyhood's dearest friends. The latter, I grieve to say, was a pure invention of the Colonel's—an oratorical addition to the scanty information he had obtained the previous day. The young lady," he continued, blandly, "enjoys the further distinction of being the object of such attention from you as would make this interview— really—a confidential matter—er—er—among friends and—er—er— relations in present and future. I need not say that the lady I refer to is Miss Zaidee Juno Hooker, only daughter of Almira Ann Hooker, relict of Jefferson Brown Hooker, formerly of Boone County, Kentucky, and latterly of—er—Pike County, Missouri."

The sallow, ascetic hue of Mr. Hotchkiss's face had passed through a livid and then a greenish shade, and finally settled into a sullen red. "What's all this about?" he demanded, roughly. The least touch of belligerent fire came into Starbottle's eye, but his bland courtesy did not change. "I believe," he said, politely, "I have made myself clear as between—er—gentlemen, though perhaps not as clear as I should to—er—er—jury."

Mr. Hotchkiss was apparently struck with some significance in the lawyer's reply. "I don't know," he said, in a lower and more cautious voice, "what you mean by what you call 'my attentions' to—any one—or how it concerns you. I have not exhausted half a dozen words with—the person you name—have never written her a line—nor even called at her house." He rose with an assumption of ease, pulled down his waistcoat, buttoned his coat, and took up his hat. The Colonel did not move. "I believe I have already indicated my meaning in what I have called 'your attentions,'" said the Colonel, blandly, "and given you my 'concern' for speaking as—er—er mutual friend. As to *your* statement of your relations with Miss Hooker, I may state that it is fully corroborated by the statement of the young lady herself in this very office yesterday."

"Then what does this impertinent nonsense mean? Why am I summoned here?" said Hotchkiss, furiously.

"Because," said the Colonel, deliberately, "that statement is infamously—yes, damnably to your discredit, sir!"

Mr. Hotchkiss was here seized by one of those important and inconsistent rages which occasionally betray the habitually cautious and timid man. He caught up the Colonel's stick, which was lying on the table. At the same moment the Colonel, without any apparent effort, grasped it by the handle. To Mr. Hotchkiss's astonishment, the stick separated in two pieces, leaving the handle and about two feet of narrow glittering steel in the Colonel's hand. The man recoiled, dropping the useless fragment. The Colonel picked it up, fitting the shining blade in it, clicked the spring, and then rising, with a face of courtesy yet of unmistakably genuine pain, and with even a slight tremor in his voice, said, gravely:

"Mr. Hotchkiss, I owe you a thousand apologies, sir, that—er— a weapon should be drawn by me—even through your own inadvertence— under the sacred protection of my roof, and upon an unarmed man. I beg your pardon, sir, and I even withdraw the expressions which provoked that inadvertence. Nor does this apology prevent you from holding me responsible—personally responsible— *elsewhere* for an indiscretion committed in behalf of a lady—my—er—client."

"Your client? Do you mean you have taken her case? You, the counsel for the Ditch Company?" said Mr. Hotchkiss, in trembling indignation.

"Having won *your* case, sir," said the Colonel, coolly, "the—er—usages of advocacy do not prevent me from espousing the cause of the weak and unprotected."

"We shall see, sir," said Hotchkiss, grasping the handle of the door and backing into the passage. "There are other lawyers who—"

"Permit me to see you out," interrupted the Colonel, rising politely.

"—will be ready to resist the attacks of blackmail," continued Hotchkiss, retreating along the passage.

"And then you will be able to repeat your remarks to me *in the street*," continued the Colonel, bowing, as he persisted in following his visitor to the door.

But here Mr. Hotchkiss quickly slammed it behind him, and hurried away. The Colonel returned to his office, and sitting down, took a sheet of letter paper bearing the inscription "Starbottle and Stryker, Attorneys and Counsellors," and wrote the following lines:

Hooker *versus* Hotchkiss.

DEAR MADAM,—Having had a visit from the defendant in
above, we should be pleased to have an interview with you at
2 p.m. to-morrow. Your obedient servants,
STARBOTTLE AND STRYKER.

This he sealed and despatched by his trusted servant Jim, and then devoted a few moments to reflection. It was the custom of the Colonel to act first, and justify the action by reason afterwards.

He knew that Hotchkiss would at once lay the matter before rival counsel. He knew that they would advise him that Miss Hooker had "no case"—that she would be non-suited on her own evidence, and he ought not to compromise, but be ready to stand trial. He believed, however, that Hotchkiss feared that exposure, and although his own instincts had been at first against that remedy, he was now instinctively in favor of it. He remembered his own power with a jury; his vanity and his chivalry alike approved of this heroic method; he was bound by the prosaic facts—he had his own theory of the case, which no mere evidence could gainsay. In fact, Mrs. Hooker's own words that "he was to tell the story in his own way" actually appeared to him an inspiration and a prophecy.

Perhaps there was something else, due possibly to the lady's wonderful eyes, of which he had thought much. Yet it was not her simplicity that affected him solely; on the contrary, it was her apparent intelligent reading of the character of her recreant lover—and of his own! Of all the Colonel's previous "light" or "serious" loves none had ever before flattered him in that way. And it was this, combined with the respect which he had held for their professional relations, that precluded his having a more familiar knowledge of his client, through serious questioning, or playful gallantry. I am not sure it was not part of the charm to have a rustic *femme incomprise* as a client.

Nothing could exceed the respect with which he greeted her as she entered his office the next day. He even affected not to notice that she had put on her best clothes, and he made no doubt appeared as when she had first attracted the mature yet faithless attentions of Deacon Hotchkiss at church. A white virginal muslin was belted around her slim figure by a blue ribbon, and her Leghorn hat was drawn around her oval cheek by a bow of the same color. She had a Southern girl's narrow feet, encased in white stockings and kid slippers, which were crossed primly before her as she sat in a chair, supporting her arm by her faithful parasol planted firmly on the floor. A faint odor of southernwood exhaled from her, and, oddly enough, stirred the Colonel with a far-off recollection of a pine-shaded Sunday school on a Georgia hillside and of his first love, aged ten, in a short, starched frock. Possibly it was the same recollection that revived something of the awkwardness he had felt then.

He, however, smiled vaguely and, sitting down, coughed slightly, and placed his fingertips together. "I have had an—er—interview with Mr. Hotchkiss, but—I—er—regret to say there seems to be no prospect of—er—compromise." He paused, and to his surprise her listless "company" face lit up with an adorable smile. "Of course!—ketch him!" she said. "Was he mad when you told him?" She put her knees comfortably together and leaned forward for a reply.

For all that, wild horses could not have torn from the Colonel a word about Hotchkiss's anger. "He expressed his intention of employing counsel—and defending a suit," returned the Colonel, affably basking in her smile. She dragged her chair nearer his desk. "Then you'll fight him tooth and nail?" she said eagerly; "you'll show him up? You'll tell the whole story your own way? You'll give him fits?—and you'll make him pay? Sure?" she went on, breathlessly.

"I—er—will," said the Colonel, almost as breathlessly.

She caught his fat white hand, which was lying on the table, between her own and lifted it to her lips. He felt her soft young fingers even through the lisle-thread gloves that encased them and the warm moisture of her lips upon his skin. He felt himself flushing—but was unable to break the silence or change his position. The next moment she had scuttled back with her chair to her old position.

"I—er—certainly shall do my best," stammered the Colonel, in an attempt to recover his dignity and composure.

"That's enough! You'll *do* it," said the girl, enthusiastically. "Lordy! Just you talk for *me* as ye did for *his* old Ditch Company, and you'll fetch it—every time! Why, when you made that jury sit up the other day—when you got that off about the Merrikan flag waving equally over the rights of honest citizens banded together in peaceful commercial pursuits, as well as over the fortress of official proflig—"

"Oligarchy," murmured the Colonel, courteously.

"Oligarchy," repeated the girl, quickly, "my breath was just took away. I said to maw, 'Ain't he too sweet for anything!' I did, honest Injin! And when you rolled it all off at the end—never missing a word—(you didn't need to mark 'em in a lesson-book, but had 'em all ready on your tongue), and walked out—Well! I didn't know you nor the Ditch Company from Adam, but I could have just run over and kissed you there before the whole court!"

She laughed, with her face glowing, although her strange eyes were cast down. Alack! the Colonel's face was equally flushed, and his own beady eyes were on his desk. To any other woman he would have voiced the banal gallantry that he should now, himself, look forward to that reward, but the words never reached his lips. He laughed, coughed slightly, and when he looked up again she had fallen into the same attitude as on her first visit, with her parasol point on the floor.

"I must ask you to—er—direct your memory—to—er—another point; the breaking off of the—er—er—er—engagement. Did he—er—give any reason for it? Or show any cause?"

"No; he never said anything," returned the girl.

"Not in his usual way?—er—no reproaches out of the hymn-book?—or the sacred writings?"

"No; he just *quit*."

"Er—ceased his attentions," said the Colonel, gravely. "And naturally you—er—were not conscious of any cause for his doing so." The girl raised her wonderful eyes so suddenly and so penetratingly without reply in any other way that the Colonel could only hurriedly say: "I see! None, of course!"

At which she rose, the Colonel rising also. "We—shall begin proceedings at once. I must, however, caution you to answer no questions nor say anything about this case to any one until you are in court."

She answered his request with another intelligent look and a nod. He accompanied her to the door. As he took her proffered hand he raised the lisle-thread fingers to his lips with old-fashioned gallantry. As if that act had condoned for his first omissions and awkwardness, he became his old-fashioned self again, buttoned his coat, pulled out his shirt frill, and strutted back to his desk.

A day or two later it was known throughout the town that Zaidee Hooker had sued Adoniram Hotchkiss for breach of promise, and that the damages were laid at five thousand dollars. As in those bucolic days the Western press was under the secure censorship of a revolver, a cautious tone of criticism prevailed, and any gossip was confined to personal expression, and even then at the risk of the gossiper. Nevertheless, the situation provoked the intensest curiosity. The Colonel was approached—until his statement that he should consider any attempt to overcome his professional secrecy a personal reflection withheld further advances. The community were left to the more ostentatious information of the defendant's counsel, Messrs. Kitcham and Bilser, that the case was "ridiculous" and "rotten," that the plaintiff would be nonsuited, and the fire-eating Starbottle would be taught a lesson that he could not "bully" the law—and there were some dark hints of a conspiracy. It was even hinted that the "case" was the revengeful and preposterous outcome of the refusal of Hotchkiss to pay Starbottle an extravagant fee for his late services to the Ditch Company. It is unnecessary to say that these words were not reported to the Colonel. It was, however, an unfortunate circumstance for the calmer, ethical consideration of the subject that the church sided with Hotchkiss, as this provoked an equal adherence to the plaintiff and Starbottle on the part of the larger body of non-church-goers, who were delighted at a possible exposure of the weakness of religious rectitude. "I've allus had my suspicions o' them early candle-light meetings down at that gospel shop," said one critic, "and I reckon Deacon Hotchkiss didn't rope in the gals to attend jest for psalm-singing." "Then for him to get up and leave the board afore the game's finished and try to sneak out of it," said another. "I suppose that's what they call *religious*."

It was therefore not remarkable that the courthouse three weeks later was crowded with an excited multitude of the curious and sympathizing. The fair plaintiff, with her mother, was early in attendance, and under the Colonel's advice appeared in the same modest garb in which she had first visited his office. This and her downcast modest demeanor were perhaps at first disappointing to the crowd, who had evidently expected a paragon of loveliness—as the Circe of the grim ascetic defendant, who sat beside his counsel. But presently all eyes were fixed on the Colonel, who certainly made up in *his* appearance any deficiency of his fair client. His portly figure was clothed in a blue dress-coat with brass buttons, a buff waistcoat which permitted his frilled shirt front to become erectile above it, a black satin stock which confined a boyish turned-down collar around his full neck, and immaculate drill trousers, strapped over varnished boots. A murmur ran round the court. "Old 'Personally Responsible' had got his war-paint on," "The Old War-Horse is smelling powder," were whispered comments. Yet for all that the most irreverent among them recognized vaguely, in this bizarre figure, something of an honored past in their country's history, and possibly felt the spell of old deeds and old names that had once thrilled their boyish pulses. The new District Judge returned Colonel Starbottle's profoundly punctilious bow. The Colonel was followed by his negro servant, carrying a parcel of hymn-books and Bibles, who, with a courtesy evidently imitated from his master, placed one before the opposite counsel. This, after a first curious glance, the lawyer somewhat superciliously tossed aside. But when Jim, proceeding to the jury-box, placed with equal politeness the remaining copies before the jury, the opposite counsel sprang to his feet.

"I want to direct the attention of the Court to this unprecedented tampering with the jury, by this gratuitous exhibition of matter impertinent and irrelevant to the issue."

The Judge cast an inquiring look at Colonel Starbottle.

"May it please the Court," returned Colonel Starbottle with dignity, ignoring the counsel, "the defendant's counsel will observe that he is already furnished with the matter—which I regret to say he has treated—in the presence of the Court—and of his client, a deacon of the church—with—er—-great superciliousness. When I state to your Honor that the books in question are hymn-books and copies of the *Holy Scriptures*, and that they are for the instruction of the jury, to whom I shall have to refer them in the course of my opening, I believe I am within my rights."

"The act is certainly unprecedented," said the Judge, dryly, "but unless the counsel for the plaintiff expects the jury to *sing* from these hymn-books, their introduction is not improper, and I cannot admit the objection. As defendant's counsel are furnished with copies also, they cannot plead 'surprise,' as in the introduction of new matter, and as plaintiff's counsel relies evidently upon the jury's attention to his opening, he would not be the first person to distract it." After a pause he added, addressing the Colonel, who remained standing, "The Court is with you, sir; proceed."

But the Colonel remained motionless and statuesque, with folded arms.

"I have overruled the objection," repeated the Judge; "you may go on."

"I am waiting, your Honor, for the—er—withdrawal by the defendant's counsel of the word 'tampering,' as refers to myself, and of 'impertinent,' as refers to the sacred volumes."

"The request is a proper one, and I have no doubt will be acceded to," returned the Judge, quietly. The defendant's counsel rose and mumbled a few words of apology, and the incident closed. There was, however, a general feeling that the Colonel had in some way "scored," and if his object had been to excite the greatest curiosity about the books, he had made his point.

But impassive of his victory, he inflated his chest, with his right hand in the breast of his buttoned coat, and began. His usual high color had paled slightly, but the small pupils of his prominent eyes glittered like steel. The young girl leaned forward in her chair with an attention so breathless, a sympathy so quick, and an admiration so artless and unconscious that in an instant she divided with the speaker the attention of the whole assemblage. It was very hot; the court was crowded to suffocation; even the open windows revealed a crowd of faces outside the building, eagerly following the Colonel's words.

He would remind the jury that only a few weeks ago he stood there as the advocate of a powerful company, then represented by the present defendant. He spoke then as the champion of strict justice against legal oppression; no less should he to-day champion the cause of the unprotected and the comparatively defenseless—save for that paramount power which surrounds beauty and innocence—even though the plaintiff of yesterday was the defendant of to-day. As he approached the court a moment ago he had raised his eyes and beheld the starry flag flying from its dome—

and he knew that glorious banner was a symbol of the perfect equality, under the Constitution, of the rich and the poor, the strong and the weak—an equality which made the simple citizen taken from the plough in the veld, the pick in the gulch, or from behind the counter in the mining town, who served on that jury, the equal arbiters of justice with that highest legal luminary whom they were proud to welcome on the bench to-day. The Colonel paused, with a stately bow to the impassive Judge. It was this, he continued, which lifted his heart as he approached the building. And yet—he had entered it with an uncertain—he might almost say—a timid step. And why? He knew, gentlemen, he was about to confront a profound—aye! a sacred responsibility! Those hymn-books and holy writings handed to the jury were *not*, as his Honor surmised, for the purpose of enabling the jury to indulge in—er—preliminary choral exercise! He might, indeed, say "alas not!" They were the damning, incontrovertible proofs of the perfidy of the defendant. And they would prove as terrible a warning to him as the fatal characters upon Belshazzar's wall. There was a strong sensation. Hotchkiss turned a sallow green. His lawyers assumed a careless smile.

It was his duty to tell them that this was not one of those ordinary "breach-of-promise" cases which were too often the occasion of ruthless mirth and indecent levity in the courtroom. The jury would find nothing of that here, There were no love-letters with the epithets of endearment, nor those mystic crosses and ciphers which, he had been credibly informed, chastely hid the exchange of those mutual caresses known as "kisses." There was no cruel tearing of the veil from those sacred privacies of the human affection—there was no forensic shouting out of those fond confidences meant only for *one*. But there was, he was shocked to say, a new sacrilegious intrusion. The weak pipings of Cupid were mingled with the chorus of the saints—the sanctity of the temple known as the "meeting-house" was desecrated by proceedings more in keeping with the shrine of Venus—and the inspired writings themselves were used as the medium of amatory and wanton flirtation by the defendant in his sacred capacity as Deacon.

The Colonel artistically paused after this thunderous denunciation. The jury turned eagerly to the leaves of the hymn-books, but the larger gaze of the audience remained fixed upon the speaker and the girl, who sat in rapt admiration of his periods. After the hush, the Colonel continued in a lower and sadder voice: "There are, perhaps, few of us here, gentlemen—with the exception of the defendant—who can arrogate to themselves the title of regular churchgoers, or to whom these humbler functions of the prayer-meeting, the Sunday-school, and the Bible class are habitually familiar. Yet"—more solemnly—"down in your hearts is the deep conviction of our short-comings and failings, and a laudable desire that others at least should profit by the teachings we neglect. Perhaps," he continued, closing his eyes dreamily, "there is not a man here who does not recall the happy days of his boyhood, the rustic village spire, the lessons shared with some artless village maiden, with whom he later sauntered, hand in hand, through the woods, as the simple rhyme rose upon their lips,

> Always make it a point to have it a rule
> Never to be late at the Sabbath-school."

He would recall the strawberry feasts, the welcome annual picnic, redolent with hunks of gingerbread and sarsaparilla. How would they feel to know that these sacred recollections were now forever profaned in their memory by the knowledge that the defendant was capable of using such occasions to make love to the larger girls and teachers, whilst his artless companions were innocently—the Court will pardon me for introducing what I am credibly informed is the local expression 'doing gooseberry'?" The tremulous flicker of a smile passed over the faces of the listening crowd, and the Colonel slightly winced. But he recovered himself instantly, and continued:

"My client, the only daughter of a widowed mother—who has for years stemmed the varying tides of adversity—in the western precincts of this town—stands before you today invested only in her own innocence. She wears no—er—rich gifts of her faithless admirer—is panoplied in no jewels, rings, nor mementoes of affection such as lovers delight to hang upon the shrine of their affections; hers is not the glory with which Solomon decorated the Queen of Sheba, though the defendant, as I shall show later, clothed her in the less expensive flowers of the king's poetry. No! gentlemen! The defendant exhibited in this affair a certain frugality of—er—pecuniary investment, which I am willing to admit may be commendable in his class. His only gift was characteristic alike of his methods and his economy. There is, I understand, a certain not unimportant feature of religious exercise known as 'taking a collection.' The defendant, on this occasion, by the mute presentation of a tip plate covered with baize, solicited the pecuniary contributions of the faithful. On approaching the plaintiff, however, he himself slipped a love-token upon the plate and pushed it towards her. That love-token was a lozenge—a small disk, I have reason to believe, concocted of peppermint and sugar, bearing upon its reverse surface the simple words, 'I love you!' I have since ascertained that these disks may be bought for five cents a dozen—or at considerably less than one half-cent for the single lozenge. Yes, gentlemen, the words 'I love you!'—the oldest legend of all; the refrain, 'when the morning stars sang together'—were presented to the plaintiff by a medium so insignificant that there is, happily, no coin in the republic low enough to represent its value.

"I shall prove to you, gentlemen of the jury," said the Colonel, solemnly, drawing a *Bible* from his coat-tail pocket, "that the defendant, for the last twelve months, conducted an amatory correspondence with the plaintiff by means of underlined words of sacred writ and church psalmody, such as 'beloved,' 'precious,' and 'dearest,' occasionally appropriating whole passages which seemed apposite to his tender passion. I shall call your attention to one of them. The defendant, while professing to be a total abstainer—a man who, in my own knowledge, has refused spirituous refreshment as an inordinate weakness of the flesh, with shameless hypocrisy underscores with his pencil the following passage and presents it to the plaintiff. The gentlemen of the jury will find it in the *Song of Solomon*, page 548, chapter II, verse 5." After a pause, in which the rapid rustling of leaves was heard in the jury-box, Colonel Starbottle declaimed in a pleading, stentorian voice, "'Stay me with —er—*flagons*, comfort me with—er—apples—for I am—er—sick of love.' Yes, gentlemen!—yes, you may well turn from those accusing pages and look at the double-faced defendant. He desires—to—er—be —'stayed with flagons'! I am not aware, at present, what kind of liquor is habitually dispensed at these meetings, and for which the defendant so urgently clamored; but it will be my duty before this trial is over to discover it, if I have to summon every barkeeper in this district. For the moment, I will simply call your attention to the *quantity*. It is not a single drink that the defendant asks for —not a glass of light and generous wine, to be shared with his inamorata—but a number of flagons or vessels, each possibly holding a pint measure—*for himself!*"

The smile of the audience had become a laugh. The Judge looked up warningly, when his eye caught the fact that the Colonel had again winced at this mirth. He regarded him seriously. Mr. Hotchkiss's counsel had joined in the laugh affectedly, but Hotchkiss himself was ashy pale. There was also a commotion in the jury-box, a hurried turning over of leaves, and an excited discussion.

"The gentlemen of the jury," said the Judge, with official gravity, "will please keep order and attend only to the speeches of counsel. Any discussion *here* is irregular and premature—and must be reserved for the jury-room—after they have retired."

The foreman of the jury struggled to his feet. He was a powerful man, with a good-humored face, and, in spite of his unfelicitous nickname of "The Bone-Breaker," had a kindly, simple, but somewhat emotional nature. Nevertheless, it appeared as if he were laboring under some powerful indignation.

"Can we ask a question, Judge?" he said, respectfully, although his voice had the unmistakable Western-American ring in it, as of one who was unconscious that he could be addressing any but his peers.

"Yes," said the Judge, good-humoredly.

"We're finding in this yere piece, out of which the Kernel hes just bin a-quotin', some language that me and my pardners allow hadn't orter to be read out afore a young lady in court—and we want to know of you—ez a fair-minded and impartial man—ef this is the reg'lar kind o' book given to gals and babies down at the meetin'-house."

"The jury will please follow the counsel's speech, without comment," said the Judge, briefly, fully aware that the defendant's counsel would spring to his feet, as he did promptly. "The Court will allow us to explain to the gentlemen that the language they seem to object to has been accepted by the best theologians for the last thousand years as being purely mystic. As I will explain later, those are merely symbols of the Church—"

"Of wot?" interrupted the foreman, in deep scorn.

"Of the Church!"

"We ain't askin' any questions o' *you*—and we ain't takin' any answers," said the foreman, sitting down promptly.

"I must insist," said the Judge, sternly, "that the plaintiff's counsel be allowed to continue his opening without interruption. You" (to defendant's counsel) "will have your opportunity to reply later."

The counsel sank down in his seat with the bitter conviction that the jury was manifestly against him, and the case as good as lost. But his face was scarcely as disturbed as his client's, who, in great agitation, had begun to argue with him wildly, and was apparently pressing some point against the lawyer's vehement opposal. The Colonel's murky eyes brightened as he still stood erect with his hand thrust in his breast.

"It will be put to you, gentlemen, when the counsel on the other side refrains from mere interruption and confines himself to reply, that my unfortunate client has no action—no remedy at law—because there were no spoken words of endearment. But, gentlemen, it will depend upon *you* to say what are and what are not articulate expressions of love. We all know that among the lower animals, with whom you may possibly be called upon to classify the defendant, there are certain signals more or less harmonious, as the case may be. The ass brays, the horse neighs, the sheep bleats—the feathered denizens of the grove call to their mates in more musical roundelays. These are recognized facts, gentlemen, which you yourselves, as dwellers among nature in this beautiful land, are all cognizant of. They are facts that no one would deny—and we should have a poor opinion of the ass who, at— er—such a supreme moment, would attempt to suggest that his call was unthinking and without significance. But, gentlemen, I shall prove to you that such was the foolish, self-convicting custom of the defendant. With the greatest reluctance, and the—er—greatest pain, I succeeded in wresting from the maidenly modesty of my fair client the innocent confession that the defendant had induced her to correspond with him in these methods. Picture to yourself, gentlemen, the lonely moonlight road beside the widow's humble cottage. It is a beautiful night, sanctified to the affections, and the innocent girl is leaning from her casement. Presently there appears upon the road a slinking, stealthy figure—the defendant, on his way to church. True to the instruction she has received from him, her lips part in the musical utterance" (the Colonel lowered his voice in a faint falsetto, presumably in fond imitation of his fair client),"'Kerree!' Instantly the night became resonant with the impassioned reply" (the Colonel here lifted his voice in stentorian tones),

"'Kerrow.' Again, as he passes, rises the soft 'Kerree'; again, as his form is lost in the distance, comes back the deep 'Kerrow.'"

A burst of laughter, long, loud, and irrepressible, struck the whole courtroom, and before the Judge could lift his half-composed face and take his handkerchief from his mouth, a faint "Kerree" from some unrecognized obscurity of the courtroom was followed by a loud "Kerrow" from some opposite locality. "The sheriff will clear the court," said the Judge, sternly; but alas, as the embarrassed and choking officials rushed hither and thither, a soft "Kerree" from the spectators at the window, *outside* the courthouse, was answered by a loud chorus of "Kerrows" from the opposite windows, filled with onlookers. Again the laughter arose everywhere—even the fair plaintiff herself sat convulsed behind her handkerchief.

The figure of Colonel Starbottle alone remained erect—white and rigid. And then the Judge, looking up, saw what no one else in the court had seen—that the Colonel was sincere and in earnest; that what he had conceived to be the pleader's most perfect acting, and most elaborate irony, were the deep, serious, mirthless *convictions* of a man without the least sense of humor. There was a touch of this respect in the Judge's voice as he said to him, gently, "You may proceed, Colonel Starbottle."

"I thank your Honor," said the Colonel, slowly, "for recognizing and doing all in your power to prevent an interruption that, during my thirty years' experience at the bar, I have never yet been subjected to without the privilege of holding the instigators thereof responsible—*personally* responsible. It is possibly my fault that I have failed, oratorically, to convey to the gentlemen of the jury the full force and significance of the defendant's signals. I am aware that my voice is singularly deficient in producing either the dulcet tones of my fair client or the impassioned vehemence of the defendant's repose. I will," continued the Colonel, with a fatigued but blind fatuity that ignored the hurriedly knit brows and warning eyes of the Judge, "try again. The note uttered by my client" (lowering his voice to the faintest of falsettos) "was 'Kerree'; the response was 'Kerrow'"—and the Colonel's voice fairly shook the dome above him.

Another uproar of laughter followed this apparently audacious repetition, but was interrupted by an unlooked-for incident. The defendant rose abruptly, and tearing himself away from the withholding hand and pleading protestations of his counsel, absolutely fled from the courtroom, his appearance outside being recognized by a prolonged "Kerrow" from the bystanders, which again and again followed him in the distance. In the momentary silence which followed, the Colonel's voice was heard saying, "We rest here, your Honor," and he sat down. No less white, but more agitated, was the face of the defendant's counsel, who instantly rose.

"For some unexplained reason, your Honor, my client desires to suspend further proceedings, with a view to effect a peaceable compromise with the plaintiff. As he is a man of wealth and position, he is able and willing to pay liberally for that privilege. While I, as his counsel, am still convinced of his legal irresponsibility, as he has chosen, however, to publicly abandon his rights here, I can only ask your Honor's permission to suspend further proceedings until I can confer with Colonel Starbottle."

"As far as I can follow the pleadings," said the Judge, gravely, "the case seems to be hardly one for litigation, and I approve of the defendant's course, while I strongly urge the plaintiff to accept it."

Colonel Starbottle bent over his fair client. Presently he rose, unchanged in look or demeanor. "I yield, your Honor, to the wishes of my client, and—er—lady. We accept."

Before the court adjourned that day it was known throughout the town that Adoniram K. Hotchkiss had compromised the suit for four thousand dollars and costs.

Colonel Starbottle had so far recovered his equanimity as to strut jauntily towards his office, where he was to meet his fair client. He was surprised, however, to find her already there, and in company with a somewhat sheepish-looking young man—a stranger. If the Colonel had any disappointment in meeting a third party to the interview, his old-fashioned courtesy did not permit him to show it. He bowed graciously, and politely motioned them each to a seat.

"I reckoned I'd bring Hiram round with me," said the young lady, lifting her searching eyes, after a pause, to the Colonel's, "though he was awful shy, and allowed that you didn't know him from Adam—or even suspected his existence. But I said, 'That's just where you slip up, Hiram; a pow'ful man like the Colonel knows everything—and I've seen it in his eye.' Lordy!" she continued, with a laugh, leaning forward over her parasol, as her eyes again sought the Colonel's, "don't you remember when you asked me if I loved that old Hotchkiss, and I told you 'That's tellin',' and you looked at me, Lordy! I knew *then* you suspected there was a Hiram *somewhere*—as good as if I'd told you. Now, you, jest get up, Hiram, and give the Colonel a good handshake. For if it wasn't for *him* and *his* searchin' ways, and *his* awful power of language, I wouldn't hev got that four thousand dollars out o' that flirty fool Hotchkiss—enough to buy a farm, so as you and me could get married! That's what you owe to *him*. Don't stand there like a stuck fool starin' at him. He won't eat you—though he's killed many a better man. Come, have *I* got to do *all* the kissin'!"

It is of record that the Colonel bowed so courteously and so profoundly that he managed not merely to evade the proffered hand of the shy Hiram, but to only lightly touch the franker and more impulsive fingertips of the gentle Zaidee. "I—er—offer my sincerest congratulations—though I think you—er—overestimate—my—er—powers of penetration. Unfortunately, a pressing engagement, which may oblige me also to leave town to-night, forbids my saying more. I have—er—left the—er—business settlement of this—er—case in the hands of the lawyers who do my office-work, and who will show you every attention. And now let me wish you a very good afternoon."

Nevertheless, the Colonel returned to his private room, and it was nearly twilight when the faithful Jim entered, to find him sitting meditatively before his desk. "'Fo' God! Kernel—I hope dey ain't nuffin de matter, but you's lookin' mightly solemn! I ain't seen you look dat way, Kernel, since de day pooh Marse Stryker was fetched home shot froo de head."

"Hand me down the whiskey, Jim," said the Colonel, rising slowly.

The negro flew to the closet joyfully, and brought out the bottle. The Colonel poured out a glass of the spirit and drank it with his old deliberation.

"You're quite right, Jim," he said, putting down his glass, "but I'm—er—getting old—and—somehow—I am missing poor Stryker damnably!"

THE DUPLICITY OF HARGRAVES
By O. Henry (1862-1910)

[From *The Junior Munsey*, February, 1902. Republished in the volume,
Sixes and Sevens (1911), by O. Henry; copyright, 1911, by Doubleday,
Page & Co.; reprinted by their permission.]

WHEN Major Pendleton Talbot, of Mobile, sir, and his daughter, Miss Lydia Talbot, came to Washington to reside, they selected for a boarding place a house that stood fifty yards back from one of the quietest avenues. It was an old-fashioned brick building, with a portico upheld by tall white pillars. The yard was shaded by stately locusts and elms, and a catalpa tree in season rained its pink and white blossoms upon the grass. Rows of high box bushes lined the fence and walks. It was the Southern style and aspect of the place that pleased the eyes of the Talbots.

In this pleasant private boarding house they engaged rooms, including a study for Major Talbot, who was adding the finishing chapters to his book, *Anecdotes and Reminiscences of the Alabama Army, Bench, and Bar*.

Major Talbot was of the old, old South. The present day had little interest or excellence in his eyes. His mind lived in that period before the Civil War when the Talbots owned thousands of acres of fine cotton land and the slaves to till them; when the family mansion was the scene of princely hospitality, and drew its guests from the aristocracy of the South. Out of that period he had brought all its old pride and scruples of honor, an antiquated and punctilious politeness, and (you would think) its wardrobe.

Such clothes were surely never made within fifty years. The Major was tall, but whenever he made that wonderful, archaic genuflexion he called a bow, the corners of his frock coat swept the floor. That garment was a surprise even to Washington, which has long ago ceased to shy at the frocks and broad-brimmed hats of Southern Congressmen. One of the boarders christened it a "Father Hubbard," and it certainly was high in the waist and full in the skirt.

But the Major, with all his queer clothes, his immense area of plaited, raveling shirt bosom, and the little black string tie with the bow always slipping on one side, both was smiled at and liked in Mrs. Vardeman's select boarding house. Some of the young department clerks would often "string him," as they called it, getting him started upon the subject dearest to him—the traditions and history of his beloved Southland. During his talks he would quote freely from the *Anecdotes and Reminiscences*. But they were very careful not to let him see their designs, for in spite of his sixty-eight years he could make the boldest of them uncomfortable under the steady regard of his piercing gray eyes.

Miss Lydia was a plump, little old maid of thirty-five, with smoothly drawn, tightly twisted hair that made her look still older. Old-fashioned, too, she was; but antebellum glory did not radiate from her as it did from the Major. She possessed a thrifty common sense, and it was she who handled the finances of the family, and met all comers when there were bills to pay. The Major regarded board bills and wash bills as contemptible nuisances. They kept coming in so persistently and so often. Why, the Major wanted to know, could they not be filed and paid in a lump sum at some convenient period—say when the *Anecdotes and Reminiscences* had been published and paid for? Miss Lydia would calmly go on with her sewing and say, "We'll pay as we go as long as the money lasts, and then perhaps they'll have to lump it."

Most of Mrs. Vardeman's boarders were away during the day, being nearly all department clerks and business men; but there was one of them who was about the house a great deal from morning to night. This was a young man named Henry Hopkins Hargraves—every one in the house addressed him by his full name—who was engaged at one of the popular vaudeville theaters. Vaudeville has risen to such a respectable plane in the last few years, and Mr. Hargraves was such a modest and well-mannered person, that Mrs. Vardeman could find no objection to enrolling him upon her list of boarders.

At the theater Hargraves was known as an all-round dialect comedian, having a large repertoire of German, Irish, Swede, and black-face specialties. But Mr. Hargraves was ambitious, and often spoke of his great desire to succeed in legitimate comedy.

This young man appeared to conceive a strong fancy for Major Talbot. Whenever that gentleman would begin his Southern reminiscences, or repeat some of the liveliest of the anecdotes, Hargraves could always be found, the most attentive among his listeners.

For a time the Major showed an inclination to discourage the advances of the "play actor," as he privately termed him; but soon the young man's agreeable manner and indubitable appreciation of the old gentleman's stories completely won him over.

It was not long before the two were like old chums. The Major set apart each afternoon to read to him the manuscript of his book. During the anecdotes Hargraves never failed to laugh at exactly the right point. The Major was moved to declare to Miss Lydia one day that young Hargraves possessed remarkable perception and a gratifying respect for the old regime. And when it came to talking of those old days—if Major Talbot liked to talk, Mr. Hargraves was entranced to listen.

Like almost all old people who talk of the past, the Major loved to linger over details. In describing the splendid, almost royal, days of the old planters, he would hesitate until he had recalled the name of the negro who held his horse, or the exact date of certain minor happenings, or the number of bales of cotton raised in such a year; but Hargraves never grew impatient or lost interest. On the contrary, he would advance questions on a variety of subjects connected with the life of that time, and he never failed to extract ready replies.

The fox hunts, the 'possum suppers, the hoe-downs and jubilees in the negro quarters, the banquets in the plantation-house hall, when invitations went for fifty miles around; the occasional feuds with the neighboring gentry; the Major's duel with Rathbone Culbertson about Kitty Chalmers, who afterward married a Thwaite of South Carolina; and private yacht races for fabulous sums on Mobile Bay; the quaint beliefs, improvident habits, and loyal virtues of the old slaves—all these were subjects that held both the Major and Hargraves absorbed for hours at a time.

Sometimes, at night, when the young man would be coming upstairs to his room after his turn at the theater was over, the Major would appear at the door of his study and beckon archly to him. Going in, Hargraves would find a little table set with a decanter, sugar bowl, fruit, and a big bunch of fresh green mint.

"It occurred to me," the Major would begin—he was always ceremonious— "that perhaps you might have found your duties at the—at your place of occupation—sufficiently arduous to enable you, Mr. Hargraves, to appreciate what the poet might well have had in his mind when he wrote, 'tired Nature's sweet restorer'—one of our Southern juleps."

It was a fascination to Hargraves to watch him make it. He took rank among artists when he began, and he never varied the process. With what delicacy he bruised the mint; with what exquisite nicety he estimated the ingredients; with what solicitous care he capped the compound with the scarlet fruit glowing against the dark green fringe! And then the hospitality and grace with which he offered it, after the selected oat straws had been plunged into its tinkling depths!

After about four months in Washington, Miss Lydia discovered one morning that they were almost without money. The *Anecdotes and Reminiscences* was completed, but publishers had not jumped at the collected gems of Alabama sense and wit. The rental of a small house which they still owned in Mobile was two months in arrears. Their board money for the month would be due in three days. Miss Lydia called her father to a consultation.

"No money?" said he with a surprised look. "It is quite annoying to be called on so frequently for these petty sums, Really, I—"

The Major searched his pockets. He found only a two-dollar bill, which he returned to his vest pocket.

"I must attend to this at once, Lydia," he said. "Kindly get me my umbrella and I will go downtown immediately. The congressman from our district, General Fulghum, assured me some days ago that he would use his influence to get my book published at an early date. I will go to his hotel at once and see what arrangement has been made."

With a sad little smile Miss Lydia watched him button his "Father Hubbard" and depart, pausing at the door, as he always did, to bow profoundly.

That evening, at dark, he returned. It seemed that Congressman Fulghum had seen the publisher who had the Major's manuscript for reading. That person had said that if the anecdotes, etc., were carefully pruned down about one-half, in order to eliminate the sectional and class prejudice with which the book was dyed from end to end, he might consider its publication.

The Major was in a white heat of anger, but regained his equanimity, according to his code of manners, as soon as he was in Miss Lydia's presence.

"We must have money," said Miss Lydia, with a little wrinkle above her nose. "Give me the two dollars, and I will telegraph to Uncle Ralph for some to-night."

The Major drew a small envelope from his upper vest pocket and tossed it on the table.

"Perhaps it was injudicious," he said mildly, "but the sum was so merely nominal that I bought tickets to the theater to-night. It's a new war drama, Lydia. I thought you would be pleased to witness its first production in Washington. I am told that the South has very fair treatment in the play. I confess I should like to see the performance myself."

Miss Lydia threw up her hands in silent despair.

Still, as the tickets were bought, they might as well be used. So that evening, as they sat in the theater listening to the lively overture, even Miss Lydia was minded to relegate their troubles, for the hour, to second place. The Major, in spotless linen, with his extraordinary coat showing only where it was closely buttoned, and his white hair smoothly roached, looked really fine and distinguished. The curtain went up on the first act of *A Magnolia Flower*, revealing a typical Southern plantation scene. Major Talbot betrayed some interest.

"Oh, see!" exclaimed Miss Lydia, nudging his arm, and pointing to her program.

The Major put on his glasses and read the line in the cast of characters that her fingers indicated.

Col. Webster Calhoun .... Mr. Hopkins Hargraves.

"It's our Mr. Hargraves," said Miss Lydia. "It must be his first appearance in what he calls 'the legitimate.' I'm so glad for him."

Not until the second act did Col. Webster Calhoun appear upon the stage. When he made his entry Major Talbot gave an audible sniff, glared at him, and seemed to freeze solid. Miss Lydia uttered a little, ambiguous squeak and crumpled her program in her hand. For Colonel Calhoun was made up as nearly resembling Major Talbot as one pea does another. The long, thin white hair, curly at the ends, the aristocratic beak of a nose, the crumpled, wide, raveling shirt front, the string tie, with the bow nearly under one ear, were almost exactly duplicated. And then, to clinch the imitation, he wore the twin to the Major's supposed to be unparalleled coat. High-collared, baggy, empire-waisted, ample-skirted, hanging a foot lower in front than behind, the garment could have been designed from no other pattern. From then on, the Major and Miss Lydia sat bewitched, and saw the counterfeit presentment of a haughty Talbot "dragged," as the Major afterward expressed it, "through the slanderous mire of a corrupt stage."

Mr. Hargraves had used his opportunities well. He had caught the Major's little idiosyncrasies of speech, accent, and intonation and his pompous courtliness to perfection—exaggerating all to the purpose of the stage. When he performed that marvelous bow that the Major fondly imagined to be the pink of all salutations, the audience sent forth a sudden round of hearty applause.

Miss Lydia sat immovable, not daring to glance toward her father. Sometimes her hand next to him would be laid against her cheek, as if to conceal the smile which, in spite of her disapproval, she could not entirely suppress.

The culmination of Hargraves audacious imitation took place in the third act. The scene is where Colonel Calhoun entertains a few of the neighboring planters in his "den."

Standing at a table in the center of the stage, with his friends grouped about him, he delivers that inimitable, rambling character monologue so famous in *A Magnolia Flower*, at the same time that he deftly makes juleps for the party.

Major Talbot, sitting quietly, but white with indignation, heard his best stories retold, his pet theories and hobbies advanced and expanded, and the dream of the *Anecdotes and Reminiscences* served, exaggerated and garbled. His favorite narrative—that of his duel with Rathbone Culbertson—was not omitted, and it was delivered with more fire, egotism, and gusto than the Major himself put into it.

The monologue concluded with a quaint, delicious, witty little lecture on the art of concocting a julep, illustrated by the act. Here Major Talbot's delicate but showy science was reproduced to a hair's breadth—from his dainty handling of the fragrant weed—"the one-thousandth part of a grain too much pressure, gentlemen, and you extract the bitterness, instead of the aroma, of this heaven-bestowed plant"—to his solicitous selection of the oaten straws.

At the close of the scene the audience raised a tumultuous roar of appreciation. The portrayal of the type was so exact, so sure and thorough, that the leading characters in the play were forgotten. After repeated calls, Hargraves came before the curtain and bowed, his rather boyish face bright and flushed with the knowledge of success.

At last Miss Lydia turned and looked at the Major. His thin nostrils were working like the gills of a fish. He laid both shaking hands upon the arms of his chair to rise.

"We will go, Lydia," he said chokingly. "This is an abominable—desecration."

Before he could rise, she pulled him back into his seat.

"We will stay it out," she declared. "Do you want to advertise the copy by exhibiting the original coat?" So they remained to the end.

Hargraves's success must have kept him up late that night, for neither at the breakfast nor at the dinner table did he appear.

About three in the afternoon he tapped at the door of Major Talbot's study. The Major opened it, and Hargraves walked in with his hands full of the morning papers—too full of his triumph to notice anything unusual in the Major's demeanor.

"I put it all over 'em last night, Major," he began exultantly. "I had my inning, and, I think, scored. Here's what *The Post* says:

"'His conception and portrayal of the old-time Southern colonel, with his absurd grandiloquence, his eccentric garb, his quaint idioms and phrases, his moth-eaten pride of family, and his really kind heart, fastidious sense of honor, and lovable simplicity, is the best delineation of a character role on the boards to-day. The coat worn by Colonel Calhoun is itself nothing less than an evolution of genius. Mr. Hargraves has captured his public.'

"How does that sound, Major, for a first-nighter?"

"I had the honor"—the Major's voice sounded ominously frigid—"of witnessing your very remarkable performance, sir, last night."

Hargraves looked disconcerted.

"You were there? I didn't know you ever—I didn't know you cared for the theater. Oh, I say, Major Talbot," he exclaimed frankly, "don't you be offended. I admit

I did get a lot of pointers from you that helped out wonderfully in the part. But it's a type, you know—not individual. The way the audience caught on shows that. Half the patrons of that theater are Southerners. They recognized it."

"Mr. Hargraves," said the Major, who had remained standing, "you have put upon me an unpardonable insult. You have burlesqued my person, grossly betrayed my confidence, and misused my hospitality. If I thought you possessed the faintest conception of what is the sign manual of a gentleman, or what is due one, I would call you out, sir, old as I am. I will ask you to leave the room, sir."

The actor appeared to be slightly bewildered, and seemed hardly to take in the full meaning of the old gentleman's words.

"I am truly sorry you took offense," he said regretfully. "Up here we don't look at things just as you people do. I know men who would buy out half the house to have their personality put on the stage so the public would recognize it."

"They are not from Alabama, sir," said the Major haughtily.

"Perhaps not. I have a pretty good memory, Major; let me quote a few lines from your book. In response to a toast at a banquet given in—Milledgeville, I believe—you uttered, and intend to have printed, these words:

"'The Northern man is utterly without sentiment or warmth except in so far as the feelings may be turned to his own commercial profit. He will suffer without resentment any imputation cast upon the honor of himself or his loved ones that does not bear with it the consequence of pecuniary loss. In his charity, he gives with a liberal hand; but it must be heralded with the trumpet and chronicled in brass.'

"Do you think that picture is fairer than the one you saw of Colonel Calhoun last night?"

"The description," said the Major, frowning, "is—not without grounds. Some exag—latitude must be allowed in public speaking."

"And in public acting," replied Hargraves.

"That is not the point," persisted the Major, unrelenting. "It was a personal caricature. I positively decline to overlook it, sir."

"Major Talbot," said Hargraves, with a winning smile, "I wish you would understand me. I want you to know that I never dreamed of insulting you. In my profession, all life belongs to me. I take what I want, and what I can, and return it over the footlights. Now, if you will, let's let it go at that. I came in to see you about something else. We've been pretty good friends for some months, and I'm going to take the risk of offending you again. I know you are hard up for money—never mind how I found out, a boarding house is no place to keep such matters secret—and I want you to let me help you out of the pinch. I've been there often enough myself. I've been getting a fair salary all the season, and I've saved some money. You're welcome to a couple hundred—or even more—until you get——"

"Stop!" commanded the Major, with his arm outstretched. "It seems that my book didn't lie, after all. You think your money salve will heal all the hurts of honor. Under no circumstances would I accept a loan from a casual acquaintance; and as to you, sir, I would starve before I would consider your insulting offer of a financial adjustment of the circumstances we have discussed. I beg to repeat my request relative to your quitting the apartment."

Hargraves took his departure without another word. He also left the house the same day, moving, as Mrs. Vardeman explained at the supper table, nearer the vicinity of the downtown theater, where *A Magnolia Flower* was booked for a week's run.

Critical was the situation with Major Talbot and Miss Lydia. There was no one in Washington to whom the Major's scruples allowed him to apply for a loan. Miss Lydia wrote a letter to Uncle Ralph, but it was doubtful whether that relative's constricted affairs would permit him to furnish help. The Major was forced to make an apologetic address to Mrs. Vardeman regarding the delayed payment for board, referring to "delinquent rentals" and "delayed remittances" in a rather confused strain.

Deliverance came from an entirely unexpected source.

Late one afternoon the door maid came up and announced an old colored man who wanted to see Major Talbot. The Major asked that he be sent up to his study. Soon an old darkey appeared in the doorway, with his hat in hand, bowing, and scraping with one clumsy foot. He was quite decently dressed in a baggy suit of black. His big, coarse shoes shone with a metallic luster suggestive of stove polish. His bushy wool was gray—almost white. After middle life, it is difficult to estimate the age of a negro. This one might have seen as many years as had Major Talbot.

"I be bound you don't know me, Mars' Pendleton," were his first words.

The Major rose and came forward at the old, familiar style of address. It was one of the old plantation darkeys without a doubt; but they had been widely scattered, and he could not recall the voice or face.

"I don't believe I do," he said kindly—"unless you will assist my memory."

"Don't you 'member Cindy's Mose, Mars' Pendleton, what 'migrated 'mediately after de war?"

"Wait a moment," said the Major, rubbing his forehead with the tips of his fingers. He loved to recall everything connected with those beloved days. "Cindy's Mose," he reflected. "You worked among the horses—breaking the colts. Yes, I remember now. After the surrender, you took the name of—don't prompt me—Mitchell, and went to the West—to Nebraska."

"Yassir, yassir,"—the old man's face stretched with a delighted grin—"dat's him, dat's it. Newbraska. Dat's me—Mose Mitchell. Old Uncle Mose Mitchell, dey calls me now. Old mars', your pa, gimme a pah of dem mule colts when I lef' fur to staht me goin' with. You 'member dem colts, Mars' Pendleton?"

"I don't seem to recall the colts," said the Major. "You know. I was married the first year of the war and living at the old Follinsbee place. But sit down, sit down, Uncle Mose. I'm glad to see you. I hope you have prospered."

Uncle Mose took a chair and laid his hat carefully on the floor beside it.

"Yessir; of late I done mouty famous. When I first got to Newbraska, dey folks come all roun' me to see dem mule colts. Dey ain't see no mules like dem in Newbraska. I sold dem mules for three hundred dollars. Yessir—three hundred.

"Den I open a blacksmith shop, suh, and made some money and bought some lan'. Me and my old 'oman done raised up seb'm chillun, and all doin' well 'cept two of 'em what died. Fo' year ago a railroad come along and staht a town slam ag'inst my lan', and, suh, Mars' Pendleton, Uncle Mose am worth leb'm thousand dollars in money, property, and lan'."

"I'm glad to hear it," said the Major heartily. "Glad to hear it."

"And dat little baby of yo'n, Mars' Pendleton—one what you name Miss Lyddy—I be bound dat little tad done growed up tell nobody wouldn't know her."

The Major stepped to the door and called: "Lydie, dear, will you come?"

Miss Lydia, looking quite grown up and a little worried, came in from her room.

"Dar, now! What'd I tell you? I knowed dat baby done be plum growed up. You don't 'member Uncle Mose, child?"

"This is Aunt Cindy's Mose, Lydia," explained the Major. "He left Sunnymead for the West when you were two years old."

"Well," said Miss Lydia, "I can hardly be expected to remember you, Uncle Mose, at that age. And, as you say, I'm 'plum growed up,' and was a blessed long time ago. But I'm glad to see you, even if I can't remember you."

And she was. And so was the Major. Something alive and tangible had come to link them with the happy past. The three sat and talked over the olden times, the Major and Uncle Mose correcting or prompting each other as they reviewed the plantation scenes and days.

The Major inquired what the old man was doing so far from his home.

"Uncle Mose am a delicate," he explained, "to de grand Baptis' convention in dis city. I never preached none, but bein' a residin' elder in de church, and able fur to pay my own expenses, dey sent me along."

"And how did you know we were in Washington?" inquired Miss Lydia.

"Dey's a cullud man works in de hotel whar I stops, what comes from Mobile. He told me he seen Mars' Pendleton comin' outen dish here house one mawnin'.

"What I come fur," continued Uncle Mose, reaching into his pocket—"besides de sight of home folks—was to pay Mars' Pendleton what I owes him.

"Yessir—three hundred dollars." He handed the Major a roll of bills. "When I lef' old mars' says: 'Take dem mule colts, Mose, and, if it be so you gits able, pay fur 'em.' Yessir—dem was his words. De war had done lef' old mars' po' hisself. Old mars' bein' long ago dead, de debt descends to Mars' Pendleton. Three hundred dollars. Uncle Mose is plenty able to pay now. When dat railroad buy my lan' I laid off to pay fur dem mules. Count de money, Mars' Pendleton. Dat's what I sold dem mules fur. Yessir."

Tears were in Major Talbot's eyes. He took Uncle Mose's hand and laid his other upon his shoulder.

"Dear, faithful, old servitor," he said in an unsteady voice, "I don't mind saying to you that 'Mars' Pendleton spent his last dollar in the world a week ago. We will accept this money, Uncle Mose, since, in a way, it is a sort of payment, as well as a token of the loyalty and devotion of the old regime. Lydia, my dear, take the money. You are better fitted than I to manage its expenditure."

"Take it, honey," said Uncle Mose. "Hit belongs to you. Hit's Talbot money."

After Uncle Mose had gone, Miss Lydia had a good cry—-for joy; and the Major turned his face to a corner, and smoked his clay pipe volcanically.

The succeeding days saw the Talbots restored to peace and ease. Miss Lydia's face lost its worried look. The major appeared in a new frock coat, in which he looked like a wax figure personifying the memory of his golden age. Another publisher who read the manuscript of the *Anecdotes and Reminiscences* thought that, with a little retouching and toning down of the high lights, he could make a really bright and salable volume of it. Altogether, the situation was comfortable, and not without the touch of hope that is often sweeter than arrived blessings.

One day, about a week after their piece of good luck, a maid brought a letter for Miss Lydia to her room. The postmark showed that it was from New York. Not knowing any one there, Miss Lydia, in a mild flutter of wonder, sat down by her table and opened the letter with her scissors. This was what she read:

DEAR MISS TALBOT:

I thought you might be glad to learn of my good fortune. I have received and accepted an offer of two hundred dollars per week by a New York stock company to play Colonel Calhoun in *A Magnolia Flower*.

There is something else I wanted you to know. I guess you'd better not tell Major Talbot. I was anxious to make him some amends for the great help he was to me in studying the part, and for the bad humor he was in about it. He refused to let me, so I did it anyhow. I could easily spare the three hundred.

Sincerely yours, H. HOPKINS HARGRAVES.

P.S. How did I play Uncle Mose?

Major Talbot, passing through the hall, saw Miss Lydia's door open and stopped.

"Any mail for us this morning, Lydia, dear?" he asked.

Miss Lydia slid the letter beneath a fold of her dress.

"*The Mobile Chronicle* came," she said promptly. "It's on the table in your study."

BARGAIN DAY AT TUTT HOUSE
By George Randolph Chester (1869-)

[From McClure's Magazine, June, 1905; copyright, 1905,
by the S.S. McClure Co.; republished by the author's permission.]

I

JUST as the stage rumbled over the rickety old bridge, creaking and groaning, the sun came from behind the clouds that had frowned all the way, and the passengers cheered up a bit. The two richly dressed matrons who had been so utterly and unnecessarily oblivious to the presence of each other now suspended hostilities for the moment by mutual and unspoken consent, and viewed with relief the little, golden-tinted valley and the tree-clad road just beyond. The respective husbands of these two ladies exchanged a mere glance, no more, of comfort. They, too, were relieved, though more by the momentary truce than by anything else. They regretted very much to be compelled to hate each other, for each had reckoned up his vis-a-vis as a rather proper sort of fellow, probably a man of some achievement, used to good living and good company.

Extreme iciness was unavoidable between them, however. When one stranger has a splendidly preserved blonde wife and the other a splendidly preserved brunette wife, both of whom have won social prominence by years of hard fighting and aloofness, there remains nothing for the two men but to follow the lead, especially when directly under the eyes of the leaders.

The son of the blonde matron smiled cheerfully as the welcome light flooded the coach.

He was a nice-looking young man, of about twenty-two, one might judge, and he did his smiling, though in a perfectly impersonal and correct sort of manner, at the pretty daughter of the brunette matron. The pretty daughter also smiled, but her smile was demurely directed at the trees outside, clad as they were in all the flaming glory of their autumn tints, glistening with the recent rain and dripping with gems that sparkled and flashed in the noonday sun as they fell.

It is marvelous how much one can see out of the corner of the eye, while seeming to view mere scenery.

The driver looked down, as he drove safely off the bridge, and shook his head at the swirl of water that rushed and eddied, dark and muddy, close up under the rotten planking; then he cracked his whip, and the horses sturdily attacked the little hill.

Thick, overhanging trees on either side now dimmed the light again, and the two plump matrons once more glared past the opposite shoulders, profoundly unaware of each other. The husbands took on the politely surly look required of them. The blonde son's eyes still sought the brunette daughter, but it was furtively done and quite unsuccessfully, for the daughter was now doing a little glaring on her own account. The blonde matron had just swept her eyes across the daughter's skirt, estimating the fit and material of it with contempt so artistically veiled that it could almost be understood in the dark.

II

The big bays swung to the brow of the hill with ease, and dashed into a small circular clearing, where a quaint little two-story building, with a mossy watering-trough out in front, nestled under the shade of majestic old trees that reared their brown and scarlet crowns proudly into the sky. A long, low porch ran across the front of the structure, and a complaining sign hung out announcing, in dim, weather-flecked letters on a cracked board, that this was the "Tutt House." A gray-headed man, in brown overalls and faded blue jumper, stood on the porch and shook his fist at the stage as it whirled by.

"What a delightfully old-fashioned inn!" exclaimed the pretty daughter. "How

I should like to stop there over night!"

"You would probably wish yourself away before morning, Evelyn," replied her mother indifferently. "No doubt it would be a mere siege of discomfort."

The blonde matron turned to her husband. The pretty daughter had been looking at the picturesque "inn" between the heads of this lady and her son.

"Edward, please pull down the shade behind me," she directed. "There is quite a draught from that broken window."

The pretty daughter bit her lip. The brunette matron continued to stare at the shade in the exact spot upon which her gaze had been before directed, and she never quivered an eyelash. The young man seemed very uncomfortable, and he tried to look his apologies to the pretty daughter, but she could not see him now, not even if her eyes had been all corners.

They were bowling along through another avenue of trees when the driver suddenly shouted, "Whoa there!"

The horses were brought up with a jerk that was well nigh fatal to the assortment of dignity inside the coach. A loud roaring could be heard, both ahead and in the rear, a sharp splitting like a fusillade of pistol shots, then a creaking and tearing of timbers. The driver bent suddenly forward.

"Gid ap!" he cried, and the horses sprang forward with a lurch. He swung them around a sharp bend with a skillful hand and poised his weight above the brake as they plunged at terrific speed down a steep grade. The roaring was louder than ever now, and it became deafening as they suddenly emerged from the thick underbrush at the bottom of the declivity.

"Caught, by gravy!" ejaculated the driver, and, for the second time, he brought the coach to an abrupt stop.

"Do see what is the matter, Ralph," said the blonde matron impatiently.

Thus commanded, the young man swung out and asked the driver about it.

"Paintsville dam's busted," he was informed. "I been a-lookin' fer it this many a year, an' this here freshet done it. You see the holler there? Well, they's ten foot o' water in it, an' it had ort to be stone dry. The bridge is tore out behind us, an' we're stuck here till that water runs out. We can't git away till to-morry, anyways."

He pointed out the peculiar topography of the place, and Ralph got back in the coach.

"We're practically on a flood-made island," he exclaimed, with one eye on the pretty daughter, "and we shall have to stop over night at that quaint, old-fashioned inn we passed a few moments ago."

The pretty daughter's eyes twinkled, and he thought he caught a swift, direct gleam from under the long lashes—but he was not sure.

"Dear me, how annoying," said the blonde matron, but the brunette matron still stared, without the slightest trace of interest in anything else, at the infinitesimal spot she had selected on the affronting window-shade.

The two men gave sighs of resignation, and cast carefully concealed glances at each other, speculating on the possibility of a cigar and a glass, and maybe a good story or two, or possibly even a game of poker after the evening meal. Who could tell what might or might not happen?

III

When the stage drew up in front of the little hotel, it found Uncle Billy Tutt prepared for his revenge. In former days the stage had always stopped at the Tutt House for the noonday meal. Since the new railway was built through the adjoining county, however, the stage trip became a mere twelve-mile, cross-country transfer from one railroad to another, and the stage made a later trip, allowing the passengers plenty of time for "dinner" before they started. Day after day, as the coach flashed by with its money-laden passengers, Uncle Billy had hoped that it would break down. But this was better, much better. The coach might be quickly mended, but not the flood.

"I'm a-goin' t' charge 'em till they squeal," he declared to the timidly protesting Aunt Margaret, "an' then I'm goin' t' charge 'em a least mite more, drat 'em!"

He retreated behind the rough wooden counter that did duty as a desk, slammed open the flimsy, paper-bound "cash book" that served as a register, and planted his elbows uncompromisingly on either side of it.

"Let 'em bring in their own traps," he commented, and Aunt Margaret fled, ashamed and conscience-smitten, to the kitchen. It seemed awful.

The first one out of the coach was the husband of the brunette matron, and, proceeding under instructions, he waited neither for luggage nor women folk, but hurried straight into the Tutt House. The other man would have been neck and neck with him in the race, if it had not been that he paused to seize two suitcases and had the misfortune to drop one, which burst open and scattered a choice assortment of lingerie from one end of the dingy coach to the other.

In the confusion of rescuing the fluffery, the owner of the suitcase had to sacrifice her hauteur and help her husband and son block up the aisle, while the other matron had the ineffable satisfaction of being *kept waiting*, at last being enabled to say, sweetly and with the most polite consideration:

"Will you kindly allow me to pass?"

The blonde matron raised up and swept her skirts back perfectly flat. She was pale but collected. Her husband was pink but collected. Her son was crimson and uncollected. The brunette daughter could not have found an eye anywhere in his countenance as she rustled out after her mother.

"I do hope that Belmont has been able to secure choice quarters," the triumphing matron remarked as her daughter joined her on the ground. "This place looked so very small that there can scarcely be more than one comfortable suite in it."

It was a vital thrust. Only a splendidly cultivated self-control prevented the blonde matron from retaliating upon the unfortunate who had muddled things. Even so, her eyes spoke whole shelves of volumes.

The man who first reached the register wrote, in a straight black scrawl, "J. Belmont Van Kamp, wife, and daughter." There being no space left for his address, he put none down.

"I want three adjoining rooms, en suite if possible," he demanded.

"Three!" exclaimed Uncle Billy, scratching his head. "Won't two do ye? I ain't got but six bedrooms in th' house. Me an' Marg't sleeps in one, an' we're a-gittin' too old fer a shake-down on th' floor. I'll have t' save one room fer th' driver, an' that leaves four. You take two now——"

Mr. Van Kamp cast a hasty glance out of the window, The other man was getting out of the coach. His own wife was stepping on the porch.

"What do you ask for meals and lodging until this time to-morrow?" he interrupted.

The decisive moment had arrived. Uncle Billy drew a deep breath.

"Two dollars a head!" he defiantly announced. There! It was out! He wished

Margaret had stayed to hear him say it.

The guest did not seem to be seriously shocked, and Uncle Billy was beginning to be sorry he had not said three dollars, when Mr. Van Kamp stopped the landlord's own breath.

"I'll give you fifteen dollars for the three best rooms in the house," he calmly said, and Landlord Tutt gasped as the money fluttered down under his nose.

"Jis' take yore folks right on up, Mr. Kamp," said Uncle Billy, pouncing on the money. "Th' rooms is th' three right along th' hull front o' th' house. I'll be up and make on a fire in a minute. Jis' take th' *Jonesville Banner* an' th' *Uticky Clarion* along with ye."

As the swish of skirts marked the passage of the Van Kamps up the wide hall stairway, the other party swept into the room.

The man wrote, in a round flourish, "Edward Eastman Ellsworth, wife, and son."

"I'd like three choice rooms, en suite," he said.

"Gosh!" said Uncle Billy, regretfully. "That's what Mr. Kamp wanted, fust off, an' he got it. They hain't but th' little room over th' kitchen left. I'll have to put you an' your wife in that, an' let your boy sleep with th' driver."

The consternation in the Ellsworth party was past calculating by any known standards of measurement. The thing was an outrage! It was not to be borne! They would not submit to it!

Uncle Billy, however, secure in his mastery of the situation, calmly quartered them as he had said. "An' let 'em splutter all they want to," he commented comfortably to himself.

IV

The Ellsworths were holding a family indignation meeting on the broad porch when the Van Ramps came contentedly down for a walk, and brushed by them with unseeing eyes.

"It makes a perfectly fascinating suite," observed Mrs. Van Kamp, in a pleasantly conversational tone that could be easily overheard by anyone impolite enough to listen. "That delightful old-fashioned fireplace in the middle apartment makes it an ideal sitting-room, and the beds are so roomy and comfortable."

"I just knew it would be like this!" chirruped Miss Evelyn. "I remarked as we passed the place, if you will remember, how charming it would be to stop in this dear, quaint old inn over night. All my wishes seem to come true this year."

These simple and, of course, entirely unpremeditated remarks were as vinegar and wormwood to Mrs. Ellsworth, and she gazed after the retreating Van Kamps with a glint in her eye that would make one understand Lucretia Borgia at last.

Her son also gazed after the retreating Van Kamp. She had an exquisite figure, and she carried herself with a most delectable grace. As the party drew away from the inn she dropped behind the elders and wandered off into a side path to gather autumn leaves.

Ralph, too, started off for a walk, but naturally not in the same direction.

"Edward!" suddenly said Mrs. Ellsworth. "I want you to turn those people out of that suite before night!"

"Very well," he replied with a sigh, and got up to do it. He had wrecked a railroad and made one, and had operated successful corners in nutmegs and chicory. No task seemed impossible. He walked in to see the landlord.

"What are the Van Kamps paying you for those three rooms?" he asked.

"Fifteen dollars," Uncle Billy informed him, smoking one of Mr. Van Kamp's good cigars and twiddling his thumbs in huge content.

"I'll give you thirty for them. Just set their baggage outside and tell them the rooms are occupied."

"No sir-ree!" rejoined Uncle Billy. "A bargain's a bargain, an' I allus stick to one I make."

Mr. Ellsworth withdrew, but not defeated. He had never supposed that such an absurd proposition would be accepted. It was only a feeler, and he had noticed a wince of regret in his landlord. He sat down on the porch and lit a strong cigar. His wife did not bother him. She gazed complacently at the flaming foliage opposite, and allowed him to think. Getting impossible things was his business in life, and she had confidence in him.

"I want to rent your entire house for a week," he announced to Uncle Billy a few minutes later. It had occurred to him that the flood might last longer than they anticipated.

Uncle Billy's eyes twinkled.

"I reckon it kin be did," he allowed. "I reckon a *ho*-tel man's got a right to rent his hull house ary minute."

"Of course he has. How much do you want?"

Uncle Billy had made one mistake in not asking this sort of folks enough, and he reflected in perplexity.

"Make me a offer," he proposed. "Ef it hain't enough I'll tell ye. You want to rent th' hull place, back lot an' all?"

"No, just the mere house. That will be enough," answered the other with a smile. He was on the point of offering a hundred dollars, when he saw the little wrinkles about Mr. Tutt's eyes, and he said seventy-five.

"Sho, ye're jokin'!" retorted Uncle Billy. He had been considered a fine horse-trader in that part of the country. "Make it a hundred and twenty-five, an' I'll go ye."

Mr. Ellsworth counted out some bills.

"Here's a hundred," he said. "That ought to be about right."

"Fifteen more," insisted Uncle Billy.

With a little frown of impatience the other counted off the extra money and handed it over. Uncle Billy gravely handed it back.

"Them's the fifteen dollars Mr. Kamp give me," he explained. "You've got the hull house fer a week, an' o' course all th' money that's tooken in is your'n. You kin do as ye please about rentin' out rooms to other folks, I reckon. A bargain's a bargain, an' I allus stick to one I make."

V

Ralph Ellsworth stalked among the trees, feverishly searching for squirrels, scarlet leaves, and the glint of a brown walking-dress, this last not being so easy to locate in sunlit autumn woods. Time after time he quickened his pace, only to find that he had been fooled by a patch of dogwood, a clump of haw bushes or even a leaf-strewn knoll, but at last he unmistakably saw the dress, and then he slowed down to a careless saunter.

She was reaching up for some brilliantly colored maple leaves, and was entirely unconscious of his presence, especially after she had seen him. Her pose showed her pretty figure to advantage, but, of course, she did not know that. How should she?

Ralph admired the picture very much. The hat, the hair, the gown, the dainty shoes, even the narrow strip of silken hose that was revealed as she stood a-uptoe, were all of a deep, rich brown that proved an exquisite foil for the pink and cream of her cheeks. He remembered that her eyes were almost the same shade, and wondered how it was that women-folk happened on combinations in dress that so well set off their natural charms. The fool!

He was about three trees away, now, and a panic akin to that which hunters describe as "buck ague" seized him. He decided that he really had no excuse for coming any nearer. It would not do, either, to be seen staring at her if she should happen to turn her head, so he veered off, intending to regain the road. It would be impossible to do this without passing directly in her range of vision, and he did not intend to try to avoid it. He had a fine, manly figure of his own.

He had just passed the nearest radius to her circle and was proceeding along the tangent that he had laid out for himself, when the unwitting maid looked carefully down and saw a tangle of roots at her very feet. She was so unfortunate, a second later, as to slip her foot in this very tangle and give her ankle ever so slight a twist.

"Oh!" cried Miss Van Kamp, and Ralph Ellsworth flew to the rescue. He had not been noticing her at all, and yet he had started to her side before she had even cried out, which was strange. She had a very attractive voice.

"May I be of assistance?" he anxiously inquired.

"I think not, thank you," she replied, compressing her lips to keep back the intolerable pain, and half-closing her eyes to show the fine lashes. Declining the proffered help, she extricated her foot, picked up her autumn branches, and turned away. She was intensely averse to anything that could be construed as a flirtation, even of the mildest, he could certainly see that. She took a step, swayed slightly, dropped the leaves, and clutched out her hand to him.

"It is nothing," she assured him in a moment, withdrawing the hand after he had held it quite long enough. "Nothing whatever. I gave my foot a slight wrench, and turned the least bit faint for a moment."

"You must permit me to walk back, at least to the road, with you," he insisted, gathering up her armload of branches. "I couldn't think of leaving you here alone."

As he stooped to raise the gay woodland treasures he smiled to himself, ever so slightly. This was not *his* first season out, either.

"Delightful spot, isn't it?" he observed as they regained the road and sauntered in the direction of the Tutt House.

"Quite so," she reservedly answered. She had noticed that smile as he stooped. He must be snubbed a little. It would be so good for him.

"You don't happen to know Billy Evans, of Boston, do you?" he asked.

"I think not. I am but very little acquainted in Boston."

"Too bad," he went on. "I was rather in hopes you knew Billy. All sorts of a splendid fellow, and knows everybody."

"Not quite, it seems," she reminded him, and he winced at the error. In spite of the sly smile that he had permitted to himself, he was unusually interested.

He tried the weather, the flood, the accident, golf, books and three good, substantial, warranted jokes, but the conversation lagged in spite of him. Miss Van Kamp would not for the world have it understood that this unconventional meeting, made allowable by her wrenched ankle, could possibly fulfill the functions of a formal introduction.

"What a ripping, queer old building that is!" he exclaimed, making one more brave effort as they came in sight of the hotel.

"It is, rather," she assented. "The rooms in it are as quaint and delightful as the exterior, too."

She looked as harmless and innocent as a basket of peaches as she said it, and never the suspicion of a smile deepened the dimple in the cheek toward him. The smile was glowing cheerfully away inside, though. He could feel it, if he could not see it, and he laughed aloud.

"Your crowd rather got the better of us there," he admitted with the keen appreciation of one still quite close to college days.

"Of course, the mater is furious, but I rather look on it as a lark."

She thawed like an April icicle.

"It's perfectly jolly," she laughed with him. "Awfully selfish of us, too, I know, but such loads of fun."

They were close to the Tutt House now, and her limp, that had entirely disappeared as they emerged from the woods, now became quite perceptible. There might be people looking out of the windows, though it is hard to see why that should affect a limp.

Ralph was delighted to find that a thaw had set in, and he made one more attempt to establish at least a proxy acquaintance.

"You don't happen to know Peyson Kingsley, of Philadelphia, do you?"

"I'm afraid I don't," she replied. "I know so few Philadelphia people, you see." She was rather regretful about it this time. He really was a clever sort of a fellow, in spite of that smile.

The center window in the second floor of the Tutt House swung open, its little squares of glass flashing jubilantly in the sunlight. Mrs. Ellsworth leaned out over the sill, from the quaint old sitting-room of the *Van Kamp apartments*!

"Oh, Ralph!" she called in her most dulcet tones. "Kindly excuse yourself and come right on up to our suite for a few moments!"

VI

It is not nearly so easy to take a practical joke as to perpetrate one. Evelyn was sitting thoughtfully on the porch when her father and mother returned. Mrs. Ellsworth was sitting at the center window above, placidly looking out. Her eyes swept carelessly over the Van Kamps, and unconcernedly passed on to the rest of the landscape.

Mrs. Van Kamp gasped and clutched the arm of her husband. There was no need. He, too, had seen the apparition. Evelyn now, for the first time, saw the real humor of the situation. She smiled as she thought of Ralph. She owed him one, but she never worried about her debts. She always managed to get them paid, principal and interest.

Mr. Van Kamp suddenly glowered and strode into the Tutt House. Uncle Billy met him at the door, reflectively chewing a straw, and handed him an envelope. Mr. Van Kamp tore it open and drew out a note. Three five-dollar bills came out with it and fluttered to the porch floor. This missive confronted him:

MR. J. BELMONT VAN KAMP,

DEAR SIR: This is to notify you that I have rented the entire Tutt House for the ensuing week, and am compelled to assume possession of the three second-floor front rooms. Herewith I am enclosing the fifteen dollars you paid to secure the suite. You are quite welcome to make use, as my guest, of the small room over the kitchen. You will find your luggage in that room. Regretting any inconvenience that this transaction may cause you, I am,

Yours respectfully, EDWARD EASTMAN ELLSWORTH.

Mr. Van Kamp passed the note to his wife and sat down or a large chair. He was glad that the chair was comfortable and roomy. Evelyn picked up the bills and tucked them into her waist. She never overlooked any of her perquisites. Mrs. Van Kamp read the note, and the tip of her nose became white. She also sat down, but she was the first to find her voice.

"Atrocious!" she exclaimed. "Atrocious! Simply atrocious, Belmont. This is a house of public entertainment. They *can't* turn us out in this high-minded manner! Isn't there a law or something to that effect?"

"It wouldn't matter if there was," he thoughtfully replied. "This fellow Ellsworth would be too clever to be caught by it. He would say that the house was not a hotel but a private residence during the period for which he has rented it."

Personally, he rather admired Ellsworth. Seemed to be a resourceful sort of chap who knew how to make money behave itself, and do its little tricks without balking in the harness.

"Then you can make him take down the sign!" his wife declared.

He shook his head decidedly.

"It wouldn't do, Belle," he replied. "It would be spite, not retaliation, and not at all sportsmanlike. The course you suggest would belittle us more than it would annoy them. There must be some other way."

He went in to talk with Uncle Billy.

"I want to buy this place," he stated. "Is it for sale?"

"It sartin is!" replied Uncle Billy. He did not merely twinkle this time. He grinned.

"How much?"

"Three thousand dollars." Mr. Tutt was used to charging by this time, and he betrayed no hesitation.

"I'll write you out a check at once," and Mr. Van Kamp reached in his pocket with the reflection that the spot, after all, was an ideal one for a quiet summer retreat.

"Air you a-goin' t' scribble that there three thou-san' on a piece o' paper?" inquired Uncle Billy, sitting bolt upright. "Ef you air a-figgerin' on that, Mr. Kamp, jis' you save yore time. I give a man four dollars fer one o' them check things oncet, an' I owe myself them four dollars yit."

Mr. Van Kamp retired in disorder, but the thought of his wife and daughter waiting confidently on the porch stopped him. Moreover, the thing had resolved itself rather into a contest between Ellsworth and himself, and he had done a little making and breaking of men and things in his own time. He did some gatling-gun thinking out by the newel-post, and presently rejoined Uncle Billy.

"Mr. Tutt, tell me just exactly what Mr. Ellsworth rented, please," he requested.

"Th' hull house," replied Billy, and then he somewhat sternly added: "Paid me spot cash fer it, too."

Mr. Van Kamp took a wad of loose bills from his trousers pocket, straightened them out leisurely, and placed them in his bill book, along with some smooth yellowbacks of eye-bulging denominations. Uncle Billy sat up and stopped twiddling his thumbs.

"Nothing was said about the furniture, was there?" suavely inquired Van Kamp.

Uncle Billy leaned blankly back in his chair. Little by little the light dawned on the ex-horse-trader. The crow's feet reappeared about his eyes, his mouth twitched, he smiled, he grinned, then he slapped his thigh and haw-hawed.

"No!" roared Uncle Billy. "No, there wasn't, by gum!"

"Nothing but the house?"

"His very own words!" chuckled Uncle Billy. "'Jis' th' mere house,' says he, an' he gits it. A bargain's a bargain, an' I allus stick to one I make."

"How much for the furniture for the week?"

"Fifty dollars!" Mr. Tutt knew how to do business with this kind of people now, you bet.

Mr. Van Kamp promptly counted out the money.

"Drat it!" commented Uncle Billy to himself. "I could 'a' got more!"

"Now where can we make ourselves comfortable with this furniture?"

Uncle Billy chirked up. All was not yet lost.

"Waal," he reflectively drawled, "there's th' new barn. It hain't been used for nothin' yit, senct I built it two years ago. I jis' hadn't th' heart t' put th' critters in it as long as th' ole one stood up."

The other smiled at this flashlight on Uncle Billy's character, and they went out to look at the barn.

VII

Uncle Billy came back from the "Tutt House Annex," as Mr. Van Kamp dubbed the barn, with enough more money to make him love all the world until he got used to having it. Uncle Billy belongs to a large family.

Mr. Van Kamp joined the women on the porch, and explained the attractively novel situation to them. They were chatting gaily when the Ellsworths came down the stairs. Mr. Ellsworth paused for a moment to exchange a word with Uncle Billy.

"Mr. Tutt," said he, laughing, "if we go for a bit of exercise will you guarantee us the possession of our rooms when we come back?"

"Yes sir-ree!" Uncle Billy assured him. "They shan't nobody take them rooms away from you fer money, marbles, ner chalk. A bargain's a bargain, an' I allus stick to one I make," and he virtuously took a chew of tobacco while he inspected the afternoon sky with a clear conscience.

"I want to get some of those splendid autumn leaves to decorate our cozy apartments," Mrs. Ellsworth told her husband as they passed in hearing of the Van Kamps. "Do you know those oldtime rag rugs are the most oddly decorative effects that I have ever seen. They are so rich in color and so exquisitely blended."

There were reasons why this poisoned arrow failed to rankle, but the Van Kamps did not trouble to explain. They were waiting for Ralph to come out and join his parents. Ralph, it seemed, however, had decided not to take a walk. He had already fatigued himself, he had explained, and his mother had favored him with a significant look. She could readily believe him, she had assured him, and had then left him in scorn.

The Van Kamps went out to consider the arrangement of the barn. Evelyn returned first and came out on the porch to find a handkerchief. It was not there, but Ralph was. She was very much surprised to see him, and she intimated as much.

"It's dreadfully damp in the woods," he explained. "By the way, you don't happen to know the Whitleys, of Washington, do you? Most excellent people."

"I'm quite sorry that I do not," she replied. "But you will have to excuse me. We shall be kept very busy with arranging our apartments."

Ralph sprang to his feet with a ludicrous expression.

"Not the second floor front suite!" he exclaimed.

"Oh, no! Not at all," she reassured him.

He laughed lightly.

"Honors are about even in that game," he said.

"Evelyn," called her mother from the hall. "Please come and take those front suite curtains down to the barn."

"Pardon me while we take the next trick," remarked Evelyn with a laugh quite as light and gleeful as his own, and disappeared into the hall.

He followed her slowly, and was met at the door by her father.

"You are the younger Mr. Ellsworth, I believe," politely said Mr. Van Kamp.

"Ralph Ellsworth. Yes, sir."

"Here is a note for your father. It is unsealed. You are quite at liberty to read it."

Mr. Van Kamp bowed himself away, and Ralph opened the note, which read:
EDWARD EASTMAN ELLSWORTH, ESQ.,

Dear Sir: This is to notify you that I have rented the entire furniture of the Tutt House for the ensuing week, and am compelled to assume possession of that in the three second floor front rooms, as well as all the balance not in actual use by Mr. and Mrs. Tutt and the driver of the stage. You are quite welcome, however, to make use of the furnishings in the small room over the kitchen. Your luggage you will find undisturbed. Regretting any inconvenience that this transaction may cause you, I remain,

Yours respectfully,

J. BELMONT VAN KAMP.

Ralph scratched his head in amused perplexity. It devolved upon him to even up the affair a little before his mother came back. He must support the family reputation for resourcefulness, but it took quite a bit of scalp irritation before he aggravated the right idea into being. As soon as the idea came, he went in and made a hide-bound bargain with Uncle Billy, then he went out into the hall and waited until Evelyn came down with a huge armload of window curtains.

"Honors are still even," he remarked. "I have just bought all the edibles about the place, whether in the cellar, the house or any of the surrounding structures, in the ground, above the ground, dead or alive, and a bargain's a bargain as between man and man."

"Clever of you, I'm sure," commented Miss Van Kamp, reflectively. Suddenly her lips parted with a smile that revealed a double row of most beautiful teeth. He meditatively watched the curve of her lips.

"Isn't that rather a heavy load?" he suggested. "I'd be delighted to help you move the things, don't you know."

"It is quite kind of you, and what the men would call 'game,' I believe, under the circumstances," she answered, "but really it will not be necessary. We have hired Mr. Tutt and the driver to do the heavier part of the work, and the rest of it will be really a pleasant diversion."

"No doubt," agreed Ralph, with an appreciative grin. "By the way, you don't happen to know Maud and Dorothy Partridge, of Baltimore, do you? Stunning pretty girls, both of them, and no end of swells."

"I know so very few people in Baltimore," she murmured, and tripped on down to the barn.

Ralph went out on the porch and smoked. There was nothing else that he could do.

VIII

It was growing dusk when the elder Ellsworths returned, almost hidden by great masses of autumn boughs.

"You should have been with us, Ralph," enthusiastically said his mother. "I never saw such gorgeous tints in all my life. We have brought nearly the entire woods with us."

"It was a good idea," said Ralph. "A stunning good idea. They may come in handy to sleep on."

Mrs. Ellsworth turned cold.

"What do you mean?" she gasped.

"Ralph," sternly demanded his father, "you don't mean to tell us that you let the Van Kamps jockey us out of those rooms after all?"

"Indeed, no," he airily responded. "Just come right on up and see."

He led the way into the suite and struck a match. One solitary candle had been left upon the mantel shelf. Ralph thought that this had been overlooked, but his mother afterwards set him right about that. Mrs. Van Kamp had cleverly left it so that the Ellsworths could see how dreadfully bare the place was. One candle in three rooms is drearier than darkness anyhow.

Mrs. Ellsworth took in all the desolation, the dismal expanse of the now enormous apartments, the shabby walls, the hideous bright spots where pictures had hung, the splintered flooring, the great, gaunt windows—and she gave in. She had met with snub after snub, and cut after cut, in her social climb, she had had the cook quit in the middle of an important dinner, she had had every disconcerting thing possible happen to her, but this—this was the last *bale* of straw. She sat down on a suitcase, in the middle of the biggest room, and cried!

Ralph, having waited for this, now told about the food transaction, and she hastily pushed the last-coming tear back into her eye.

"Good!" she cried. "They will be up here soon. They will be compelled to compromise, and they must not find me with red eyes."

She cast a hasty glance around the room, then, in a sudden panic, seized the candle and explored the other two. She went wildly out into the hall, back into the little room over the kitchen, downstairs, everywhere, and returned in consternation.

"There's not a single mirror left in the house!" she moaned.

Ralph heartlessly grinned. He could appreciate that this was a characteristic woman trick, and wondered admiringly whether Evelyn or her mother had thought of it. However, this was a time for action.

"I'll get you some water to bathe your eyes," he offered, and ran into the little room over the kitchen to get a pitcher. A cracked shaving-mug was the only vessel that had been left, but he hurried down into the yard with it. This was no time for fastidiousness.

He had barely creaked the pump handle when Mr. Van Kamp hurried up from the barn.

"I beg your pardon, sir," said Mr. Van Kamp, "but this water belongs to us. My daughter bought it, all that is in the ground, above the ground, or that may fall from the sky upon these premises."

IX

The mutual siege lasted until after seven o'clock, but it was rather one-sided. The Van Kamps could drink all the water they liked, it made them no hungrier. If the Ellsworths ate anything, however, they grew thirstier, and, moreover, water was necessary if anything worth while was to be cooked. They knew all this, and resisted until Mrs. Ellsworth was tempted and fell. She ate a sandwich and choked. It was heartbreaking, but Ralph had to be sent down with a plate of sandwiches and an offer to trade them for water.

Halfway between the pump and the house he met Evelyn coming with a small pail of the precious fluid. They both stopped stock still; then, seeing that it was too late to retreat, both laughed and advanced.

"Who wins now?" bantered Ralph as they made the exchange.

"It looks to me like a misdeal," she gaily replied, and was moving away when he called her back.

"You don't happen to know the Gately's, of New York, do you?" he was quite anxious to know.

"I am truly sorry, but I am acquainted with so few people in New York. We are from Chicago, you know."

"Oh," said he blankly, and took the water up to the Ellsworth suite.

Mrs. Ellsworth cheered up considerably when she heard that Ralph had been met halfway, but her eyes snapped when he confessed that it was Miss Van Kamp who had met him.

"I hope you are not going to carry on a flirtation with that overdressed creature," she blazed.

"Why mother," exclaimed Ralph, shocked beyond measure. "What right have you to accuse either this young lady or myself of flirting? Flirting!"

Mrs. Ellsworth suddenly attacked the fire with quite unnecessary energy.

X

Down at the barn, the wide threshing floor had been covered with gay rag-rugs, and strewn with tables, couches, and chairs in picturesque profusion. Roomy box-stalls had been carpeted deep with clean straw, curtained off with gaudy bed-quilts, and converted into cozy sleeping apartments. The mow and the stalls had been screened off with lace curtains and blazing counterpanes, and the whole effect was one of Oriental luxury and splendor. Alas, it was only an "effect"! The red-hot parlor stove smoked abominably, the pipe carried other smoke out through the hawmow window, only to let it blow back again. Chill cross-draughts whistled in from cracks too numerous to be stopped up, and the miserable Van Kamps could only cough and shiver, and envy the Tutts and the driver, non-combatants who had been fed two hours before.

Up in the second floor suite there was a roaring fire in the big fireplace, but there was a chill in the room that no mere fire could drive away—the chill of absolute emptiness.

A man can outlive hardships that would kill a woman, but a woman can endure discomforts that would drive a man crazy.

Mr. Ellsworth went out to hunt up Uncle Billy, with an especial solace in mind. The landlord was not in the house, but the yellow gleam of a lantern revealed his presence in the woodshed, and Mr. Ellsworth stepped in upon him just as he was pouring something yellow and clear into a tumbler from a big jug that he had just taken from under the flooring.

"How much do you want for that jug and its contents?" he asked, with a sigh of gratitude that this supply had been overlooked.

Before Mr. Tutt could answer, Mr. Van Kamp hurried in at the door.

"Wait a moment!" he cried. "I want to bid on that!"

"This here jug hain't fer sale at no price," Uncle Billy emphatically announced, nipping all negotiations right in the bud. "It's too pesky hard to sneak this here licker in past Marge't, but I reckon it's my treat, gents. Ye kin have all ye want."

One minute later Mr. Van Kamp and Mr. Ellsworth were seated, one on a saw-buck and the other on a nail-keg, comfortably eyeing each other across the work bench, and each was holding up a tumbler one-third filled with the golden yellow liquid.

"Your health, sir," courteously proposed Mr. Ellsworth.

"And to you, sir," gravely replied Mr. Van Kamp.

XI

Ralph and Evelyn happened to meet at the pump, quite accidentally, after the former had made half a dozen five-minute-apart trips for a drink. It was Miss Van Kamp, this time, who had been studying on the mutual acquaintance problem.

"You don't happen to know the Tylers, of Parkersburg, do you?" she asked.

"The Tylers! I should say I do!" was the unexpected and enthusiastic reply. "Why, we are on our way now to Miss Georgiana Tyler's wedding to my friend Jimmy Carston. I'm to be best man."

"How delightful!" she exclaimed. "We are on the way there, too. Georgiana was my dearest chum at school, and I am to be her 'best girl.'"

"Let's go around on the porch and sit down," said Ralph.

XII

Mr. Van Kamp, back in the woodshed, looked about him with an eye of content.

"Rather cozy for a woodshed," he observed. "I wonder if we couldn't scare up a little session of dollar limit?"

Both Uncle Billy and Mr. Ellsworth were willing. Death and poker level all Americans. A fourth hand was needed, however. The stage driver was in bed and asleep, and Mr. Ellsworth volunteered to find the extra player.

"I'll get Ralph," he said. "He plays a fairly stiff game." He finally found his son on the porch, apparently alone, and stated his errand.

"Thank you, but I don't believe I care to play this evening," was the astounding reply, and Mr. Ellsworth looked closer. He made out, then, a dim figure on the other side of Ralph.

"Oh! Of course not!" he blundered, and went back to the woodshed.

Three-handed poker is a miserable game, and it seldom lasts long. It did not in this case. After Uncle Billy had won the only jack-pot deserving of the name, he was allowed to go blissfully to sleep with his hand on the handle of the big jug.

After poker there is only one other always available amusement for men, and that is business. The two travelers were quite well acquainted when Ralph put his head in at the door.

"Thought I'd find you here," he explained. "It just occurred to me to wonder whether you gentlemen had discovered, as yet, that we are all to be house guests at the Carston-Tyler wedding."

"Why, no!" exclaimed his father in pleased surprise. "It is a most agreeable coincidence. Mr. Van Kamp, allow me to introduce my son, Ralph. Mr. Van Kamp and myself, Ralph, have found out that we shall be considerably thrown together in a business way from now on. He has just purchased control of the Metropolitan and Western string of interurbans."

"Delighted, I'm sure," murmured Ralph, shaking hands, and then he slipped out as quickly as possible. Some one seemed to be waiting for him.

Perhaps another twenty minutes had passed, when one of the men had an illuminating idea that resulted, later on, in pleasant relations for all of them. It was about time, for Mrs. Ellsworth, up in the bare suite, and Mrs. Van Kamp, down in the draughty barn, both wrapped up to the chin and both still chilly, had about reached the limit of patience and endurance.

"Why can't we make things a little more comfortable for all concerned?" suggested Mr. Van Kamp. "Suppose, as a starter, that we have Mrs. Van Kamp give a shiver party down in the barn?"

"Good idea," agreed Mr. Ellsworth. "A little diplomacy will do it. Each one of us will have to tell his wife that the other fellow made the first abject overtures."

Mr. Van Kamp grinned understandingly, and agreed to the infamous ruse.

"By the way," continued Mr. Ellsworth, with a still happier thought, "you must allow Mrs. Ellsworth to furnish the dinner for Mrs. Van Kamp's shiver party."

"Dinner!" gasped Mr. Van Kamp. "By all means!"

Both men felt an anxious yawning in the region of the appetite, and a yearning moisture wetted their tongues. They looked at the slumbering Uncle Billy and decided to see Mrs. Tutt themselves about a good, hot dinner for six.

"Law me!" exclaimed Aunt Margaret when they appeared at the kitchen door. "I swan I thought you folks 'u'd never come to yore senses. Here I've had a big pot o' stewed chicken ready on the stove fer two mortal hours. I kin give ye that, an' smashed taters an' chicken gravy, an' dried corn, an' hot corn-pone, an' currant jell, an' strawberry preserves, an' my own cannin' o' peaches, an' pumpkin-pie an' coffee. Will that do ye?" Would it *do*! *Would* it do!!

As Aunt Margaret talked, the kitchen door swung wide, and the two men were stricken speechless with astonishment. There, across from each other at the kitchen table, sat the utterly selfish and traitorous younger members of the rival houses of Ellsworth and Van Kamp, deep in the joys of chicken, and mashed potatoes, and gravy, and hot corn-pone, and all the other "fixings," laughing and chatting gaily like chums of years' standing. They had seemingly just come to an agreement about something or other, for Evelyn, waving the shorter end of a broken wishbone, was vivaciously saying to Ralph:

"A bargain's a bargain, and I always stick to one I make."

A CALL
By Grace MacGowan Cooke (1863-)

[From *Harper's Magazine*, August, 1906. Copyright, 1906, by Harper & Brothers. Republished by the author's permission.]

A boy in an unnaturally clean, country-laundered collar walked down a long white road. He scuffed the dust up wantonly, for he wished to veil the all-too-brilliant polish of his cowhide shoes. Also the memory of the whiteness and slipperiness of his collar oppressed him. He was fain to look like one accustomed to social diversions, a man hurried from hall to hall of pleasure, without time between to change collar or polish boot. He stooped and rubbed a crumb of earth on his overfresh neck-linen.

This did not long sustain his drooping spirit. He was mentally adrift upon the *Hints and Helps to Young Men in Business and Social Relations*, which had suggested to him his present enterprise, when the appearance of a second youth, taller and broader than himself, with a shock of light curling hair and a crop of freckles that advertised a rich soil threw him a lifeline. He put his thumbs to his lips and whistled in a peculiarly ear-splitting way. The two boys had sat on the same bench at Sunday-school not three hours before; yet what a change had come over the world for one of them since then!

"Hello! Where you goin', Ab?" asked the newcomer, gruffly.

"Callin'," replied the boy in the collar, laconically, but with carefully averted gaze.

"On the girls?" inquired the other, awestruck. In Mount Pisgah you saw the girls home from night church, socials, or parties; you could hang over the gate; and you might walk with a girl in the cemetery of a Sunday afternoon; but to ring a front-door bell and ask for Miss Heart's Desire one must have been in long trousers at least three years—and the two boys confronted in the dusty road had worn these dignifying garments barely six months.

"Girls," said Abner, loftily; "I don't know about girls—I'm just going to call on one girl—Champe Claiborne." He marched on as though the conversation was at an end; but Ross hung upon his flank. Ross and Champe were neighbors, comrades in all sorts of mischief; he was in doubt whether to halt Abner and pummel him, or propose to enlist under his banner.

"Do you reckon you could?" he debated, trotting along by the irresponsive Jilton boy.

"Run home to your mother," growled the originator of the plan, savagely. "You ain't old enough to call on girls; anybody can see that; but I am, and I'm going to call on Champe Claiborne."

Again the name acted as a spur on Ross. "With your collar and boots all dirty?" he jeered. "They won't know you're callin'."

The boy in the road stopped short in his dusty tracks. He was an intense creature, and he whitened at the tragic insinuation, longing for the wholesome stay and companionship of freckle-faced Ross. "I put the dirt on o' purpose so's to look kind of careless," he half whispered, in an agony of doubt. "S'pose I'd better go into your house and try to wash it off? Reckon your mother would let me?"

"I've got two clean collars," announced the other boy, proudly generous. "I'll lend you one. You can put it on while I'm getting ready. I'll tell mother that we're just stepping out to do a little calling on the girls."

Here was an ally worthy of the cause. Abner welcomed him, in spite of certain jealous twinges. He reflected with satisfaction that there were two Claiborne girls, and though Alicia was so stiff and prim that no boy would ever think of calling on her, there was still the hope that she might draw Ross's fire, and leave him, Abner, to make the numerous remarks he had stored up in his mind from *Hints and Helps to Young Men in Social and Business Relations* to Champe alone.

Mrs. Pryor received them with the easy-going kindness of the mother of one son. She followed them into the dining-room to kiss and feed him, with an absent

"Howdy, Abner; how's your mother?"

Abner, big with the importance of their mutual intention, inclined his head stiffly and looked toward Ross for explanation. He trembled a little, but it was with delight, as he anticipated the effect of the speech Ross had outlined. But it did not come.

"I'm not hungry, mother," was the revised edition which the freckle-faced boy offered to the maternal ear. "I—we are going over to Mr. Claiborne's—on—er—on an errand for Abner's father."

The black-eyed boy looked reproach as they clattered up the stairs to Ross's room, where the clean collar was produced and a small stock of ties.

"You'd wear a necktie—wouldn't you?" Ross asked, spreading them upon the bureau-top.

"Yes. But make it fall carelessly over your shirt-front," advised the student of *Hints and Helps*. "Your collar is miles too big for me. Say! I've got a wad of white chewing-gum; would you flat it out and stick it over the collar button? Maybe that would fill up some. You kick my foot if you see me turning my head so's to knock it off."

"Better button up your vest," cautioned Ross, laboring with the "careless" fall of his tie.

"Huh-uh! I want 'that easy air which presupposes familiarity with society'— that's what it says in my book," objected Abner.

"Sure!" Ross returned to his more familiar jeering attitude. "Loosen up all your clothes, then. Why don't you untie your shoes? Flop a sock down over one of 'em— that looks 'easy' all right."

Abner buttoned his vest. "It gives a man lots of confidence to know he's good-looking," he remarked, taking all the room in front of the mirror.

Ross, at the wash-stand soaking his hair to get the curl out of it, grumbled some unintelligible response. The two boys went down the stairs with tremulous hearts.

"Why, you've put on another clean shirt, Rossie!" Mrs. Pryor called from her chair—mothers' eyes can see so far! "Well—don't get into any dirty play and soil it." The boys walked in silence—but it was a pregnant silence; for as the roof of the Claiborne house began to peer above the crest of the hill, Ross plumped down on a stone and announced, "I ain't goin'."

"Come on," urged the black-eyed boy. "It'll be fun—and everybody will respect us more. Champe won't throw rocks at us in recess-time, after we've called on her. She couldn't."

"Called!" grunted Ross. "I couldn't make a call any more than a cow. What'd I say? What'd I do? I can behave all right when you just go to people's houses—but a call!"

Abner hesitated. Should he give away his brilliant inside information, drawn from the *Hints and Helps* book, and be rivalled in the glory of his manners and bearing? Why should he not pass on alone, perfectly composed, and reap the field of glory unsupported? His knees gave way and he sat down without intending it.

"Don't you tell anybody and I'll put you on to exactly what grown-up gentlemen say and do when they go calling on the girls," he began.

"Fire away," retorted Ross, gloomily. "Nobody will find out from me. Dead men tell no tales. If I'm fool enough to go, I don't expect to come out of it alive."

Abner rose, white and shaking, and thrusting three fingers into the buttoning of his vest, extending the other hand like an orator, proceeded to instruct the freckled, perspiring disciple at his feet.

"'Hang your hat on the rack, or give it to a servant.'" Ross nodded intelligently. He could do that.

"'Let your legs be gracefully disposed, one hand on the knee, the other—'"

Abner came to an unhappy pause. "I forget what a fellow does with the other hand. Might stick it in your pocket, loudly, or expectorate on the carpet. Indulge in little frivolity. Let a rich stream of conversation flow.'"

Ross mentally dug within himself for sources of rich streams of conversation. He found a dry soil. "What you goin' to talk about?" he demanded, fretfully. "I won't go a step farther till I know what I'm goin' to say when I get there."

Abner began to repeat paragraphs from *Hints and Helps*. "'It is best to remark,'" he opened, in an unnatural voice, "'How well you are looking!' although fulsome compliments should be avoided. When seated ask the young lady who her favorite composer is.'"

"What's a composer?" inquired Ross, with visions of soothing-syrup in his mind.

"A man that makes up music. Don't butt in that way; you put me all out—

'composer is. Name yours. Ask her what piece of music she likes best. Name yours. If the lady is musical, here ask her to play or sing.'"

This chanted recitation seemed to have a hypnotic effect on the freckled boy; his big pupils contracted each time Abner came to the repetend, "Name yours."

"I'm tired already," he grumbled; but some spell made him rise and fare farther.

When they had entered the Claiborne gate, they leaned toward each other like young saplings weakened at the root and locking branches to keep what shallow foothold on earth remained.

"You're goin' in first," asserted Ross, but without conviction. It was his custom to tear up to this house a dozen times a week, on his father's old horse or afoot; he was wont to yell for Champe as he approached, and quarrel joyously with her while he performed such errand as he had come upon; but he was gagged and hamstrung now by the hypnotism of Abner's scheme.

"'Walk quietly up the steps; ring the bell and lay your card on the servant,'" quoted Abner, who had never heard of a server.

"'Lay your card on the servant!'" echoed Ross. "Cady'd dodge. There's a porch to cross after you go up the steps—does it say anything about that?"

"It says that the card should be placed on the servant," Abner reiterated, doggedly. "If Cady dodges, it ain't any business of mine. There are no porches in my book. Just walk across it like anybody. We'll ask for Miss Champe Claiborne."

"We haven't got any cards," discovered Ross, with hope.

"I have," announced Abner, pompously. "I had some struck off in Chicago. I ordered 'em by mail. They got my name Pillow, but there's a scalloped gilt border around it. You can write your name on my card. Got a pencil?"

He produced the bit of cardboard; Ross fished up a chewed stump of lead pencil, took it in cold, stiff fingers, and disfigured the square with eccentric scribblings.

"They'll know who it's meant for," he said, apologetically, "because I'm here. What's likely to happen after we get rid of the card?"

"I told you about hanging your hat on the rack and disposing your legs."

"I remember now," sighed Ross. They had been going slower and slower. The angle of inclination toward each other became more and more pronounced.

"We must stand by each other," whispered Abner.

"I will—if I can stand at all," murmured the other boy, huskily.

"Oh, Lord!" They had rounded the big clump of evergreens and found Aunt Missouri Claiborne placidly rocking on the front porch! Directed to mount steps and ring bell, to lay cards upon the servant, how should one deal with a rosy-faced, plump lady of uncertain years in a rocking-chair. What should a caller lay upon her? A lion in the way could not have been more terrifying. Even retreat was cut off. Aunt Missouri had seen them. "Howdy, boys; how are you?" she said, rocking peacefully. The two stood before her like detected criminals.

Then, to Ross's dismay, Abner sank down on the lowest step of the porch, the westering sun full in his hopeless eyes. He sat on his cap. It was characteristic that the freckled boy remained standing. He would walk up those steps according to plan and agreement, if at all. He accepted no compromise. Folding his straw hat into a battered cone, he watched anxiously for the delivery of the card. He was not sure what Aunt Missouri's attitude might be if it were laid on her. He bent down to his companion. "Go ahead," he whispered. "Lay the card."

Abner raised appealing eyes. "In a minute. Give me time," he pleaded.

"Mars' Ross—Mars' Ross! Head 'em off!" sounded a yell, and Babe, the house-boy, came around the porch in pursuit of two half-grown chickens.

"Help him, Rossie," prompted Aunt Missouri, sharply. "You boys can stay to supper and have some of the chicken if you help catch them."

Had Ross taken time to think, he might have reflected that gentlemen making formal calls seldom join in a chase after the main dish of the family supper. But the needs of Babe were instant. The lad flung himself sidewise, caught one chicken in his hat, while Babe fell upon the other in the manner of a football player. Ross handed the pullet to the house-boy, fearing that he had done something very much out of character, then pulled the reluctant negro toward to the steps.

"Babe's a servant," he whispered to Abner, who had sat rigid through the entire performance. "I helped him with the chickens, and he's got to stand gentle while you lay the card on."

Confronted by the act itself, Abner was suddenly aware that he knew not how to begin. He took refuge in dissimulation.

"Hush!" he whispered back. "Don't you see Mr. Claiborne's come out?—He's going to read something to us."

Ross plumped down beside him. "Never mind the card; tell 'em," he urged.

"Tell 'em yourself."

"No—let's cut and run."

"I—I think the worst of it is over. When Champe sees us she'll—"

Mention of Champe stiffened Ross's spine. If it had been glorious to call upon her, how very terrible she would make it should they attempt calling, fail, and the failure come to her knowledge! Some things were easier to endure than others; he resolved to stay till the call was made.

For half an hour the boys sat with drooping heads, and the old gentleman read aloud, presumably to Aunt Missouri and themselves. Finally their restless eyes discerned the two Claiborne girls walking serene in Sunday trim under the trees at the edge of the lawn. Arms entwined, they were whispering together and giggling a little. A caller, Ross dared not use his voice to shout nor his legs to run toward them.

"Why don't you go and talk to the girls, Rossie?" Aunt Missouri asked, in the kindness of her heart. "Don't be noisy—it's Sunday, you know—and don't get to playing anything that'll dirty up your good clothes."

Ross pressed his lips hard together; his heart swelled with the rage of the misunderstood. Had the card been in his possession, he would, at that instant, have laid it on Aunt Missouri without a qualm.

"What is it?" demanded the old gentleman, a bit testily.

"The girls want to hear you read, father," said Aunt Missouri, shrewdly; and she got up and trotted on short, fat ankles to the girls in the arbor. The three returned together, Alicia casting curious glances at the uncomfortable youths, Champe threatening to burst into giggles with every breath.

Abner sat hard on his cap and blushed silently. Ross twisted his hat into a three-cornered wreck.

The two girls settled themselves noisily on the upper step. The old man read on and on. The sun sank lower. The hills were red in the west as though a brush fire flamed behind their crests. Abner stole a furtive glance at his companion in misery, and the dolor of Ross's countenance somewhat assuaged his anguish. The freckle-faced boy was thinking of the village over the hill, a certain pleasant white house set back in a green yard, past whose gate, the two-plank sidewalk ran. He knew lamps were beginning to wink in the windows of the neighbors about, as though the houses said, "Our boys are all at home—but Ross Pryor's out trying to call on the girls, and can't get anybody to understand it." Oh, that he were walking down those two planks, drawing a stick across the pickets, lifting high happy feet which could turn in at that gate! He wouldn't care what the lamps said then. He wouldn't even mind if the whole Claiborne family died laughing at him—if only some power would raise him up from this paralyzing spot and put him behind the safe barriers of his own home!

The old man's voice lapsed into silence; the light was becoming too dim for his reading. Aunt Missouri turned and called over her shoulder into the shadows of the big hall: "You Babe! Go put two extra plates on the supper-table."

The boys grew red from the tips of their ears, and as far as any one could see under their wilting collars. Abner felt the lump of gum come loose and slip down a cold spine. Had their intentions but been known, this inferential invitation would have been most welcome. It was but to rise up and thunder out, "We came to call on the young ladies."

They did not rise. They did not thunder out anything. Babe brought a lamp and set it inside the window, and Mr. Claiborne resumed his reading. Champe giggled and said that Alicia made her. Alcia drew her skirts about her, sniffed, and looked virtuous, and said she didn't see anything funny to laugh at. The supper-bell rang. The family, evidently taking it for granted that the boys would follow, went in.

Alone for the first time, Abner gave up. "This ain't any use," he complained. "We ain't calling on anybody."

"Why didn't you lay on the card?" demanded Ross, fiercely. "Why didn't you say: 'We've-just-dropped-into-call-on-Miss-Champe. It's-a -pleasant-evening. We-feel-we-must-be-going,' like you said you would? Then we could have lifted our hats and got away decently."

Abner showed no resentment.

"Oh, if it's so easy, why didn't you do it yourself?" he groaned.

"Somebody's coming," Ross muttered, hoarsely. "Say it now. Say it quick."

The somebody proved to be Aunt Missouri, who advanced only as far as the end of the hall and shouted cheerfully: "The idea of a growing boy not coming to meals when the bell rings! I thought you two would be in there ahead of us. Come on." And clinging to their head-coverings as though these contained some charm whereby the owners might be rescued, the unhappy callers were herded into the dining-room. There were many things on the table that boys like. Both were becoming fairly cheerful, when Aunt Missouri checked the biscuit-plate with: "I treat my neighbors' children just like I'd want children of my own treated. If your mothers let you eat all you want, say so, and I don't care; but if either of them is a little bit particular, why, I'd stop at six!"

Still reeling from this blow, the boys finally rose from the table and passed out with the family, their hats clutched to their bosoms, and clinging together for mutual aid and comfort. During the usual Sunday-evening singing Champe laughed till Aunt Missouri threatened to send her to bed. Abner's card slipped from his hand and dropped face up on the floor. He fell upon it and tore it into infinitesimal pieces.

"That must have been a love-letter," said Aunt Missouri, in a pause of the music. "You boys are getting 'most old enough to think about beginning to call on the girls." Her eyes twinkled.

Ross growled like a stoned cur. Abner took a sudden dive into *Hints and Helps*, and came up with, "You flatter us, Miss Claiborne," whereat Ross snickered out like a human boy. They all stared at him.

"It sounds so funny to call Aunt Missouri 'Mis' Claiborne,'" the lad of the freckles explained.

"Funny?" Aunt Missouri reddened. "I don't see any particular joke in my having my maiden name."

Abner, who instantly guessed at what was in Ross's mind, turned white at the thought of what they had escaped. Suppose he had laid on the card and asked for Miss Claiborne!

"What's the matter, Champe?" inquired Ross, in a fairly natural tone. The air he had drawn into his lungs when he laughed at Abner seemed to relieve him from the numbing gentility which had bound his powers since he joined Abner's ranks.

"Nothing. I laughed because you laughed," said the girl.

The singing went forward fitfully. Servants traipsed through the darkened yard, going home for Sunday night. Aunt Missouri went out and held some low-toned parley with them. Champe yawned with insulting enthusiasm. Presently both girls quietly disappeared. Aunt Missouri never returned to the parlor—evidently thinking that the girls would attend to the final amenities with their callers. They were left alone with old Mr. Claiborne. They sat as though bound in their chairs, while the old man read in silence for a while. Finally he closed his book, glanced about him, and observed absently:

"So you boys were to spend the night?" Then, as he looked at their startled faces: "I'm right, am I not? You are to spent the night?"

Oh, for courage to say: "Thank you, no. We'll be going now. We just came over to call on Miss Champe." But thought of how this would sound in face of the facts, the painful realization that they dared not say it because they *had* not said it, locked their lips. Their feet were lead; their tongues stiff and too large for their mouths. Like creatures in a nightmare, they moved stiffly, one might have said creakingly, up the stairs and received each—a bedroom candle!

"Good night, children," said the absent-minded old man. The two gurgled out some sounds which were intended for words and doged behind the bedroom door.

"They've put us to bed!" Abner's black eyes flashed fire. His nervous hands clutched at the collar Ross had lent him. "That's what I get for coming here with you, Ross Pryor!" And tears of humiliation stood in his eyes.

In his turn Ross showed no resentment. "What I'm worried about is my mother," he confessed. "She's so sharp about finding out things. She wouldn't tease me—she'd just be sorry for me. But she'll think I went home with you."

"I'd like to see my mother make a fuss about my calling on the girls!" growled Abner, glad to let his rage take a safe direction.

"Calling on the girls! Have we called on any girls?" demanded clear-headed, honest Ross.

"Not exactly—yet," admitted Abner, reluctantly. "Come on—let's go to bed. Mr. Claiborne asked us, and he's the head of this household. It isn't anybody's business what we came for."

"I'll slip off my shoes and lie down till Babe ties up the dog in the morning," said Ross. "Then we can get away before any of the family is up."

Oh, youth—youth—youth, with its rash promises! Worn out with misery the boys slept heavily. The first sound that either heard in the morning was Babe hammering upon their bedroom door. They crouched guiltily and looked into each other's eyes. "Let pretend we ain't here and he'll go away," breathed Abner.

But Babe was made of sterner stuff. He rattled the knob. He turned it. He put in a black face with a grin which divided it from ear to ear. "Cady say I mus' call dem fool boys to breakfus'," he announced. "I never named you-all dat. Cady, she say dat."

"Breakfast!" echoed Ross, in a daze.

"Yessuh, breakfus'," reasserted Babe, coming entirely into the room and look-ing curiously about him. "Ain't you-all done been to bed at all?" wrapping his arms about his shoulders and shaking with silent ecstasies of mirth. The boys threw themselves upon him and ejected him.

"Sent up a servant to call us to breakfast," snarled Abner. "If they'd only sent their old servant to the door in the first place, all this wouldn't 'a' happened. I'm just that way when I get thrown off the track. You know how it was when I tried to repeat those things to you—I had to go clear back to the beginning when I got interrupted."

"Does that mean that you're still hanging around here to begin over and make a call?" asked Ross, darkly. "I won't go down to breakfast if you are."

Abner brightened a little as he saw Ross becoming wordy in his rage. "I dare you to walk downstairs and say, 'We-just-dropped-in-to-call-on-Miss-Champe'!" he said.

"I—oh—I—darn it all! there goes the second bell. We may as well trot down."

"Don't leave me, Ross," pleaded the Jilton boy. "I can't stay here—and I can't go down."

The tone was hysterical. The boy with freckles took his companion by the arm without another word and marched him down the stairs. "We may get a chance yet to call on Champe all by herself out on the porch or in the arbor before she goes to school," he suggested, by way of putting some spine into the black-eyed boy.

An emphatic bell rang when they were half-way down the stairs. Clutching their hats, they slunk into the dining-room. Even Mr. Claiborne seemed to notice something unusual in their bearing as they settled into the chairs assigned to them, and asked them kindly if they had slept well.

It was plain that Aunt Missouri had been posting him as to her understanding of the intentions of these young men. The state of affairs gave an electric hilarity to the atmosphere. Babe travelled from the sideboard to the table, trembling like chocolate pudding. Cady insisted on bringing in the cakes herself, and grinned as she whisked her starched blue skirts in and out of the dining-room. A dimple even showed itself at the corners of pretty Alicia's prim little mouth. Champe giggled, till Ross heard Cady whisper:

"Now you got one dem snickerin' spells agin. You gwine bust yo' dress buttons off in the back ef you don't mind."

As the spirits of those about them mounted, the hearts of the two youths sank—if it was like this among the Claibornes, what would it be at school and in the world at large when their failure to connect intention with result became village talk? Ross bit fiercely upon an unoffending batter-cake, and resolved to make a call single-handed before he left the house.

They went out of the dining-room, their hats as ever pressed to their breasts. With no volition of their own, their uncertain young legs carried them to the porch. The Claiborne family and household followed like small boys after a circus procession. When the two turned, at bay, yet with nothing between them and liberty but a hypnotism of their own suggestion, they saw the black faces of the servants peering over the family shoulders.

Ross was the boy to have drawn courage from the desperation of their case, and made some decent if not glorious ending. But at the psychological moment there came around the corner of the house that most contemptible figure known to the Southern plantation, a shirt-boy—a creature who may be described, for the benefit of those not informed, as a pickaninny clad only in a long, coarse cotton shirt. While all eyes were fastened upon him this inglorious ambassador bolted forth his message:

"Yo' ma say"—his eyes were fixed upon Abner—"ef yo' don' come home, she gwine come after yo'—an' cut yo' into inch pieces wid a rawhide when she git yo'. Dat jest what Miss Hortense say."

As though such a book as *Hints and Helps* had never existed, Abner shot for the gate—he was but a hobbledehoy fascinated with the idea of playing gentleman. But in Ross there were the makings of a man. For a few half-hearted paces, under the first impulse of horror, he followed his deserting chief, the laughter of the family, the unrestrainable guffaws of the negroes, sounding in the rear. But when Champe's high, offensive giggle, topping all the others, insulted his ears, he stopped dead, wheeled, and ran to the porch faster than he had fled from it. White as paper, shaking with inexpressible rage, he caught and kissed the tittering girl, violently, noisily, before them all.

The negroes fled—they dared not trust their feelings; even Alicia sniggered unobtrusively; Grandfather Claiborne chuckled, and Aunt Missouri frankly collapsed into her rocking-chair, bubbling with mirth, crying out:

"Good for you, Ross! Seems you did know how to call on the girls, after all."

But Ross, paying no attention, walked swiftly toward the gate. He had served his novitiate. He would never be afraid again. With cheerful alacrity he dodged the stones flung after him with friendly, erratic aim by the girl upon whom, yesterday afternoon, he had come to make a social call.

HOW THE WIDOW WON THE DEACON
By William James Lampton (-1917)

[From Harper's Bazaar, April, 1911; copyright, 1911, by Harper & Brothers; republished by permission.]

OF course the Widow Stimson never tried to win Deacon Hawkins, nor any other man, for that matter. A widow doesn't have to try to win a man; she wins without trying. Still, the Widow Stimson sometimes wondered why the deacon was so blind as not to see how her fine farm adjoining his equally fine place on the outskirts of the town might not be brought under one management with mutual benefit to both parties at interest. Which one that management might become was a matter of future detail. The widow knew how to run a farm successfully, and a large farm is not much more difficult to run than one of half the size. She had also had one husband, and knew something more than running a farm successfully. Of all of which the deacon was perfectly well aware, and still he had not been moved by the merging spirit of the age to propose consolidation.

This interesting situation was up for discussion at the Wednesday afternoon meeting of the Sisters' Sewing Society.

"For my part," Sister Susan Spicer, wife of the Methodist minister, remarked as she took another tuck in a fourteen-year-old girl's skirt for a ten-year-old—"for my part, I can't see why Deacon Hawkins and Kate Stimson don't see the error of their ways and depart from them."

"I rather guess *she* has," smiled Sister Poteet, the grocer's better half, who had taken an afternoon off from the store in order to be present.

"Or is willing to," added Sister Maria Cartridge, a spinster still possessing faith, hope, and charity, notwithstanding she had been on the waiting list a long time.

"Really, now," exclaimed little Sister Green, the doctor's wife, "do you think it is the deacon who needs urging?"

"It looks that way to me," Sister Poteet did not hesitate to affirm.

"Well, I heard Sister Clark say that she had heard him call her 'Kitty' one night when they were eating ice-cream at the Mite Society," Sister Candish, the druggist's wife, added to the fund of reliable information on hand.

"'Kitty,' indeed!" protested Sister Spicer. "The idea of anybody calling Kate Stimson 'Kitty'! The deacon will talk that way to 'most any woman, but if she let him say it to her more than once, she must be getting mighty anxious, I think."

"Oh," Sister Candish hastened to explain, "Sister Clark didn't say she had heard him say it twice.'"

"Well, I don't think she heard him say it once," Sister Spicer asserted with confidence.

"I don't know about that," Sister Poteet argued. "From all I can see and hear I think Kate Stimson wouldn't object to 'most anything the deacon would say to her, knowing as she does that he ain't going to say anything he shouldn't say."

"And isn't saying what he should," added Sister Green, with a sly snicker, which went around the room softly.

"But as I was saying—" Sister Spicer began, when Sister Poteet, whose rocker, near the window, commanded a view of the front gate, interrupted with a warning, "'Sh-'sh."

"Why shouldn't I say what I wanted to when—" Sister Spicer began.

"There she comes now," explained Sister Poteet, "and as I live the deacon drove her here in his sleigh, and he's waiting while she comes in. I wonder what next," and Sister Poteet, in conjunction with the entire society, gasped and held their eager breaths, awaiting the entrance of the subject of conversation.

Sister Spicer went to the front door to let her in, and she was greeted with the greatest cordiality by everybody.

"We were just talking about you and wondering why you were so late coming," cried Sister Poteet. "Now take off your things and make up for lost time. There's a pair of pants over there to be cut down to fit that poor little Snithers boy."

The excitement and curiosity of the society were almost more than could be borne, but never a sister let on that she knew the deacon was at the gate waiting. Indeed, as far as the widow could discover, there was not the slightest indication that anybody had ever heard there was such a person as the deacon in existence.

"Oh," she chirruped, in the liveliest of humors, "you will have to excuse me for today. Deacon Hawkins overtook me on the way here, and here said I had simply got to go sleigh-riding with him. He's waiting out at the gate now."

"Is that so?" exclaimed the society unanimously, and rushed to the window to see if it were really true.

"Well, did you ever?" commented Sister Poteet, generally.

"Hardly ever," laughed the widow, good-naturedly, "and I don't want to lose the chance. You know Deacon Hawkins isn't asking somebody every day to go sleighing with him. I told him I'd go if he would bring me around here to let you know what had become of me, and so he did. Now, good-by, and I'll be sure to be present at the next meeting. I have to hurry because he'll get fidgety."

The widow ran away like a lively schoolgirl. All the sisters watched her get into the sleigh with the deacon, and resumed the previous discussion with greatly increased interest.

But little recked the widow and less recked the deacon. He had bought a new horse and he wanted the widow's opinion of it, for the Widow Stimson was a competent judge of fine horseflesh. If Deacon Hawkins had one insatiable ambition it was to own a horse which could fling its heels in the face of the best that Squire Hopkins drove. In his early manhood the deacon was no deacon by a great deal. But as the years gathered in behind him he put off most of the frivolities of youth and held now only to the one of driving a fast horse. No other man in the county drove anything faster except Squire Hopkins, and him the deacon had not been able to throw the dust over. The deacon would get good ones, but somehow never could he find one that the squire didn't get a better. The squire had also in the early days beaten the deacon in the race for a certain pretty girl he dreamed about. But the girl and the squire had lived happily ever after and the deacon, being a philosopher, might have forgotten the squire's superiority had it been manifested in this one regard only. But in horses, too—that graveled the deacon.

"How much did you give for him?" was the widow's first query, after they had reached a stretch of road that was good going and the deacon had let him out for a length or two.

"Well, what do you suppose? You're a judge."

"More than I would give, I'll bet a cookie."

"Not if you was as anxious as I am to show Hopkins that he can't drive by everything on the pike."

"I thought you loved a good horse because he was a good horse," said the widow, rather disapprovingly.

"I do, but I could love him a good deal harder if he would stay in front of Hopkins's best."

"Does he know you've got this one?"

"Yes, and he's been blowing round town that he is waiting to pick me up on the road some day and make my five hundred dollars look like a pewter quarter."

"So you gave five hundred dollars for him, did you?" laughed the widow.

"Is it too much?"

"Um-er," hesitated the widow, glancing along the graceful lines of the powerful trotter, "I suppose not if you can beat the squire."

"Right you are," crowed the deacon, "and I'll show him a thing or two in getting over the ground," he added with swelling pride.

"Well, I hope he won't be out looking for you today, with me in your sleigh," said the widow, almost apprehensively, "because, you know, deacon, I have always wanted you to beat Squire Hopkins."

The deacon looked at her sharply. There was a softness in her tones that appealed to him, even if she had not expressed such agreeable sentiments. Just what the deacon might have said or done after the impulse had been set going must remain unknown, for at the crucial moment a sound of militant bells, bells of defiance, jangled up behind them, disturbing their personal absorption, and they looked around simultaneously. Behind the bells was the squire in his sleigh drawn by his fastest stepper, and he was alone, as the deacon was not. The widow weighed one hundred and sixty pounds, net—which is weighting a horse in a race rather more than the law allows.

But the deacon never thought of that. Forgetting everything except his cherished ambition, he braced himself for the contest, took a twist hold on the lines, sent a sharp, quick call to his horse, and let him out for all that was in him. The squire followed suit and the deacon. The road was wide and the snow was worn down smooth. The track couldn't have been in better condition. The Hopkins colors were not five rods behind the Hawkins colors as they got away. For half a mile it was nip and tuck, the deacon encouraging his horse and the widow encouraging the deacon, and then the squire began creeping up. The deacon's horse was a good one, but he was not accustomed to hauling freight in a race. A half-mile of it was as much as he could stand, and he weakened under the strain.

Not handicapped, the squire's horse forged ahead, and as his nose pushed up to the dashboard of the deacon's sleigh, that good man groaned in agonized disappointment and bitterness of spirit. The widow was mad all over that Squire Hopkins should take such a mean advantage of his rival. Why didn't he wait till another time when the deacon was alone, as he was? If she had her way she never would, speak to Squire Hopkins again, nor to his wife, either. But her resentment was not helping the deacon's horse to win.

Slowly the squire pulled closer to the front; the deacon's horse, realizing what it meant to his master and to him, spurted bravely, but, struggle as gamely as he might, the odds were too many for him, and he dropped to the rear. The squire shouted in triumph as he drew past the deacon, and the dejected Hawkins shrivelled into a heap on the seat, with only his hands sufficiently alive to hold the lines. He had been beaten again, humiliated before a woman, and that, too, with the best horse that he could hope to put against the ever-conquering squire. Here sank his fondest hopes, here ended his ambition. From this on he would drive a mule or an automobile. The fruit of his desire had turned to ashes in his mouth.

But no. What of the widow? She realized, if the deacon did not, that she, not the squire's horse, had beaten the deacon's, and she was ready to make what atonement she could. As the squire passed ahead of the deacon she was stirred by a noble resolve. A deep bed of drifted snow lay close by the side of the road not far in front. It was soft and safe and she smiled as she looked at it as though waiting for her. Without a hint of her purpose, or a sign to disturb the deacon in his final throes, she rose as the sleigh ran near its edge, and with a spring which had many a time sent her lightly from the ground to the bare back of a horse in the meadow, she cleared the robes and lit plump in the drift. The deacon's horse knew before the deacon did that something had happened in his favor, and was quick to respond. With his first jump of relief the deacon suddenly revived, his hopes came fast again, his blood retingled, he gathered himself, and, cracking his lines, he shot forward, and three minutes later he had passed the squire as though he were hitched to the fence. For a quarter of a mile the squire made heroic efforts to recover his vanished prestige, but effort was useless, and finally concluding that he was practically left standing, he veered off from the main road down a farm lane to find some spot in which to hide the humiliation of his defeat. The deacon, still going at a clipping gait, had one eye over his shoulder as wary drivers always have on such occasions, and when he saw the squire was off the track he slowed down and jogged along with the apparent intention of continuing indefinitely. Presently an idea struck him, and he looked around for the widow. She was not where he had seen her last. Where was she? In the enthusiasm of victory he had forgotten her. He was so dejected at the moment she had leaped that he did not realize what she had done, and two minutes later he was so elated that, shame on him! he did not care. With her, all was lost; without her, all was won, and the deacon's greatest ambition was to win. But now, with victory perched on his horse-collar, success his at last, he thought of the widow, and he did care. He cared so much that he almost threw his horse off his feet by the abrupt turn he gave him, and back down the pike he flew as if a legion of squires were after him.

He did not know what injury she might have sustained; She might have been seriously hurt, if not actually killed. And why? Simply to make it possible for him to win. The deacon shivered as he thought of it, and urged his horse to greater speed. The squire, down the lane, saw him whizzing along and accepted it profanely as an exhibition for his especial benefit. The deacon now had forgotten the squire as he had only so shortly before forgotten the widow. Two hundred yards from the drift into which she had jumped there was a turn in the road, where some trees shut off the sight, and the deacon's anxiety increased momentarily until he reached this point. From here he could see ahead, and down there in the middle of the road stood the widow waving her shawl as a banner of triumph, though she could only guess at results. The deacon came on with a rush, and pulled up alongside of her in a condition of nervousness he didn't think possible to him.

"Hooray! hooray!" shouted the widow, tossing her shawl into the air. "You beat him. I know you did. Didn't you? I saw you pulling ahead at the turn yonder. Where is he and his old plug?"

"Oh, bother take him and his horse and the race and everything. Are you hurt?" gasped the deacon, jumping out, but mindful to keep the lines in his hand. "Are you hurt?" he repeated, anxiously, though she looked anything but a hurt woman.

"If I am," she chirped, cheerily, "I'm not hurt half as bad as I would have been if the squire had beat you, deacon. Now don't you worry about me. Let's hurry back to town so the squire won't get another chance, with no place for me to jump."

And the deacon? Well, well, with the lines in the crook of his elbow the deacon held out his arms to the widow and——. The sisters at the next meeting of the Sewing Society were unanimously of the opinion that any woman who would risk her life like that for a husband was mighty anxious.

GIDEON
By Wells Hastings (1878-)

[From *The Century Magazine*, April, 1914; copyright, 1914,
by The Century Co.; republished by the author's permission.]

A N' de next' frawg dat houn' pup seen, he pass him by wide."

The house, which had hung upon every word, roared with laughter, and shook with a storming volley of applause. Gideon bowed to right and to left, low, grinning, assured comedy obeisances; but as the laughter and applause grew he shook his head, and signaled quietly for the drop. He had answered many encores, and he was an instinctive artist. It was part of the fuel of his vanity that his audience had never yet had enough of him. Dramatic judgment, as well as dramatic sense of delivery, was native to him, qualities which the shrewd Felix Stuhk, his manager and exultant discoverer, recognized and wisely trusted in. Off stage Gideon was watched over like a child and a delicate investment, but once behind the footlights he was allowed to go his own triumphant gait.

It was small wonder that Stuhk deemed himself one of the cleverest managers in the business; that his narrow, blue-shaven face was continually chiseled in smiles of complacent self-congratulation. He was rapidly becoming rich, and there were bright prospects of even greater triumphs, with proportionately greater reward. He had made Gideon a national character, a headliner, a star of the first magnitude in the firmament of the vaudeville theater, and all in six short months. Or, at any rate, he had helped to make him all this; he had booked him well and given him his opportunity. To be sure, Gideon had done the rest; Stuhk was as ready as any one to do credit to Gideon's ability. Still, after all, he, Stuhk, was the discoverer, the theatrical Columbus who had had the courage and the vision.

A now-hallowed attack of tonsilitis had driven him to Florida, where presently Gideon had been employed to beguile his convalescence, and guide him over the intricate shallows of that long lagoon known as the Indian River in search of various fish. On days when fish had been reluctant Gideon had been lured into conversation, and gradually into narrative and the relation of what had appeared to Gideon as humorous and entertaining; and finally Felix, the vague idea growing big within him, had one day persuaded his boatman to dance upon the boards of a long pier where they had made fast for lunch. There, with all the sudden glory of crystallization, the vague idea took definite form and became the great inspiration of Stuhk's career.

Gideon had grown to be to vaudeville much what *Uncle Remus* is to literature: there was virtue in his very simplicity. His artistry itself was native and natural. He loved a good story, and he told it from his own sense of the gleeful morsel upon his tongue as no training could have made him. He always enjoyed his story and himself in the telling. Tales never lost their savor, no matter how often repeated; age was powerless to dim the humor of the thing, and as he had shouted and gurgled and laughed over the fun of things when all alone, or holding forth among the men and women and little children of his color, so he shouted and gurgled and broke from sonorous chuckles to musical, falsetto mirth when he fronted the sweeping tiers of faces across the intoxicating glare of the footlights. He had that rare power of transmitting something of his own enjoyments. When Gideon was on the stage, Stuhk used to enjoy peeping out at the intent, smiling faces of the audience, where men and women and children, hardened theater-goers and folk fresh from the country, sat with moving lips and faces lit with an eager interest and sympathy for the black man strutting in loose-footed vivacity before them.

"He's simply unique," he boasted to wondering local managers—"unique, and it took me to find him. There he was, a little black gold-mine, and all of 'em passed him by until I came. Some eye? What? I guess you'll admit you have to hand it some to your Uncle Felix. If that coon's health holds out, we'll have all the money there is in the mint."

That was Felix's real anxiety—"If his health holds out." Gideon's health was watched over as if he had been an ailing prince. His bubbling vivacity was the foundation upon which his charm and his success were built. Stuhk became a sort of vicarious neurotic, eternally searching for symptoms in his protege; Gideon's tongue, Gideon's liver, Gideon's heart were matters to him of an unfailing and anxious interest. And of late—of course it might be imagination —Gideon had shown a little physical falling off. He ate a bit less, he had begun to move in a restless way, and, worst of all, he laughed less frequently.

As a matter of fact, there was ground for Stuhk's apprehension. It was not all a matter of managerial imagination: Gideon was less himself. Physically there was nothing the matter with him; he could have passed his rigid insurance scrutiny as easily as he had done months before, when his life and health had been insured for a sum that made good copy for his press-agent. He was sound in every organ, but there was something lacking in general tone. Gideon felt it himself, and was certain that a "misery," that embracing indisposition of his race, was creeping upon him. He had been fed well, too well; he was growing rich, too rich; he had all the praise, all the flattery that his enormous appetite for approval desired, and too much of it. White men sought him out and made much of him; white women talked to him about his career; and wherever he went, women of color—black girls, brown girls, yellow girls—wrote him of their admiration, whispered, when he would listen, of their passion and hero-worship. "City niggers" bowed down before him; the high gallery was always packed with them. Musk-scented notes scrawled upon barbaric, "high-toned" stationery poured in upon him. Even a few white women, to his horror and embarrassment, had written him of love, letters which he straightway destroyed. His sense of his position was strong in him; he was proud of it. There might be "folks outer their haids," but he had the sense to remember. For months he had lived in a heaven of gratified vanity, but at last his appetite had begun to falter. He was sated; his soul longed to wipe a spiritual mouth on the back of a spiritual hand, and have done. His face, now that the curtain was down and he was leaving the stage, was doleful, almost sullen.

Stuhk met him anxiously in the wings, and walked with him to his dressing-room. He felt suddenly very weary of Stuhk.

"Nothing the matter, Gideon, is there? Not feeling sick or anything?"

"No, Misteh Stuhk; no, seh. Jes don' feel extry pert, that's all."

"But what is it—anything bothering you?"

Gideon sat gloomily before his mirror.

"Misteh Stuhk," he said at last, "I been steddyin' it oveh, and I about come to the delusion that I needs a good po'k-chop. Seems foolish, I know, but it do' seem as if a good po'k-chop, fried jes right, would he'p consid'able to disumpate this misery feelin' that's crawlin' and creepin' round my sperit."

Stuhk laughed.

"Pork-chop, eh? Is that the best you can think of? I know what you mean, though. I've thought for some time that you were getting a little overtrained. What you need is—let me see—yes, a nice bottle of wine. That's the ticket; it will ease things up and won't do you any harm. I'll go, with you. Ever had any champagne, Gideon?"

Gideon struggled for politeness.

"Yes, seh, I's had champagne, and it's a nice kind of lickeh sho enough; but, Misteh Stuhk, seh, I don' want any of them high-tone drinks to-night, an' ef yo' don' mind, I'd rather amble off 'lone, or mebbe eat that po'k-chop with some otheh cullud man, ef I kin fin' one that ain' one of them no-'count Carolina niggers. Do you s'pose yo' could let me have a little money to-night, Misteh Stuhk?"

Stuhk thought rapidly. Gideon had certainly worked hard, and he was not dissipated. If he wanted to roam the town by himself, there was no harm in it. The sullenness still showed in the black face; Heaven knew what he might do if he suddenly began to balk. Stuhk thought it wise to consent gracefully.

"Good!" he said. "Fly to it. How much do you want? A hundred?"

"How much is coming to me?"

"About a thousand, Gideon."

"Well, I'd moughty like five hun'red of it, ef that's 'greeable to yo'."

Felix whistled.

"Five hundred? Pork-chops must be coming high. You don't want to carry all that money around, do you?"

Gideon did not answer; he looked very gloomy.

Stuhk hastened to cheer him.

"Of course you can have anything you want. Wait a minute, and I will get it for you.

"I'll bet that coon's going to buy himself a ring or something," he reflected as he went in search of the local manager and Gideon's money.

But Stuhk was wrong. Gideon had no intention of buying himself a ring. For the matter of that, he had several that were amply satisfactory. They had size and sparkle and luster, all the diamond brilliance that rings need to have; and for none of them had he paid much over five dollars. He was amply supplied with jewelry in which he felt perfect satisfaction. His present want was positive, if nebulous; he desired a fortune in his pocket, bulky, tangible evidence of his miraculous success. Ever since Stuhk had found him, life had had an unreal quality for him. His Monte Cristo wealth was too much like a fabulous, dream-found treasure, money that could not be spent without danger of awakening. And he had dropped into the habit of storing it about him, so that in any pocket into which he plunged his hand he might find a roll of crisp evidence of reality. He liked his bills to be of all denominations, and some so large as exquisitely to stagger imagination, others charming by their number and crispness—the dignified, orange paper of a man of assured position and wealth-crackling greenbacks the design of which tinged the whole with actuality. He was specially partial to engravings of President Lincoln, the particular savior and patron of his race. This five hundred dollars he was adding to an unreckoned sum of about two thousand, merely as extra fortification against a growing sense of gloom. He wished to brace his flagging spirits with the gay wine of possession, and he was glad, when the money came, that it was in an elastic-bound roll, so bulky that it was pleasantly uncomfortable in his pocket as he left his manager.

As he turned into the brilliantly lighted street from the somber alleyway of the stage entrance, he paused for a moment to glance at his own name, in three-foot letters of red, before the doors of the theater. He could read, and the large block type always pleased him. "THIS WEEK: GIDEON." That was all. None of the fulsome praise, the superlative, necessary definition given to lesser performers. He had been, he remembered, "GIDEON, America's Foremost Native Comedian," a title that was at once boast and challenge. That necessity was now past, for he was a national character; any explanatory qualification would have been an insult to the public intelligence. To the world he was just "Gideon"; that was enough. It gave him pleasure, as he sauntered along, to see the announcement repeated on window cards and hoardings.

Presently he came to a window before which he paused in delighted wonder. It was not a large window; to the casual eye of the passer-by there was little to draw attention. By day it lighted the fractional floor space of a little stationer, who supplemented a slim business by a sub-agency for railroad and steamship lines; but to-night this window seemed the framework of a marvel of coincidence. On the broad, dusty sill inside were propped two cards: the one on the left was his own red-lettered announcement for the week; the one at the right—oh, world of wonders!—was a photogravure of that exact stretch of the inner coast of Florida which Gideon knew best, which was home.

There it was, the Indian River, rippling idly in full sunlight, palmettos leaning over the water, palmettos standing as irregular sentries along the low, reeflike island which stretched away out of the picture. There was the gigantic, lonely pine he knew well, and, yes—he could just make it out—there was his own ramshackle little pier, which stretched in undulating fashion, like a long-legged, wading caterpillar, from the abrupt shore-line of eroded coquina into deep water.

He thought at first that this picture of his home was some new and delicate device put forth by his press-agent. His name on one side of a window, his birthplace upon the other—what could be more tastefully appropriate? Therefore, as he spelled out the reading-matter beneath the photogravure, he was sharply disappointed. It read:

Spend this winter in balmy Florida.
Come to the Land of Perpetual Sunshine.
Golf, tennis, driving, shooting, boating, fishing, all of the best.

There was more, but he had no heart for it; he was disappointed and puzzled. This picture had, after all, nothing to do with him. It was a chance, and yet, what a strange chance! It troubled and upset him. His black, round-featured face took on deep wrinkles of perplexity. The "misery" which had hung darkly on his horizon for weeks engulfed him without warning. But in the very bitterness of his melancholy he knew at last his disease. It was not champagne or recreation that he needed, not even a "po'k-chop," although his desire for it had been a symptom, a groping for a too homeopathic remedy: he was homesick.

Easy, childish tears came into his eyes, and ran over his shining cheeks. He shivered forlornly with a sudden sense of cold, and absently clutched at the lapels of his gorgeous, fur-lined ulster.

Then in abrupt reaction he laughed aloud, so that the shrill, musical falsetto startled the passers-by, and in another moment a little semicircle of the curious watched spellbound as a black man, exquisitely appareled, danced in wild, loose grace before the dull background of a somewhat grimy and apparently vacant window. A newsboy recognized him.

He heard his name being passed from mouth to mouth, and came partly to his senses. He stopped dancing, and grinned at them.

"Say, you are Gideon, ain't you?" his discoverer demanded, with a sort of reverent audacity.

"Yaas, *seh*," said Gideon; "that's me. Yo' shu got it right." He broke into a joyous peal of laughter—the laughter that had made him famous, and bowed deeply before him. "Gideon—posi-*tive*-ly his las' puffawmunce." Turning, he dashed for a passing trolley, and, still laughing, swung aboard.

He was naturally honest. In a land of easy morality his friends had accounted him something of a paragon; nor had Stuhk ever had anything but praise for him. But now he crushed aside the ethics of his intent without a single troubled thought. Running away has always been inherent in the negro. He gave one regretful thought to the gorgeous wardrobe he was leaving behind him; but he dared not return for it. Stuhk might have taken it into his head to go back to their rooms. He must content himself with the reflection that he was at that moment wearing his best.

The trolley seemed too slow for him, and, as always happened nowadays, he was recognized; he heard his name whispered, and was aware of the admiring glances of the curious. Even popularity had its drawbacks. He got down in front of a big hotel and chose a taxicab from the waiting rank, exhorting the driver to make his best speed to the station. Leaning back in the soft depths of the cab, he savored his independence, cheered already by the swaying, lurching speed. At the station he tipped the driver in lordly fashion, very much pleased with himself and anxious to give pleasure. Only the sternest prudence and an unconquerable awe of uniform had kept him from tossing bills to the various traffic policemen who had seemed to smile upon his hurry.

No through train left for hours; but after the first disappointment of momentary check, he decided that he was more pleased than otherwise. It would save embarrassment. He was going South, where his color would be more considered than his reputation, and on the little local he chose there was a "Jim Crow" car—one, that is, specially set aside for those of his race. That it proved crowded and full of smoke did not trouble him at all, nor did the admiring pleasantries which the splendor of his apparel immediately called forth. No one knew him; indeed, he was naturally enough mistaken for a prosperous gambler, a not unflattering supposition. In the yard, after the train pulled out, he saw his private car under a glaring arc light, and grinned to see it left behind.

He spent the night pleasantly in a noisy game of high-low-jack, and the next morning slept more soundly than he had slept for weeks, hunched upon a wooden bench in the boxlike station of a North Carolina junction. The express would have brought him to Jacksonville in twenty-four hours; the journey, as he took it, boarding any local that happened to be going south, and leaving it for meals or sometimes for sleep or often as the whim possessed him, filled five happy days. There he took a night train, and dozed from Jacksonville until a little north of New Smyrna.

He awoke to find it broad daylight, and the car half empty. The train was on a siding, with news of a freight wreck ahead. Gideon stretched himself, and looked out of the window, and emotion seized him. For all his journey the South had seemed to welcome him, but here at last was the country he knew. He went out upon the platform and threw back his head, sniffing the soft breeze, heavy with the mysterious thrill of unplowed acres, the wondrous existence of primordial jungle, where life has rioted unceasingly above unceasing decay. It was dry with the fine dust of waste places, and wet with the warm mists of slumbering swamps; it seemed to Gideon to tremble with the songs of birds, the dry murmur of palm leaves, and the almost inaudible whisper of the gray moss that festooned the live-oaks.

"Um-m-m," he murmured, apostrophizing it, "yo' 's the right kind o' breeze, yo' is. Yo'-all's healthy." Still sniffing, he climbed down to the dusty road-bed.

The negroes who had ridden with him were sprawled about him on the ground; one of them lay sleeping, face up, in the sunlight. The train had evidently been there for some time, and there were no signs of an immediate departure. He bought some oranges of a little, bowlegged black boy, and sat down on a log to eat them and to give up his mind to enjoyment. The sun was hot upon him, and his thoughts were vague and drowsy. He was glad that he was alive, glad to be back once more among familiar scenes. Down the length of the train he saw white passengers from the Pullmans restlessly pacing up and down, getting into their cars and out of them, consulting watches, attaching themselves with gesticulatory expostulation to various officials; but their impatience found no echo in his thought. What was the hurry? There was plenty of time. It was sufficient to have come to his own land; the actual walls of home could wait. The delay was pleasant, with its opportunity for drowsy sunning, its relief from the grimy monotony of travel. He glanced at the orange-colored "Jim Crow" with distaste, and inspiration, dawning slowly upon him, swept all other thought before it in its great and growing glory.

A brakeman passed, and Gideon leaped to his feet and pursued him.

"Misteh, how long yo'-all reckon this train goin' to be?"

"About an hour."

The question had been a mere matter of form. Gideon had made up his mind, and if he had been told that they started in five minutes he would not have changed it. He climbed back into the car for his coat and his hat, and then almost furtively stole down the steps again and slipped quietly into the palmetto scrub.

"'Most made the mistake of ma life," he chuckled, "stickin' to that ol' train fo-heveh. 'T isn't the right way at, all foh Gideon to come home."

The river was not far away. He could catch the dancing blue of it from time to time in ragged vista, and for this beacon he steered directly. His coat was heavy on his arm, his thin patent-leather ties pinched and burned and demanded detours around swampy places, but he was happy.

As he went along, his plan perfected itself. He would get into loose shoes again, old ones, if money could buy them, and old clothes, too. The bull-briers snatching at his tailored splendor suggested that.

He laughed when the Florida partridge, a small quail, whirred up from under his feet; he paused to exchange affectionate mockery with red squirrels; and once, even when he was brought up suddenly to a familiar and ominous, dry reverberation, the small, crisp sound of the rolling drums of death, he did not look about him for some instrument of destruction, as at any other time he would have done, but instead peered cautiously over the log before him, and spoke in tolerant admonition:

"Now, Misteh Rattlesnake, yo' jes min' yo' own business. Nobody's goin' step on yo', ner go triflin' roun' yo' in no way whatsomeveh. Yo' jes lay there in the sun an' git 's fat 's yo' please. Don' yo' tu'n yo' weeked li'l' eyes on Gideon. He's jes goin' 'long home, an' ain' lookin' foh no muss."

He came presently to the water, and, as luck would have it, to a little group of negro cabins, where he was able to buy old clothes and, after much dickering, a long and somewhat leaky rowboat rigged out with a tattered leg-of-mutton sail. This he provisioned with a jug of water, a starch box full of white corn-meal, and a wide strip of lean razorback bacon.

As he pushed out from shore and set his sail to the small breeze that blew down from the north, an absolute contentment possessed him. The idle waters of the lagoon, lying without tide or current in eternal indolence, rippled and sparkled in breeze and sunlight with a merry surface activity, and seemed to lap the leaky little boat more swiftly on its way. Mosquito Inlet opened broadly before him, and skirting the end of Merritt's Island he came at last into that longest lagoon, with which he was most familiar, the Indian River. Here the wind died down to a mere breath, which barely kept his boat in motion; but he made no attempt to row. As long as he moved at all, he was satisfied. He was living the fulfilment of his dreams in exile, lounging in the stern in the ancient clothes he had purchased, his feet stretched comfortably before him in their broken shoes, one foot upon a thwart, the other hanging overside so laxly that occasional ripples lapped the run-over heel. From time to time he scanned shore and river for familiar points of interest—some remembered snag that showed the tip of one gnarled branch. Or he marked a newly fallen palmetto, already rotting in the water, which must be added to that map of vast detail that he carried in his head. But for the most part his broad black face was turned up to the blue brilliance above him in unblinking contemplation; his keen eyes, brilliant despite their sun-muddied whites, reveled in the heights above him, swinging from horizon to horizon in the wake of an orderly file of little bluebill ducks, winging their way across the river, or brightening with interest at the rarer sight of a pair of mallards or redheads, lifting with the soaring circles of the great bald-headed eagle, or following the scattered squadron of heron—white heron, blue heron, young and old, trailing, sunlit, brilliant patches, clear even against the bright white and blue of the sky above them.

Often he laughed aloud, sending a great shout of mirth across the water in fresh relish of those comedies best known and best enjoyed. It was as excruciatingly funny as it had ever been, when his boat nosed its way into a great flock of ducks idling upon the water, to see the mad paddling haste of those nearest him, the reproachful turn of their heads, or, if he came too near, their spattering run out of water, feet and wings pumping together as they rose from the surface, looking for all the world like fat little women, scurrying with clutched skirts across city streets. The pelicans, too, delighted him as they perched with pedantic solemnity upon wharf-piles, or sailed in hunched and huddled gravity twenty feet above the river's surface in swift, dignified flight, which always ended suddenly in an abrupt, up-ended plunge that threw dignity to the winds in its greedy haste, and dropped them crashing into the water.

When darkness came suddenly at last, he made in toward shore, mooring to the warm-fretted end of a fallen and forgotten landing. A straggling orange-grove was here, broken lines of vanquished cultivation, struggling little trees swathed and choked in the festooning gray moss, still showing here and there the valiant golden gleam of fruit. Gideon had seen many such places, had seen settlers come and clear themselves a space in the jungle, plant their groves, and live for a while in lazy independence; and then for some reason or other they would go, and before they had scarcely turned their backs, the jungle had crept in again, patiently restoring its ancient sovereignty. The place was eery with the ghost of dead effort; but it pleased him.

He made a fire and cooked supper, eating enormously and with relish. His conscience did not trouble him at all. Stuhk and his own career seemed already distant; they took small place in his thoughts, and served merely as a background for his present absolute content. He picked some oranges, and ate them in meditative enjoyment. For a while he nodded, half asleep, beside his fire, watching the darkened river, where the mullet, shimmering with phosphorescence, still leaped starkly above the surface, and fell in spattering brilliance. Midnight found him sprawled asleep beside his fire.

Once he awoke. The moon had risen, and a little breeze waved the hanging moss, and whispered in the glossy foliage of orange and palmetto with a sound like falling rain. Gideon sat up and peered about him, rolling his eyes hither and thither at the menacing leap and dance of the jet shadows. His heart was beating thickly, his muscles twitched, and the awful terrors of night pulsed and shuddered over him. Nameless specters peered at him from every shadow, ingenerate familiars of his wild, forgotten blood. He groaned aloud in a delicious terror; and presently, still twitching and shivering, fell asleep again. It was as if something magical had happened; his fear remembered the fear of centuries, and yet with the warm daylight was absolutely forgotten.

He got up a little after sunrise, and went down to the river to bathe, diving deep with a joyful sense of freeing himself from the last alien dust of travel. Once ashore again, however, he began to prepare his breakfast with some haste. For the first time in his journey he was feeling a sense of loneliness and a longing for his kind. He was still happy, but his laughter began to seem strange to him in the solitude. He tried the defiant experiment of laughing for the effect of it, an experiment which brought him to his feet in startled terror; for his laughter was echoed. As he stood peering about him, the sound came again, not laughter this time, but a suppressed giggle. It was human beyond a doubt. Gideon's face shone with relief and sympathetic amusement; he listened for a moment, and then strode surely forward toward a clump of low palms. There he paused, every sense alert. His ear caught a soft rustle, a little gasp of fear; the sound of a foot moved cautiously.

"Missy," he said tentatively, "I reckon yo'-all's come jes 'bout 'n time foh breakfus. Yo' betteh have some. Ef yo' ain' too white to sit down with a black man."

The leaves parted, and a smiling face as black as Gideon's own regarded him in shy amusement.

"Who is yo', man?"

"I mought be king of Kongo," he laughed, "but I ain't. Yo' see befo' yo' jes Gideon—at yo'r 'steemed sehvice." He bowed elaborately in the mock humility of assured importance, watching her face in pleasant anticipation.

But neither awe nor rapture dawned there. She repeated the name, inclining her head coquettishly; but it evidently meant nothing to her. She was merely trying its sound. "Gideon, Gideon. I don' call to min' any sech name ez that. Yo'-all's f'om up No'th likely." He was beyond the reaches of fame.

"No," said Gideon, hardly knowing whether he was glad or sorry—"no, I live south of heah. What-all's yo' name?"

The girl giggled deliciously.

"Man," she said, "I shu got the mos' reediculoustest name you eveh did heah. They call me Vashti—yo' bacon's bu'nin'." She stepped out, and ran past him to snatch his skillet deftly from the fire.

"Vashti"—a strange and delightful name. Gideon followed her slowly. Her romantic coming and her romantic name pleased him; and, too, he thought her beautiful. She was scarcely more than a girl, slim and strong and almost of his own height. She was barefooted, but her blue-checked gingham was clean and belted smartly about a small waist. He remembered only one woman who ran as lithely as she did, one of the numerous "diving beauties" of the vaudeville stage.

She cooked their breakfast, but he served her with an elaborate gallantry, putting forward all his new and foreign graces, garnishing his speech with imposing polysyllables, casting about their picnic breakfast a radiant aura of grandeur borrowed from the recent days of his fame. And he saw that he pleased her, and with her open admiration essayed still greater flights of polished manner.

He made vague plans for delaying his journey as they sat smoking in pleasant conversational ease; and when an interruption came it vexed him.

"Vashty! Vashty!" a woman's voice sounded thin and far away. "Vashty-y! Yo' heah me, chile?"

Vashti rose to her feet with a sigh.

"That's my ma," she said regretfully.

"What do yo' care?" asked Gideon. "Let her yell awhile."

The girl shook her head.

"Ma's a moughty pow'ful 'oman, and she done got a club 'bout the size o' my wrist." She moved off a step or so, and glanced back at him.

Gideon leaped to his feet.

"When yo' comin' back? Yo'—yo' ain' goin' without——" He held out his arms to her, but she only giggled and began to walk slowly away. With a bound he was after her, one hand catching her lightly by the shoulder. He felt suddenly that he must not lose sight of her.

"Let me go! Tu'n me loose, yo'!" The girl was still laughing, but evidently troubled. She wrenched herself away with an effort, only to be caught again a moment later. She screamed and struck at him as he kissed her; for now she was really in terror.

The blow caught Gideon squarely in the mouth, and with such force that he staggered back, astonished, while the girl took wildly to her heels. He stood for a moment irresolute, for something was happening to him. For months he had evaded love with a gentle embarrassment; now, with the savage crash of that blow, he knew unreasoningly that he had found his woman.

He leaped after her again, running as he had not run in years, in savage, determined pursuit, tearing through brier and scrub, tripping, falling, rising, never losing sight of the blue-clad figure before him until at last she tripped and fell, and he stood panting above her.

He took a great breath or so, and leaned over and picked her up in his arms, where she screamed and struck and scratched at him. He laughed, for he felt no longer sensible to pain, and, still chuckling, picked his way carefully back to the shore, wading deep into the water to unmoor his boat. Then with a swift movement he dropped the girl into the bow, pushed free, and clambered actively aboard.

The light, early morning breeze had freshened, and he made out well toward the middle of the river, never even glancing around at the sound of the hallooing he now heard from shore. His exertions had quickened his breathing, but he felt strong and joyful. Vashti lay a huddle of blue in the bow, crouched in fear and desolation, shaken and torn with sobbing; but he made no effort to comfort her. He was untroubled by any sense of wrong; he was simply and unreasoningly satisfied with what he had done. Despite all his gentle, easygoing, laughter-loving existence, he found nothing incongruous or unnatural in this sudden act of violence. He was aglow with happiness; he was taking home a wife. The blind tumult of capture had passed; a great tenderness possessed him.

The leaky little boat was plunging and dancing in swift ecstasy of movement; all about them the little waves ran glittering in the sunlight, plashing and slapping against the boat's low side, tossing tiny crests to the following wind, showing rifts of white here and there, blowing handfuls of foam and spray. Gideon went softly about the business of shortening his small sail, and came quietly back to his steering-seat again. Soon he would have to be making for what lea the western shore offered; but he was holding to the middle of the river as long as he could, because with every mile the shores were growing more familiar, calling to him to make what speed he could. Vashti's sobbing had grown small and ceased; he wondered if she had fallen asleep.

Presently, however, he saw her face raised—a face still shining with tears. She saw that he was watching her, and crouched low again. A dash of spray spattered over her, and she looked up frightened, glancing fearfully overside; then once more her eyes came back to him, and this time she got up, still small and crouching, and made her way slowly and painfully down the length of the boat, until at last Gideon moved aside for her, and she sank in the bottom beside him, hiding her eyes in her gingham sleeve.

Gideon stretched out a broad hand and touched her head lightly; and with a tiny gasp her fingers stole up to his.

"Honey," said Gideon—"Honey, yo' ain' mad, is yo'?"

She shook her head, not looking at him.

"Yo' ain' grievin' foh yo' ma?"

Again she shook her head.

"Because," said Gideon, smiling down at her, "I ain' got no beeg club like she has."

A soft and smothered giggle answered him, and this time Vashti looked up and laid her head against him with a small sigh of contentment.

Gideon felt very tender, very important, at peace with himself and all the world. He rounded a jutting point, and stretched out a black hand, pointing.

THE END

The Codes Of Hammurabi And Moses
W. W. Davies

QTY

The discovery of the Hammurabi Code is one of the greatest achievements of archaeology, and is of paramount interest, not only to the student of the Bible, but also to all those interested in ancient history...

Religion   **ISBN:** *1-59462-338-4*   **Pages:132**
MSRP $12.95

The Theory of Moral Sentiments
Adam Smith

QTY

This work from 1749. contains original theories of conscience amd moral judgment and it is the foundation for systemof morals.

Philosophy **ISBN:** *1-59462-777-0*   **Pages:536**
MSRP $19.95

Jessica's First Prayer
Hesba Stretton

QTY

In a screened and secluded corner of one of the many railway-bridges which span the streets of London there could be seen a few years ago, from five o'clock every morning until half past eight, a tidily set-out coffee-stall, consisting of a trestle and board, upon which stood two large tin cans, with a small fire of charcoal burning under each so as to keep the coffee boiling during the early hours of the morning when the work-people were thronging into the city on their way to their daily toil...

Pages:84

Childrens   **ISBN:** *1-59462-373-2*   *MSRP $9.95*

My Life and Work
Henry Ford

QTY

Henry Ford revolutionized the world with his implementation of mass production for the Model T automobile. Gain valuable business insight into his life and work with his own auto-biography... "We have only started on our development of our country we have not as yet, with all our talk of wonderful progress, done more than scratch the surface. The progress has been wonderful enough but..."

Pages:300

Biographies/   **ISBN:** *1-59462-198-5*   *MSRP $21.95*

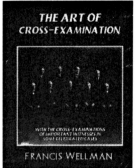

The Art of Cross-Examination
Francis Wellman

QTY

I presume it is the experience of every author, after his first book is published upon an important subject, to be almost overwhelmed with a wealth of ideas and illustrations which could readily have been included in his book, and which to his own mind, at least, seem to make a second edition inevitable. Such certainly was the case with me; and when the first edition had reached its sixth impression in five months, I rejoiced to learn that it seemed to my publishers that the book had met with a sufficiently favorable reception to justify a second and considerably enlarged edition. ..

Reference   ISBN: *1-59462-647-2*

Pages:412

MSRP *$19.95*

On the Duty of Civil Disobedience
Henry David Thoreau

QTY

Thoreau wrote his famous essay, On the Duty of Civil Disobedience, as a protest against an unjust but popular war and the immoral but popular institution of slave-owning. He did more than write—he declined to pay his taxes, and was hauled off to gaol in consequence. Who can say how much this refusal of his hastened the end of the war and of slavery ?

Law   ISBN: *1-59462-747-9*

Pages:48

MSRP *$7.45*

Dream Psychology Psychoanalysis for Beginners
Sigmund Freud

QTY

Sigmund Freud, born Sigismund Schlomo Freud (May 6, 1856 - September 23, 1939), was a Jewish-Austrian neurologist and psychiatrist who co-founded the psychoanalytic school of psychology. Freud is best known for his theories of the unconscious mind, especially involving the mechanism of repression; his redefinition of sexual desire as mobile and directed towards a wide variety of objects; and his therapeutic techniques, especially his understanding of transference in the therapeutic relationship and the presumed value of dreams as sources of insight into unconscious desires.

Psychology   ISBN: *1-59462-905-6*

Pages:196

MSRP *$15.45*

The Miracle of Right Thought
Orison Swett Marden

QTY

Believe with all of your heart that you will do what you were made to do. When the mind has once formed the habit of holding cheerful, happy, prosperous pictures, it will not be easy to form the opposite habit. It does not matter how improbable or how far away this realization may see, or how dark the prospects may be, if we visualize them as best we can, as vividly as possible, hold tenaciously to them and vigorously struggle to attain them, they will gradually become actualized, realized in the life. But a desire, a longing without endeavor, a yearning abandoned or held indifferently will vanish without realization.

Pages:360

Self Help   ISBN: *1-59462-644-8*

MSRP *$25.45*

QTY

The Rosicrucian Cosmo-Conception Mystic Christianity *by Max Heindel*   ISBN: *1-59462-188-8*   **$38.95**
The Rosicrucian Cosmo-conception is not dogmatic, neither does it appeal to any other authority than the reason of the student. It is: not controversial, but is: sent forth in the, hope that it may help to clear..   New Age/Religion Pages 646

Abandonment To Divine Providence *by Jean-Pierre de Caussade*   ISBN: *1-59462-228-0*   **$25.95**
"The Rev. Jean Pierre de Caussade was one of the most remarkable spiritual writers of the Society of Jesus in France in the 18th Century. His death took place at Toulouse in 1751. His works have gone through many editions and have been republished...   Inspirational/Religion Pages 400

Mental Chemistry *by Charles Haanel*   ISBN: *1-59462-192-6*   **$23.95**
Mental Chemistry allows the change of material conditions by combining and appropriately utilizing the power of the mind. Much like applied chemistry creates something new and unique out of careful combinations of chemicals the mastery of mental chemistry...   New Age Pages 354

The Letters of Robert Browning and Elizabeth Barret Barrett 1845-1846 vol II   ISBN: *1-59462-193-4*   **$35.95**
by Robert Browning and Elizabeth Barrett   Biographies Pages 596

Gleanings In Genesis (volume I) *by Arthur W. Pink*   ISBN: *1-59462-130-6*   **$27.45**
Appropriately has Genesis been termed "the seed plot of the Bible" for in it we have, in germ form, almost all of the great doctrines which are afterwards fully developed in the books of Scripture which follow...   Religion/Inspirational Pages 420

The Master Key *by L. W. de Laurence*   ISBN: *1-59462-001-6*   **$30.95**
In no branch of human knowledge has there been a more lively increase of the spirit of research during the past few years than in the study of Psychology, Concentration and Mental Discipline. The requests for authentic lessons in Thought Control, Mental Discipline and...   New Age/Business Pages 422

The Lesser Key Of Solomon Goetia *by L. W. de Laurence*   ISBN: *1-59462-092-X*   **$9.95**
This translation of the first book of the "Lernegton" which is now for the first time made accessible to students of Talismanic Magic was done, after careful collation and edition, from numerous Ancient Manuscripts in Hebrew, Latin, and French...   New Age/Occult Pages 92

Rubaiyat Of Omar Khayyam *by Edward Fitzgerald*   ISBN:*1-59462-332-5*   **$13.95**
Edward Fitzgerald, whom the world has already learned, in spite of his own efforts to remain within the shadow of anonymity, to look upon as one of the rarest poets of the century, was born at Bredfield, in Suffolk, on the 31st of March, 1809. He was the third son of John Purcell...   Music Pages 172

Ancient Law *by Henry Maine*   ISBN: *1-59462-128-4*   **$29.95**
The chief object of the following pages is to indicate some of the earliest ideas of mankind, as they are reflected in Ancient Law, and to point out the relation of those ideas to modern thought.   Religion/History Pages 452

Far-Away Stories *by William J. Locke*   ISBN: *1-59462-129-2*   **$19.45**
"Good wine needs no bush, but a collection of mixed vintages does. And this book is just such a collection. Some of the stories I do not want to remain buried for ever in the museum files of dead magazine-numbers an author's not unpardonable vanity..."   Fiction Pages 272

Life of David Crockett *by David Crockett*   ISBN: *1-59462-250-7*   **$27.45**
"Colonel David Crockett was one of the most remarkable men of the times in which he lived. Born in humble life, but gifted with a strong will, an indomitable courage, and unremitting perseverance...   Biographies/New Age Pages 424

Lip-Reading *by Edward Nitchie*   ISBN: *1-59462-206-X*   **$25.95**
Edward B. Nitchie, founder of the New York School for the Hard of Hearing, now the Nitchie School of Lip-Reading, Inc, wrote "LIP-READING Principles and Practice". The development and perfecting of this meritorious work on lip-reading was an undertaking...   How-to Pages 400

A Handbook of Suggestive Therapeutics, Applied Hypnotism, Psychic Science   ISBN: *1-59462-214-0*   **$24.95**
by Henry Munro   Health/New Age/Health/Self-help Pages 376

A Doll's House: and Two Other Plays *by Henrik Ibsen*   ISBN: *1-59462-112-8*   **$19.95**
Henrik Ibsen created this classic when in revolutionary 1848 Rome. Introducing some striking concepts in playwriting for the realist genre, this play has been studied the world over.   Fiction/Classics/Plays 308

The Light of Asia *by sir Edwin Arnold*   ISBN: *1-59462-204-3*   **$13.95**
In this poetic masterpiece, Edwin Arnold describes the life and teachings of Buddha. The man who was to become known as Buddha to the world was born as Prince Gautama of India but he rejected the worldly riches and abandoned the reigns of power when...   Religion/History/Biographies Pages 170

The Complete Works of Guy de Maupassant *by Guy de Maupassant*   ISBN: *1-59462-157-8*   **$16.95**
"For days and days, nights and nights, I had dreamed of that first kiss which was to consecrate our engagement, and I knew not on what spot I should put my lips..."   Fiction/Classics Pages 240

The Art of Cross-Examination *by Francis L. Wellman*   ISBN: *1-59462-309-0*   **$26.95**
Written by a renowned trial lawyer, Wellman imparts his experience and uses case studies to explain how to use psychology to extract desired information through questioning.   How-to/Science/Reference Pages 408

Answered or Unanswered? *by Louisa Vaughan*   ISBN: *1-59462-248-5*   **$10.95**
Miracles of Faith in China   Religion Pages 112

The Edinburgh Lectures on Mental Science (1909) *by Thomas*   ISBN: *1-59462-008-3*   **$11.95**
This book contains the substance of a course of lectures recently given by the writer in the Queen Street Hall, Edinburgh. Its purpose is to indicate the Natural Principles governing the relation between Mental Action and Material Conditions...   New Age/Psychology Pages 148

Ayesha *by H. Rider Haggard*   ISBN: *1-59462-301-5*   **$24.95**
Verily and indeed it is the unexpected that happens! Probably if there was one person upon the earth from whom the Editor of this, and of a certain previous history, did not expect to hear again...   Classics Pages 380

Ayala's Angel *by Anthony Trollope*   ISBN: *1-59462-352-X*   **$29.95**
The two girls were both pretty, but Lucy who was twenty-one who supposed to be simple and comparatively unattractive, whereas Ayala was credited, as her Bombwhat romantic name might show, with poetic charm and a taste for romance. Ayala when her father died was nineteen...   Fiction Pages 484

The American Commonwealth *by James Bryce*   ISBN: *1-59462-286-8*   **$34.45**
An interpretation of American democratic political theory. It examines political mechanics and society from the perspective of Scotsman James Bryce   Politics Pages 572

Stories of the Pilgrims *by Margaret P. Pumphrey*   ISBN: *1-59462-116-0*   **$17.95**
This book explores pilgrims religious oppression in England as well as their escape to Holland and eventual crossing to America on the Mayflower, and their early days in New England...   History Pages 268

QTY

The Fasting Cure *by Sinclair Upton*   ISBN: *1-59462-222-1*   **$13.95**
In the Cosmopolitan Magazine for May, 1910, and in the Contemporary Review (London) for April, 1910, I published an article dealing with my experiences in fasting. I have written a great many magazine articles, but never one which attracted so much attention... New Age/Self Help/Health Pages 164

Hebrew Astrology *by Sepharial*   ISBN: *1-59462-308-2*   **$13.45**
In these days of advanced thinking it is a matter of common observation that we have left many of the old landmarks behind and that we are now pressing forward to greater heights and to a wider horizon than that which represented the mind-content of our progenitors... Astrology Pages 144

Thought Vibration or The Law of Attraction in the Thought World   ISBN: *1-59462-127-6*   **$12.95**
by William Walker Atkinson   Psychology/Religion Pages 144

Optimism *by Helen Keller*   ISBN: *1-59462-108-X*   **$15.95**
Helen Keller was blind, deaf, and mute since 19 months old, yet famously learned how to overcome these handicaps, communicate with the world, and spread her lectures promoting optimism. An inspiring read for everyone... Biographies/Inspirational Pages 84

Sara Crewe *by Frances Burnett*   ISBN: *1-59462-360-0*   **$9.45**
In the first place, Miss Minchin lived in London. Her home was a large, dull, tall one, in a large, dull square, where all the houses were alike, and all the sparrows were alike, and where all the door-knockers made the same heavy sound... Childrens/Classic Pages 88

The Autobiography of Benjamin Franklin *by Benjamin Franklin*   ISBN: *1-59462-135-7*   **$24.95**
The Autobiography of Benjamin Franklin has probably been more extensively read than any other American historical work, and no other book of its kind has had such ups and downs of fortune. Franklin lived for many years in England, where he was agent... Biographies/History Pages 332

Name	
Email	
Telephone	
Address	
City, State ZIP	

☐ **Credit Card**   ☐ **Check / Money Order**

Credit Card Number	
Expiration Date	
Signature	

Please Mail to: Book Jungle
PO Box 2226
Champaign, IL 61825
or Fax to: 630-214-0564

ORDERING INFORMATION

web: *www.bookjungle.com*
email: *sales@bookjungle.com*
fax: *630-214-0564*
mail: *Book Jungle PO Box 2226 Champaign, IL 61825*
or PayPal *to sales@bookjungle.com*

Please contact us for bulk discounts

DIRECT-ORDER TERMS

**20% Discount if You Order
Two or More Books**
Free Domestic Shipping!
Accepted: Master Card, Visa,
Discover, American Express

CPSIA information can be obtained at www.ICGtesting.com
Printed in the USA
LVOW110915270912

300551LV00005B/80/A